MURDER,
NO DOUBT

MURDER, NO DOUBT

A Widow's Real-Life Nightmare

by Ruth Langlos
and Dennis Niemiec

New Horizon Press
Far Hills, New Jersey

Requests for permission should be addressed to:
New Horizon Press
P.O. Box 669
Far Hills, NJ 07931

Langlos, Ruth, and Dennis Niemiec.
Murder, no doubt: A widow's real-life nightmare.

Library of Congress Catalog Card Number: 93-84521

ISBN: 0-88282-078-8
New Horizon Press

Manufactured in the U.S.A.

1997 1996 1995 1994 1993 / 5 4 3 2 1

Dedication

This book is dedicated to the memory of my beloved husband Jack Langlos and my three sons, Jan, Chad, and Thad Emrick, whose love and support sustained me throughout my tragedy and many years of suffering.

I also wish to dedicate this to all victims of violent crime.

—Ruth Langlos

To Kerry and the boys, and to Mom and Dad, who made it possible.

—Dennis Niemiec

Acknowledgments

This book could not have been written without the guidance, encouragement, and love of Francois Toussaint. Dr. Mary Brenneman, my psychiatrist, helped me through many crises, for which I will be eternally grateful. I owe special thanks to Dr. Edwin Shneidman and Nancy Allen for their deep concern and interest in helping guide me.

Many others deserve thanks for their help for so many years: Rev. Ralph Osborne and Dr. Donald Buteyn for giving me spiritual guidance; Dr. Ervin Jindrich and Dr. Margaret Billingham for their sympathy and medical expertise; Mike Miller and Mike Westray of the Downey Police Department, who never gave up on the Langlos case; to Keith Rogers for his superb job as my private investigator; Patty Ecker, the reporter who broke my story on television and continued to report on it.

Thanks to my relatives and friends, who gave me their love and prayers through my many years of struggle and sorrow: Cathy, Cherie, Jeffrey, Carol, Jason, Tara, and Matthew Emrick; Richard Robinson; Eldon, Mary, Joy, Wendy, and Stacy Baker; Susan Johnson Miller; Wayne, Shawn, Debbie, and Marc Brubaker; Bert and Marion Girard; Dr. Alan Girard; Mary, Jeni, Kathy, Tad, and Sara Wheeler; Dorry, Pat, Andrea, Penny, and Lonnie Patterson; Lynn and Don Stefan; Drs. Ed and Katherine Fisher; Virginia Cartwright; Ann Rosenthal; Mimi Juarez; Violet Phelps; Hilma Bellows; Janet Werier; Fayette and Donna Richards; Patty Acord; and Midge Kent.

Thanks to those who sat with me through many hours in court: Louise McCord; Ted Shafer; Dr. Jack and Aileen Greiner; Joan McArthur; Alison Quinn; Ellen, Paula, and Lori Pirok; Kay

Wahl; Zel Loseff; Dave Kennedy; Pete Keir; and my brother Kenneth Baker.

Thanks to those in the legal system who supported me: D.D.A. Sterling Norris, D.D.A. Roger Kelly, Congressman Ed Royce, Supervisor Mike Antonovich, and many Los Angeles County and California State officials.

I also want to thank Pete Stone, Kenneth Cooper, William Bullis, Harry Simon, Jay Standing, William Masterson,

Special thanks to all of the support groups: Ellen Griffin Dunne, who founded Justice for Homicide Victims, and co-leaders Marcella and Bob Leach; Parents of Murdered Children & Other Survivors of Homicide, Dorothy Bess, Lee Bess, and Doris Tate of the Los Angeles Chapter, and Kathy Yarnell, Carol Ralph, and Betsy Amparon of the Orange County Chapter; Theresa Saldana, who founded the Victims for Victims–Los Angeles Chapter, and Orange County Chapter Leaders Betty Barclay and Debbie Huffman; Gayle Sato and Diane Lightfoot of Friends and Families of Homicide Victims; Coleen and Gary Campbell, founders of Memory of Victims Everywhere; Lori Nelson and Ivy Crawford of the Victims Witness program of the Los Angeles D.A.'s office; and Mended Hearts–Memphis and Orange County Chapters, for their care and concern during and after my heart surgery.

Thanks to all those who made this book a reality: Meredith MacRae, for her belief in my story; Dennis Niemiec, my co-author, for our excellent working relationship; Frank Weimann, my agent, who persevered when others would have given up; Joan Dunphy, my publisher and editor-in-chief, who had the wisdom and courage to let me tell my story; and my son Thad, for his advice in preparing the manuscript.

To you and all I have missed who supported and loved me during my long ordeal, my deepest gratitude and heartfelt thanks.

—Ruth Langlos

Without the help and understanding of several people, this book would never have become a reality.

A special thanks to my wife, Kerry, and my sister Denise for keeping me on track; to my mother, Cecile, for her unwavering support; to my friend Mike Hayball for his computer expertise; and to my co-author, Ruth Langlos, for her determination.

For their help and encouragement I thank *Detroit Free Press* City Editor Carole Leigh Hutton, *Free Press* photographer Steven Nickerson, and Thad Emrick.

Finally, I owe a debt of gratitude to my agent, Frank Weiman, and my publisher and editor, Joan Dunphy, for believing in me and in a compelling story about a courageous lady.

—Dennis Niemiec

Contents

• *Contents* •

Prologue

For Tom Lacey, Monday dawned sunny and bright. Tom had a new job, a new girlfriend, and most important, a new outlook.

Lacey understood mood swings. A part-time psychological consultant, he dealt with depression, schizophrenia, and even homicidal tendencies the way a doctor dealt with the flu.

But nobody, not even someone trained in the science of the mind, was immune to emotional peaks and valleys. The key was climbing out of the valleys.

At twenty-nine, Lacey felt a compelling drive to get untracked from the self-doubts that held him hostage. Lacey realized he couldn't change things simply by agonizing over them. Wasn't that what he advised patients? He nodded to himself encouragingly.

Hooking up with clinical psychologist Dr. Jack Langlos had boosted Lacey's self-confidence. Two months before, Lacey had become Langlos's part-time assistant at the Lakewood Park Health Center, a mental health and convalescent hospital in Downey, California.

It was his job to help analyze some of the patients, suggest forms of treatment, and monitor their progress. He didn't earn much, but this wasn't about money anyway. Someday Lacey hoped to have his own practice, and an association with the widely respected Dr. Langlos was great for his resume. In addition, he now was making progress on a master's degree.

Langlos let his assistant take an active role. Although in the prime of his career, Langlos wasn't overbearing in discussions with his underling. Their give and take gave Lacey a warm feeling of accomplishment.

As Lacey completed the forty-five-minute commute from his Los Angeles apartment, he noticed his boss's blue Volkswagen parked in front to the health center. Nervously he glanced at his watch: 9:05. He ran his long tapered fingers through his blond hair. Dr. Langlos had set up this meeting in his office when they had last talked Thursday night. Lacey had written "9:30" in his appointment book. Could the meeting have been for 9:00? Lacey grimaced. Quickly, he parked the car and got out. Once inside the building he headed straight for the reception desk. Needing his notes he wanted to ask for the keys to Dr. Langlos's office, which was located in an area that housed patients. Because of confidentiality and security concerns, the offices were locked at all times. Anthony the receptionist hadn't arrived yet. In fact, the reception room seemed deserted. He wondered where Eric Lortimer, the hospital administrator who always had a full set of keys, was. "He's always early except when I need him," Lacey muttered.

Lacey fumbled in the top drawer of the receptionist's desk for two keys on a silver ring with a small piece of leather attached. Unable to find them, he took a master key that unlocked several offices. Letting himself into Langlos's silent office, Lacey looked around. "Damn, I must have been wrong about the time." He stashed his briefcase on a small table near the door, sauntered toward the large oak desk, and began to walk around it to get his papers from the left bottom drawer.

Suddenly Lacey froze. Protruding from the back side of the desk was a pair of feet. Lacey began breathing irregularly. At once, he felt lightheaded and nauseous.

Steadying himself, Lacey moved closer and gasped. "My God, it's Dr. Langlos." Langlos was lying face up on the floor in a widening pool of dark red blood. Sick to his stomach, Lacey turned away. Then, slowly, he snuck another glance. A part of his friend's head was wedged underneath a corner of the desk.

Lacey's heart began racing. Hoping someone had come in, he yelled, "It's Dr. Langlos! Someone hurry!" In another office, red-haired and statuesque Coleen Fitzpatrick, the center's director of nursing who had come in early to update some patient records, heard him. His panicked voice told her it was an emergency. She came running in.

"What's wrong, Lacey?"

"It's Langlos," he said, pointing to the body. Fitzpatrick bent over the still form for a long moment.

"We'd better call the police; he's dead," Fitzpatrick said softly.

MURDER,
NO DOUBT

Chapter 1

A Floating Rose

Detective Mike Miller leaned back in his swivel chair and sighed. This week was starting like a lot of weeks. Miller was tracking teenaged punks who preferred the B&Es of homes to the three Rs of classrooms.

His district, Downey, was a California working-class community that lacked the glamour and glitz of suburbs like Beverly Hills and Malibu. Its streets featured factories and hardware stores instead of boutiques and styling salons.

Still, Detective Miller felt that the predominately blue-collar town of 89,000 and he were a nice fit. His family name was familiar throughout the city; his father was a city councilman. He had lived here for all his thirty years, and he planned to stay.

Despite his comfort with the working class, there was a touch of Hollywood about Miller. With matinee idol looks, Miller was a man's man: six-foot-one, with a strong jaw and muscular physique. His dark black hair never looked disheveled and his soft voice sounded so much like comedian Steve Martin that people always thought he was doing an impression. But Miller didn't long for the silver screen. He aspired to be the police chief someday.

Because Downey had escaped the high crime rate in surrounding Los Angeles County, Miller and his police colleagues referred to their community as a "rose floating in the toilet."

On this Monday, at 9:57, Miller's regular partner was on another assignment. Miller and Detective Mike Westray got the call: a suspicious death at the Lakewood Park Health Center.

The two very different men, who had been paired before and solved several crimes together, nodded to each other and headed for the door. Westray was an Ed Asner clone: short, gruff, and heavyset. Miller was a climber within the ranks; unlike him, Westray didn't particularly care what the bosses thought of him. At thirty-seven, he was happy in a black and white. No need to kiss somebody's butt to get a nice office.

While Miller was a sober fellow, Westray was the department's clown. His smile was omnipresent and his eyes mirrored the mischief in his soul. Straight-laced Miller made an easy target for Westray's pranks and jokes.

But even Westray, when they arrived at the crime scene only a few minutes later, didn't find anything amusing about the scene at 12023 Lakewood Boulevard.

The center was located across the street from the North American Rockwell plant that manufactured space capsules. Miller and Westray headed for Room 4 in a wing of small attached cottages on the west side of the health center. The cottages were in a minimal security area that housed patients ready for release.

The scene already was a beehive of activity. Police officers, police photographers, and identification technicians scurried about. A crew of officers was stationed on the roof of the complex, looking for clues.

Miller gazed about the office while being briefed by Detective Gary Morrow, who had already arrived on the scene. The dead man was Jack Langlos, a clinical psychologist at the center.

Miller's brown eyes settled on the north wall. He observed three blood smudges, each about four inches in diameter, about three and a half feet off the floor. Dark red rivulets of dried blood ran from the smudges to the floor. Blood was splattered on a small wall calendar and on a piece of cloth on the floor nearby.

2

"How odd," murmured Miller. During his seven years on the force he had been trained to assume nothing. Even though Miller had handled only a couple of murders, he immediately sensed this was a homicide. The large amount of blood around the room and the position of the body on the floor told him this was no natural death, no suicide either, unless the man bashed himself on the back of the head and waged a savage fight with himself. Langlos lay on the floor, a part of his head wedged under a huge oak desk. He was fully clothed. The desk appeared to have been moved, causing a hump in the green shag carpeting.

Miller bent down to see the body more closely. The man's glasses were askew, with the right ear piece indented in his right eye. Langlos' head was wedged under the three-hundred-pound desk. It rested on his right cheek.

There was a large pocket of blood at the top of the victim's head, which had suffered a deep, half-moon-shaped gash. The back of his maroon sports jacket was soaked with blood. Blood was smeared on the edge of the desk and on the ear piece of the phone. The top three buttons of Langlos's white-and-blue pinstriped shirt had been ripped off. His left rear pocket had been partially pulled out. Miller straightened up. "This poor guy took a hell of a beating," Westray declared. Several heads nodded their agreement.

◆ ◆ ◆

A thousand miles away Ruth Langlos twisted and retwisted the same strand of blond hair, gripping it with pink-tipped nails. She sighed heavily and anxiously picked up the phone once again. Why had her husband, Jack, not answered her phone calls? She hadn't been able to reach him since they parted Friday at the Los Angeles Airport. His warm kiss shortly after midnight still lingered in her mind. "See you in a week," he had said, grinning boyishly.

She missed him even before her redeye Continental Airlines flight touched down at 4:00 A.M. in Houston. But a week-long visit with her son, Jan, and his wife, Cathy, in the suburb of La Porte was long overdue.

As Ruth dialed, her hand shook. She tried to figure out where Jack could be. He would have a busy schedule Saturday. The Lakewood Park Health Center was an hour's drive from their apartment near the Pacific Ocean. He'd be seeing patients early in the day, and that night at eight o'clock when the Roger Young Auditorium in Los Angeles was packed with three hundred people, he'd be blowing the trumpet for the Scottish Thistle Band.

Sunday, Jack would be home—or so she thought. The long night passed. She tried to catch him in the morning before he headed like clockwork to ten o'clock Mass. No answer. After Mass, no answer.

Right after dinner she dialed Jack again. She wanted to see how his weekend had gone, tell him she loved him. She tried until 12:45 in the morning. But he didn't answer.

All kinds of thoughts—good and bad—churned in her mind. Maybe he had spent the weekend with one of the guys in the band. Maybe he was asleep. Maybe he had been called to work unexpectedly at a hospital in San Francisco. Still Ruth felt uneasy.

Jack was so organized that seldom did anything happen that he hadn't planned for. During their courtship, this was the guy who secretly wrote down twenty-six reasons to marry her. He wasn't about to leave an important decision like that to chance. She never told him she found the list inadvertently while emptying his pockets, before sending the pants to the dry cleaners.

Sunday night she tossed and turned under the cotton sheets. This game of "what if" was useless. Jack would be amused. "Don't worry over things you can't control," he'd say.

Now it was Monday morning. She hoped to reach Jack at 7:00 A.M. before he went to work. The phone rang and rang. Could he be in the shower? Or did he go to work straight from a friend's?

That theory seemed strange because Jack wore a plaid sport coat and black pants when he played for a Scottish dance. He wouldn't go to the Lakewood Park Center dressed like that. At 8:00 A.M. she reached Jay Kingsley, their next door neighbor. He hadn't seen Jack all weekend.

Her stomach clenching spasmatically, she waited until 10:00 A.M. California time. Jack would be at work now — punctuality

4

was one of his trademarks.

"Who's calling?" demanded Maureen Anthony, the office receptionist.

"Maureen, don't you recognize my voice?"

"We have to know who's calling."

"Maureen, it's Ruth Langlos," Ruth said. She shook her head. The long-distance connection must have disguised her voice.

"Just a minute."

"Jack, where have you been? I've been trying to reach you all weekend." The words rolled off her tongue.

"Ruth," he started. The voice wasn't Jack's. It was Eric Lortimer, the hospital administrator. "We just found your husband dead in his office," he blurted out.

She dropped the phone. "Jack's dead! Jack's dead!" she screamed.

Cathy, her daughter-in-law, rushed in and grabbed the dangling receiver. Ruth wanted to run, but she was frozen, riveted to the spot. After talking for a few minutes, Cathy hung up and came toward her. "Ruth," Cathy said softly, "Jack was dead for some time. There's evidence of foul play." Cathy saw Ruth begin shivering and covered her with a mound of wool blankets. "They thought a chaplain and a police officer had told you. They're sorry."

Ruth heard Cathy's voice but didn't understand. Her body was shaking. She felt as if she was freezing. Tears ran down her cheeks and blurred her vision. The next few hours were a living nightmare. People came in and out. As a black-garbed figure with a white collar bent over her, she murmured, "Jack's dead! How could it be?"

Jack Langlos wasn't the type of man to make enemies. His patients affectionately call him "Dr. Jack." He and Ruth had been married five years and a month. Ruth had been divorced for more than eight years when the soft-spoken, handsome bachelor rekindled a spark in her life. Their common interests—especially music—and philosophies bonded them.

Jack's career was on a meteoric rise. His patient load was growing and they had started to look for a new home in a posh neighborhood in Pacific Palisades. And because of his increasing success, Jack was eyeing a dark green Porsche.

Never had life been better for either of them, and now it was all over. Why? Why had this darling man been taken from her? What had happened to him?

Chapter 2

Bloody Assault

For six weary hours, a team of police investigators combed the Lakewood Park Health Center for clues.

Who had beaten this man? What was the murder weapon? Were there witnesses? What was the motive? Robbery? Blackmail? A woman scorned?

The Lakewood Park Center had 210 patients, who lived in minimum- or maximum-security units. Some were friendly but disoriented, others schizophrenic or senile. A few were very dangerous.

In a room adjacent to the crime scene, one of the patients, Mark Thomas, tried to comprehend what the police officer had said.

"Dr. Jack, dead? He played real good music, you know. We talked about jazz a lot," said Thomas. "I had a brother who played in our high school band. Dr. Jack played in his high school band, too."

Thomas, a fifty-four-year-old man with copper-colored skin and sleepy eyes, loved to talk, but his attention span was limited.

"Did you see or hear anything unusual over the weekend?"

Detective Morrow asked.

"Like what?"

"Like someone coming out of Dr. Langlos's office?"

"Was Dr. Jack here? He didn't drop in to say hi."

Philip Edwards, another patient, nodded when he heard the name. "Dr. Jack. Great guy. I've know him a long time."

Edwards lived in the other adjacent room on the south side. He was handsome, about thirty-five with curly blond hair and piercing blue eyes. His wife had left him, unable to cope with a manic depressive.

Edwards and Thomas had been at dinner with the other patients from 4:45 to 5:45 Saturday, about the time police estimated the murder occurred. The dining room was in another building.

After several interviews, Morrow shook his head questioningly. The residents here—young and old, black and white, men and women—liked Jack Langlos, Morrow discovered, but none could help the police.

Neither could Tom Lacey, except for a few isolated observations. Langlos didn't have marital problems or enemies, but it was difficult to check out whom he might have been with that afternoon. He often didn't write his appointments in a book but trusted them to memory. When Morrow asked Lacey to describe the death scene, Lacey quivered. "You're very pale," Morrow said quietly. "Why don't we get you some medical assistance."

He decided to talk more to Lacey later.

Meanwhile, Miller and Westray feverishly searched without success for Langlos's wallet. A metal money clip was discovered inside a black briefcase on a chair near the body. It was empty.

Amid the hubbub of investigators, fingerprint technicians, and photographers, tall, silver-haired Dominic Hernandez strode into the office.

As a deputy coroner, Hernandez's job was to make sense of crime scenes. Hernandez was well respected among cops for his investigative skills and straightforward approach. Hernandez didn't play politics. If he couldn't determine how a person died, he'd say so. But most times, he could.

Miller and Westray felt lucky. Police don't request a particular investigator when the morgue is called. Whoever's up, that's who they get. Hernandez was on call this day, and the Downey detectives knew their fortunes were picking up.

Westray and an ID technician lifted the desk off Langlos so Hernandez could do an examination. "Kill a guy, then drop a desk on him," Westray said as they slid the furniture to the side. "One sick son of a bitch."

Hernandez pointed out the deep, one-inch laceration on the top of the victim's head. "It almost forms a V with the point toward the front of his head," he observed.

He continued examining the body. "There are two bruises on the inside of his mouth," Hernandez said matter-of-factly. One was on the upper lip and the other on the lower right lip.

After Miller showed him a blood smudge on the left rear corner of the desk, Hernandez folded a piece of paper over the corner. He made an impression and compared it to the gash.

"The desk could have caused this," Hernandez said, pointing at the wound. "So could a gun." He emptied the victim's pockets, removing ninety cents, one key ring with two keys and a pocket light attached, a cigarette lighter, a stick of gum, a handkerchief, and a partial pack of Long John cigarettes—four Long John butts were in the ashtray on the desk.

"No ID or wallet," he said quizzically.

A silver ballpoint pen lay by the victim's right knee. A clear plastic Bic pen was three inches from his right hand. The three missing shirt buttons were nearby. One was under the desk, one on the chair of the seat behind the desk, and the third on the floor under a bloody cloth. Although the collar button apparently had been buttoned, no necktie was found.

As he did his investigation, Hernandez talked into a tape recorder. Case 76-1473 wasn't that unusual in Hernandez's eyes. "The victim died thirty-six to forty-eight hours ago." Which meant Langlos most likely had been killed Saturday before he had a chance to leave for the Scottish dance.

Hernandez removed the body at 1:30 and filed a simple clinical report: Dr. Jack Langlos, 5'10" and 169 pounds, had blue eyes and his own teeth. He had no mustache, beard, or deformities.

Cause of death: an assault. A homicide by unknown person(s).

◆   ◆   ◆

In Houston, Ruth Langlos's daughter-in-law, Cathy Emrick, was standing over Ruth, taking her pulse. An Emergency Medical Team member, Cathy knew she was seeing the signs of shock. She had earlier contacted her husband, Jan, a software programmer for NASA.

Next, she had called Ruth's twin sons, Chad and Thad Emrick. Now she tried to comfort her mother-in-law as best she could. Meanwhile, the awful news was coming from Downey in dribbles. Detective Morrow told Cathy they couldn't find Jack's billfold, his necktie, or his wristwatch. His money clip was empty.

By mid-afternoon as the initial shock of hearing the news set in, dark thoughts swirled through Ruth's mind. Perhaps a patient had gone berserk and murdered her husband. She kept wondering, *Which one? Which one?*

Jack treated them all with compassion and understanding. One woman thought she was Meryl Streep. Another handsome gentleman spoke perfectly normally but had to be confined. He was a pyromaniac.

Jack rarely commented on his patients to Ruth. He kept a three-by-five-inch card on each of them. One day she had noticed a red notation on a card that Jack had pulled for billing purposes. It read: "HOMICIDAL/SUICIDAL."

She expressed concern, but Jack was nonplussed. "Everything's under control. He just came over from Metro State Hospital. As long as he's on medication, he's okay."

But was he okay? Or had he killed Jack? What was his name? Eyes widening, Ruth watched and listened. The raindrops thumped on the bedroom window as an overcast sky cast a grayish pall on the last hours of daylight.

Ruth's thoughts fastened on the Lakewood Park Center. Like many of its patients, the place had a mysterious past. Before Jack had joined the staff, it went under the name Garden of Lebanon.

Two years before, the chief of the county health department had ordered the coroner to investigate several unusual deaths that had occurred there within twelve months of each other. Area newspapers reported that the home had been cited for seventeen infractions of the health code.

Downey police did their own probe and found that the nursing home staff had failed to file reports on various fights. In one case, an elderly man had lost an eye.

Conditions had improved when a new owner, David Ward, a wealthy businessman, had purchased the facility as an investment. The name of the facility was changed and a new staff hired, including Jack. They had restored an air of professionalism. The scandals had ceased, and so had the negative headlines. Until now.

At 3:30 P.M. Morrow called again with more questions. "Did Mr. Langlos wear a watch?" Ruth explained to Morrow that Jack's watch was at the local jewelry store for repair. It had been damaged five days ago when Jack tried to extinguish a suspicious fire in the garage under their apartment. Who could have set it, she wondered. Perhaps someone with a grudge?

Morrow broke into her thoughts. "We found two capsules of Benadryl; did Jack have medical problems?"

"Only a light case of asthma," she answered. "He was allergic to cats and a certain breed of dogs."

"Did your husband carry a wallet, Mrs. Langlos?" Morrow pressed.

She sighed, "Yes, it's a green plaid wallet. It's usually in his right hip pocket. But he didn't carry money there. He had his credit cards and a rare coin that looks like a penny. And two blank checks."

"Where would he keep his money?" Morrow continued.

"In a money clip in his pants pocket. It has two theatrical masks—Comedy and Tragedy."

"That was in his briefcase. Empty."

Ruth asked him to contact their bank and put stops on their checking accounts and credit cards—MasterCharge, Penney's, Saks Fifth Avenue, and Fedco. Then she started to cry again. What good were money and credit cards anyway without Jack?

• ◆ •

As Ruth struggled to accept the finality of Jack's death, at the Downey police station, Captain Frank Sanders was refereeing a verbal sparring match between Miller and Westray.

"That desk wasn't *on* his face," argued Miller. "The weight of the desk was *not on* his face. He was lodged *under* the desk."

Westray shook his head and sarcastically said: "You didn't lift that desk. It was right on top of his face."

Sanders tried to cut to the chase. "Was it murder?"

"Yeah," Miller said.

"No doubt," seconded Westray.

"Then let's not argue about the goddamn desk," said Sanders. "Let's get the killer."

An average of one murder a year occurred in Downey. With sixteen investigators on its 105-member force, the Downey police department had the manpower, if not the experience, to handle homicides.

Sanders was thankful this case was assigned to Miller and Westray. For all their arguing and shenanigans, these were two of his best cops. They'd find Jack Langlos's killer, he was confident.

At seven that evening, Miller and Westray continued a very long day by searching the Langlos apartment, with the widow's permission. The two-bedroom apartment was neatly tucked along winding Sunset Boulevard among the area's most fashionable homes.

Miller noted a small piece of paper hooked on the door. It was a note with two names and a brief message requesting Jack Langlos call them. A thorough search of the apartment and the widow's red Pontiac in the lot failed to produce the victim's wallet.

As he thumbed through checks in a blue plastic holder atop a small filing cabinet, Miller heard a loud bellow of laughter from the bathroom.

"Mike, come right away. You've got to see this," his partner called. "Look here." The wall was covered with a wallpaper that looked like crinkled aluminum foil.

"Psychedelic," Westray observed. Both cops had their first

laugh of the day. It felt good.

The detectives confiscated the three-by-five cards listing the doctor's patients. They noted that four patients were diagnosed as having homicidal tendencies. On the way back to the station, the weary twosome stopped by Langlos's office to take another look around and interview employees on the night shift. "No help here," Westray said as they left.

At the station, they sent an all-points bulletin teletype indicating that the wallet and its contents were missing. "Let's go home and get some rest," Miller said. "Tomorrow's another long day."

◆ ◆ ◆

Arriving early Tuesday morning, Miller gagged at the thoughts of the job ahead.

Police work is filled with unpleasantries. Notifying the next of kin after a death. Resisting the urge to thump some foul-mouthed drunk who questions your manhood instead of getting into the squad car. Seeing the terror on the wrinkled face of a senior citizen whose home has been vandalized.

Miller had learned to live with most of those unpleasantries. But one he still had a hard time with was the autopsy.

He could stomach watching the doctors probing and cutting in their gowns and rubber aprons, but he never got used to the rancid smell of death. The smell lingered on his clothes and in his mind, it ruined his appetite and darkened his thoughts for days.

At 9:00 A.M. Miller gritted his teeth and led a contingent of detectives and ID technicians into downtown Los Angeles for the autopsy of Jack Langlos. Miller briefed Dr. Eugene Carpenter, a deputy medical examiner, on the unusual circumstances surrounding the death.

The doctor had a sloppy look. He was in his early fifties, but his disheveled white hair, wrinkled clothes, and measured speech made him seem much older.

Before the autopsy, Carpenter looked at the gash on Langlos's head. He noted there was no swelling or bruising.

"There's a good chance he was dying when this occurred,"

Carpenter told the police.

The exam took less than a hour. It looked routine to Miller and Morrow, who stood fifteen feet away with their hands over their noses. But the results weren't routine. In a cramped office he shared with another doctor, Carpenter announced his findings.

"The head injury did not cause death," Carpenter declared. "Mr. Langlos's arteries were constricted. He appears to have been suffering from occlusive coronary artery disease."

"Are you saying he died of a heart attack?" Miller's eyebrows lifted in astonishment.

Carpenter nodded. "Yes, Mr. Langlos died a natural death."

"Didn't you find anything else on the body that would indicate foul play?"

"No."

"What about all the blood? And the buttons ripped off his shirt?"

"That would be indicative of somebody suffering shortness of breath, having a heart attack, and tearing open their collar."

"Doctor, are you sure about this?" Miller wasn't prepared for the curve the doctor had thrown.

"Death was natural," Carpenter repeated.

Miller doubted that. The more he learned of this case, the more unnatural it became.

Chapter 3

The 139th Psalm

Five days before, Jack and Ruth were sharing sweet hopes for the future. Now, having returned to California, she was shopping for his casket. She stared at one, then another. She wasn't prepared to do anything but cry. Her sons and a friend, Mary Wheeler, had come with her. With their prodding, she finally settled on a traditional casket, the bronze. The nightmare was continuing.

On Wednesday, they still couldn't set a date for the funeral, because the medical examiner had not released Jack's body.

Jack, who served in the Navy during World War II, had wanted to be buried in a Veterans Administration cemetery, but the nearest one had closed January 31, 1976. No plots were available, but they would accept his ashes. Jack hadn't believed in cremation. Neither did Ruth.

Aileen Griener, a close friend, finally came up with a solution: Jack's body could be placed in Aileen's crypt next to her deceased husband until Jack could be transferred to a new VA cemetery being constructed in nearby Riverside.

Years later, Aileen and Ruth would laugh at the notion of loaning a crypt to a friend. But it wasn't funny at the time.

Nothing was.

At their apartment Ruth had a locksmith change all the locks. Whoever had robbed Jack probably had made copies of all the keys.

One of the most difficult times for her was late at night. Getting to sleep in their bed without Jack's arms around her was agonizing. Before retiring, the family gathered and Jan read the 139th Psalm. Jack and Ruth had read that psalm to each other many nights.

"O Lord, you have examined my heart and know everything about me. . . . You both precede and follow me, and place your hand of blessing on my head. . . . This is too glorious, too wonderful to believe!"

Her mind spun back to just one week before.

The moon had rested motionless against a starry backdrop. As they sped along the highway, a California breeze steadily flowed through the sunroof of the Volkswagen. Jack talked about how much he wished he could accompany her to Texas. The next week would be lonely indeed. Ruth stared at him for a minute, wondering whether she deserved such a wonderful husband. "When was the last time I told you I love you?" she asked. He turned away from the wheel for an instant and with a gleam in his eyes answered: "When was the last time I told you I loved *you*?" They laughed. A day hardly passed that they didn't express their deep love in some way—a kiss, a smile, a compliment. They all translated into the same message: I love you.

The memory faded. Reality claimed her again. The psalm was ending.

"If I ride the morning winds to the farthest oceans, even there your hand will guide me, your strength will support me. . . . How precious it is, Lord, to realize that you are thinking about me constantly!"

Ruth took the Bible to bed with her. Between verses and memories she slipped into sleep, knowing the next night she would face the same insomnia again.

◆ ◆ ◆

Detectives Miller and Westray visited the apartment in the midst of funeral preparations. Ruth's sons and daughter-in-law were working at a feverish pace. Thad was busy on the phone notifying relatives and friends of Jack's death. Chad was writing a eulogy. Jan was polishing Jack's trumpet so it could be displayed on top of the casket.

For the police from the modest community of Downey, visiting Pacific Palisades was like going to a rich aunt's house. It was a dramatic drive along windy, hilly roads flanked by the majestic Santa Monica Mountains and the cascading Pacific Ocean. But interviewing a widow before she buried her husband was not a treat. Miller and Westray had a simple game plan: Ask basic questions, keep the interview short, and try to let the widow set the tone. This was a fishing expedition. If she wanted to talk, fine. They would prod her for details, particularly clues to where they could find the victim's wallet and credit cards. But if she kept sobbing or rambling, they would be sensitive enough to call it quits for the day.

Ruth greeted them with reddened, swollen eyes. "Please make yourself comfortable," she said, indicating the sofa.

Miller lobbed a few softballs. How long had Jack worked at the center? Why had she gone to Texas? How long had they been married?

She ran her hand across her aching forehead and tried to answer each one. Suddenly she remembered something that seemed important, "Jack always carried two blank checks in his wallet from two different accounts. One of the accounts had less than one hundred dollars, but the other had more than six thousand dollars. Checks 1104 and 163 are missing." She stared at the detectives, waiting for a response. When there was none, she went on. "Jack always carried his money clip in his right front pants pocket and his wallet in the right rear pocket," she explained.

"The money clip was in his briefcase, Mrs. Langlos," said Westray.

"No way did he carry the money clip in the briefcase," she shouted. In her mind one thought kept getting stronger: *These men don't know Jack the way I do.*

Miller moved forward on the couch and looked her in the eye. "Mrs. Langlos, who do you think robbed your husband?"

"I think a patient went berserk," she rasped, tearing the tissue in her hand into small pieces. "Then the patient gave the stolen goods to a relative."

He looked at her questioningly and changed the subject.

"Did your husband owe anybody any money?" Miller asked.

"No," she said tonelessly.

"Anybody owe him money?"

"Dr. Hartman."

"Who's he?" Miller asked, sitting up and leaning toward her.

"Dr. Eugene Hartman. He worked with Jack. Jack loaned him two hundred dollars before Christmas. That check bounced. He wanted to borrow five hundred dollars, but Jack wouldn't lend that much," she stopped, ran her fingers through her disheveled hair, and changed subjects.

"Did you find Jack's necktie in his office?"

"No," said Miller. "Maybe he didn't wear one that day."

"Jack wouldn't be caught dead without a necktie," she exclaimed, not realizing the joke. Miller and Westray started biting their lips and fidgeting in their seats. She stared at them questioningly. What was wrong? Did they doubt her?

Ruth continued: "Jack was meticulous about the way he dressed. He wouldn't even go to the doctor's without a coat and tie. At work, he always wore a tie."

The interview ended a few minutes later. For Miller and Westray, it ended just in time. They could barely contain themselves.

As they rode away, the detectives broke down and began laughing hysterically.

"Wouldn't be caught dead without a tie," Westray roared. "Well, sorry. That's the way we found him!"

Miller laughed so hard his eyes watered. "I bit the inside of my mouth, I couldn't believe she said that. I knew I couldn't look at you or I'd have lost it."

"She seemed so sincere. I thought she was gonna start bawling again. And there I was with a shit-eatin' grin."

They couldn't stop laughing.

• ◆ •

Nobody in Ruth's family laughed that night. They visited the funeral home. Ruth had ordered a closed casket because she was afraid of how Jack's battered face might look. A wreath of red roses and Jack's trumpet lay atop the bronze casket.

As Ruth and her sons walked into the so-called slumber room filled with family friends, the health center administrator, Eric Lortimer, a short man with beady eyes, a high forehead, and black curly hair, called out, "Ruth," and ran over. He thrust a dozen red roses into her arms. She forced a smile, figuring he felt guilty over the abrupt way he broke the news of Jack's death.

Before she could utter a thank you, Lortimer began to talk nonstop in a nervous, high-pitched voice.

"While Jack was having his heart attack, he stumbled around the room in a daze. Then he ripped the buttons off his shirt to loosen his collar and get air."

He not only described the scene but acted it out. He gazed toward the heavens as if in a stupor to simulate Jack's demeanor and pulled at his own shirt to show the panic of a man in deep trouble. It was eerie, seeing Lortimer feign a heart attack as though he had actually been in the office and witnessed Jack's last gasps.

"I can explain all the blood, too."

"Blood? What blood?" Ruth gasped. Lortimer began emoting again.

"Jack was losing strength. He lost his balance and hit his head on the corner of his desk. Wobbly and bleeding profusely, he brushed against the chair and wall, leaving smears of blood." Beads of sweat ran down Lortimer's face. "Jack reached for the phone but it was too late." Lortimer dropped to one knee. "He fell to the ground and wedged himself under the desk." He stood up. "That's why they found him in a pool of blood. There wasn't anybody else in the room."

Ruth screamed and ran to the lady's room. Blood. She thought Jack had been attacked by a patient and robbed. Nobody had mentioned any blood.

When Ruth returned, Lortimer stayed away from her. Ruth's sons knew the gory details but had planned to tell their mother after the funeral. "Lortimer and his theatrics," Chad said.

Word of Lortimer's revelations spread through the room. The place was abuzz.

Dr. Kathryn Fisher, a longtime friend and an internist, quickly walked up. "Jack couldn't have died from a heart attack with that much external bleeding."

Ruth's friend Aileen, a hospital lab technician in Orange County, seconded Fisher's concerns. "Ruth, you really must have another autopsy."

"How can I? The funeral is tomorrow."

"You really should. There is something wrong here."

Somehow Ruth got through the evening. Images of Jack struggling to breathe were still vivid in her mind Friday morning as Ruth dressed for the funeral.

She began putting on a two-piece black dress, a black hat, and veil. The top was trimmed with white mink cuffs. As Ruth turned the doorknob to leave, Mary Wheeler, a friend who had come to the house to help her, called out, "Ruth, I believe you forgot something." She paused. "You haven't put your skirt on."

It was another funny, sad thought of her attending the funeral in her slip. Ruth grimaced, thinking how Jack would smile at the joke.

Tears ran down her cheeks as she finished dressing. Channel 11 filmed the funeral for the evening news. And, unknown to everyone, plainclothes police officers attended to observe the crowd.

Jack had been Catholic, Ruth Presbyterian. They used to rotate churches every Sunday. Father Paul Dotson and Dr. Donald Buteyn of the Hollywood Presbyterian Church co-celebrated the funeral service in Corpus Christi Catholic Church in Pacific Palisades. Father Dotson gave the Mass and Dr. Buteyn would give the eulogy. The Scottish Thistle Band played Scottish anthems.

The eulogy traced Jack's two career paths: clinical psychologist and professional musician. Dr. Buteyn began, "Born in New York City, John Thomas Langlos was of German-Irish descent. He graduated from Fort Lauderdale High School and received

20

numerous medals for combat duty with the United States Navy. He received bachelor's and master's degrees in psychology from the University of Miami. He earned a Ph.D. in 1974.

"Dr. Langlos, or Jack as everybody knew him, can be best described by his humility and reticence," the Dr. Buteyn declared. "Given these qualities, he was not one to tell even his closest friends or relatives the many accomplishments of his life."

Ruth knew Jack would be embarrassed as the minister recited a litany of achievements: Jack had been a mental health counselor with the psychiatric unit of Los Angeles County Hospital for eight years. He testified in fifty-eight hundred cases as an officer of Los Angeles Superior Court, spoke to paramedical and civic groups, counseled thousands of adult mentally retarded patients in Los Angeles County, and evaluated two thousand executives for businesses in the Los Angeles area. He was entered in Who's Who in the West and the National Register of Health Service Providers in Psychology.

Jack's musical background also was impressive: He played trumpet and string bass for the Los Angeles Doctors' Symphony; fronted his own Dixieland band, Thee Saints, and recorded with several bands.

"Despite or because of his humility, he will not be forgotten," the minister concluded.

As the family walked outside the church, they saw musicians from throughout California had joined forces to pay tribute to one of their own by playing "Amazing Grace" and "Just a Closer Walk with Thee." As the pallbearers put the casket in the coach, the band struck up a New Orleans-style version of "When the Saints Go Marching In."

At the cemetery, Ruth turned to her son Jan. "Please put Jack's trumpet in his hands." Later Ruth pressed her hand to the cold casket, her mind in turmoil. "I don't know what Jack looks like," Ruth sobbed. "Please, I'm not ready to leave him. Not now. Not ever."

Her sons led her away.

That night, a newscaster said: "The Dixieland band set fingers snapping in the background at the unique funeral service. It was just like Dr. Langlos would have wanted it."

Yes, the funeral had been a fitting testimonial to Jack's love of life. But it had come many, many years too soon. Ruth knew she would never reconcile herself to that untimely loss.

Chapter 4

A Clue at the Market

Detective Miller had reason to be uptight. He was sure the Langlos case was a murder, but the coroner had ruled it a heart attack.

The body of Jack Langlos had been discovered seventy-two hours before. Usually a homicide is solved within seventy-two hours.

If it's going to be solved.

Miller's instincts told him what had happened. He had envisioned the scenario several times.

Langlos was grabbed by an attacker and yanked forward, hitting his head on the desk corner. Instead of scaring the attacker, the sight of blood seemed to have enraged him. The attacker bounced Langlos off the wall several times and finally threw him into a chair. During the beating, Langlos may have suffered a heart attack. He slumped out of his chair and thrashed around on the floor for a short time. When he stopped moving, the attacker dropped the desk on him.

Now all Miller had to do was prove it. He had a throbbing headache. Black coffee and adrenaline helped a murder investigation, but they were poor substitutes for sleep.

"All right, whadda we got so far?" Westray demanded, plopping into a padded chair in the Downey police conference room.

"A missing tie," Miller replied.

"Check."

"A missing wallet."

"Check."

"Missing checks, credit cards, and cash."

"Check, check, and check."

"Notice that the operative word here is *missing*."

"I'm hungry. Did Whitey bring in any bagels?" Westray couldn't solve a case on an empty stomach.

Miller didn't need to answer. Detective Fred White never brought any food to share.

"Cheap son of a bitch," Westray muttered.

"I think Langlos knew his killer," Miller declared. "We got a print off the window sill, but there's no sign of forced entry. I say whoever it was knocked on the door and Langlos let him in."

"Yeah, like one of his Looney-Toons patients," said Westray, flipping a piece of chewing gum in his mouth. "The doc might have thought the patient was coming for help and let him in."

Miller shook his head. "I don't think Langlos would let a patient in like that. He didn't treat patients in his office. From what I've been told, the only people he'd let in would be other personnel and doctors."

"Of course," Miller added, "somebody could have forced their way in when he answered the door. The center claims it's doing everything possible to help us account for all patients and employees that weekend."

"Right," Westray said sarcastically. "Like they really want to help us. All that guy Lortimer cares about is their image. Murder isn't good for PR, you know."

"Do you think they're covering up?"

"I don't know, but I don't think they're about to go out of their way to offer any leads—especially if they find something in their own backyard."

"So, a wacky patient offed him for the money?"

"The money, and maybe just for the sheer thrill of it."

Miller pored over a list of Langlos's patients for what seemed like the hundredth time. "Well, if it was a wacko patient, it doesn't look like it was one of Langlos's patients."

They had found the names of four potentially dangerous patients during their search of Langlos's apartment.

Of these, Glenn Donovan had been the most dangerous suspect. Diagnosed by Langlos as homicidal and suicidal, Donovan possibly could kill for the sake of killing, although he had never done so. His deep-seated aggression centered on his father, who had abandoned him when he was a child. Donovan's mousey features, horned-rimmed glasses, and timid voice belied the rage within his soul.

In Miller's mind, Donovan was an ex-suspect. First of all, Donovan considered Jack Langlos his friend, someone who would listen to his troubles. More important, Donovan had been locked in his room the entire weekend under tight security. He had been escorted to meals with the other high-risk patients and then escorted back to his room.

So had the other three. The most unusual interview had been with Victor Umbaro, a rock of a man at six-foot-two and 195 pounds. He had assaulted two cops while on a drinking spree, but that was when he was nineteen. At forty-two, he still had the body of a young man. His mind? That was quite a different matter.

Miller and Westray had been advised by the nurses to go easy on Umbaro. He had never recovered from the death of his wife and child in a car accident. The loss had shattered his already fragile emotions. When angry or frustrated, he exhibited a monumental temper. The next minute, he could become a whimpering child.

The Downey police never saw the temper. They never saw much of anything except for tears.

"Mr. Umbaro, Dr. Jack Langlos was found dead in his office Monday morning," Westray said. "We'd like to ask you some questions."

"Dead. Dead. Dead?" Umbaro repeated the word like it was foreign. He began crying, controllably at first. Then he sobbed, his massive chest bobbing up and down.

The nurse escorted them out. End of interview.

"We can always try to get a confession from Oscar Grant," Westray said mischievously.

Miller looked up the patient list and laughed. "Yeah, maybe that's the only way we're gonna solve this."

"Weirdest prime suspect I ever saw," laughed Westray.

Grant's name was one of three that had been jotted on a piece of paper found in the top drawer of Langlos's desk at the center. All three were patients, but none had ever been seen by Langlos. That fact baffled police.

Two of the patients, Martha Lampkin and Eva Dunbar, had airtight alibis. But when the center's staff couldn't locate Grant at first, police prepared for a massive search.

As they ran background checks and questioned staff about his family, nurse Claudia Jones sheepishly admitted that Grant was indeed in his room and not in the dining room where they had thought. The search was over almost before it started.

When they entered Grant's room in the long-term care wing of the center, Miller and Westray came face to face with a man in his late seventies. Grant couldn't dress himself properly, let alone kill someone. His cotton shirt was on backwards, and his socks didn't match.

"Senile," Jones whispered. Miller and Westray understood.

If a patient had killed Langlos, the police didn't have a clue which one did it.

"It sure wasn't a professional job," Miller said wearily. "No .38 slug to the back of the head. This killer was messy."

Westray smiled. "Maybe it was a tryout hit. You know, the mob hires a guy to see what he can do. 'Here's a simple one—do the friendly psychologist in his office.' And the hitman botched it up."

Miller stared at his partner and grinned. "You mean our murderer is a vicious hitman with the grace of Don Knotts."

"Just a theory, partner," Westray deadpanned.

"I think you're Don Knotts," Miller laughed.

"No, I'm the hungry cop who can't solve the big case without nourishment."

"You've already had enough nourishment for a lifetime," Miller replied.

They were giddy. Since Monday morning, the cops had pounded the streets—hard. They feared the killer would escape from the area, so they hopped from interview to interview and city to city at a frenzied pace.

A dietician at the health center had seen Langlos in the dining room area late Saturday afternoon. It was the last time Langlos was seen alive.

Greta Connors, a caretaker at the Lakewood Park Health Center, had checked the area where Dr. Langlos's office was located on Sunday. From three in the afternoon until eleven at night, she had walked by the office every hour. The office had been unlocked. Because the lights were out, she never entered.

Delilah Oswald hadn't been scheduled to work the Saturday shift, but she found herself patrolling the west wing anyway.

"They were shorthanded, so I got a call to come in at about five o'clock in the afternoon," she explained. "I can use the overtime, so I did it. But I never checked the door on Dr. Jack's office. We were so understaffed that I probably only got by there a couple times all night. The lights were off, so I wasn't concerned."

Miller had found an appointment book in the victim's inside jacket pocket. Only one entry was listed for the day of the murder: a musical engagement at 8:00 P.M.

Miller and Westray had found a small piece of paper in the front door of Langlos's apartment. "Jack, call Ron or Matt as soon as you get a chance," the note read. It was signed Matt H. "Sunday, P.M." was scribbled in the upper righthand corner.

Ron Chapman, leader of the six-piece Scottish Thistle Band, was eager to help police. He wracked his memory for any tidbit of information that could prove useful. Jack Langlos was more than a fellow musician to Chapman; he was like a family member. An outgoing guy with a keen wit and an ample midsection, Chapman played the accordion and string bass and organized the band's schedule. He booked them, prodded them, and inspired them. Chapman was the band's heart; Langlos was its soul. The band members respected Langlos for his incredible ability. They also liked his quiet, unflappable approach. The band could count on Langlos for a superior performance no matter how he felt or how big the crowd.

"Here we had this packed auditorium, it's twenty minutes before showtime, and Jack hadn't arrived," Chapman recalled. "Now if it was anybody else, there'd be no worry. But you could set your watch by Jack. He was never late, and I mean never."

"Did you try calling him?" Miller asked.

"Sure, but there was no answer. Matt Hayes—he's another band member—had talked to Jack at ten o'clock Saturday morning. They went over some last minute details and everything was set," said Chapman.

"What does this Hayes do for a living?"

"He's the vice principal at St. Monica High School in Santa Monica."

"So why did you go over to Langlos's apartment on Sunday?"

"Well, everybody figured he had car trouble, but he was so dependable that we expected he'd at least call," Chapman explained. "When we were finished someone said, 'Langlos better have one hell of an excuse or he better be dead.' Everyone felt awful about that remark later.

"Anyway, Hayes and I went to Jack's apartment at about four o'clock in the afternoon to see if everything was okay. His car wasn't there. We went around into the backyard and looked into the glass door. We saw his band coat and his trumpet laid out on the couch. We figured he never came home to get them."

"Which would mean he knew beforehand that he wasn't going to play that night?"

"Yeah, we thought that was odd. But we didn't know where he might have gone or who to contact because his wife was in Texas. So we left a note for him to call us."

"Did he have any enemies? Anybody he was having problems with?"

"I don't think so. Langlos wasn't the kind of guy to make enemies. He was pretty easy going." Chapman paused. "I guess being a good guy doesn't prevent you from getting murdered."

"People with and without enemies are killed every day," Miller replied while scratching a note in his pad. "Some are just harder to solve, that's all."

Another dead end. Solid leads were dwindling fast. Even the coroner had thrown a curve. "What a sham!" Miller mumbled. But he still felt the attacker would confess to somebody; criminals like to talk too much for their own good.

Miller labored in a closed society where a detective is only as good as his last case. Right now, he wasn't looking good as a cop—nor was his performance as a husband or father much better because of the extra time he was devoting to the Langlos case.

Miller already had one failed marriage, a liaison fresh out of high school that lasted less than a year. His police career had helped stretch his second marriage to the breaking point more than once.

The worst time was when he had been a narc. His shoulder-length hair and thick, flowing beard were standard in his job, but his grubby appearance embarrassed his family. During his days away from home, Miller bought dope, partied heavily, and wreaked havoc in society's underbelly. The arrests mounted. His career took off. And his marriage survived—barely.

The shifts became more stable when Miller was promoted to detective. But murder doesn't work on a nine-to-five schedule. Since responding to that dead body call on Lakewood Boulevard, Miller had been home scarcely enough to sleep a couple hours, shower, and shave. With a five-year-old son and a baby due in June, his absence wasn't appreciated. Miller could feel the tension in his temples.

Detective Westray was uptight, too. He was getting married for the second time on February 21, less than ten days away.

"I'm a typical cop," he told friends. "I got two wives, three if you count the job." He also had two kids he wouldn't see as much any more. His winsome smile hid the pain.

Before he said, "I do," Westray wanted to nab the savage who had beaten Jack Langlos to death. He didn't buy the theory that Langlos had hit his head on the desk corner. The desk was too close to the wall; Langlos would have had to be nearly standing on his head and land at a 45-degree angle on the corner.

And why weren't there any scuff marks on the floor? If Langlos had thrashed about, his black rubber-soled shoes would have left marks on the tile not covered by the rug. No, Langlos had been struck in the head with a blunt object during a bloody beating. To cap it off, the murderer had dropped the desk on him. Now that made more sense.

Miller and the coroner's investigator would find out he was right when they caught the creep, Westray figured. Meanwhile, he could tell his partner was in a deep funk over a lack of progress.

How could he shake him out of the rut? Westray smiled. Practical jokes were Westray's trademark, and Miller was his favorite target. Why? The guy was gullible and always got irritated when he couldn't think of a way to pay Westray back.

Maybe it was time for the glitter trick, Westray pondered while eyeing Miller's perfectly styled coiffure. With the massive amount of hair spray Miller applied, his thick head of hair wouldn't budge even if he got into a wrestling match in a monsoon.

Westray would fix him big-time. He'd rig a bag of brightly colored glitter in the top compartment of Miller's locker. It would spill on his perfect hair. The thought of his dignified partner driving around all day with a head sprinkled with glitter was appealing. "Aw, that'll piss him off for sure," Westray mused.

However, that trick—or any other—would have to wait. At 10:05 A.M. Thursday, as Westray plotted and Miller sulked, the telephone rang.

"We've got check #163 from the Langlos account," said George Sullivan, branch manager of the Security Pacific Bank in Pacific Palisades. "Apparently it's been forged by somebody."

"What's the amount?" Miller prodded.

"It's for one hundred dollars to the Boy's Market in Carson. Whoever cashed it used Langlos's driver's license and Mastercharge card."

"What's the date on it?"

"It was cashed on February 1 and deposited February 3. The check appears to be a poor attempt of forgery."

Miller was excited. Sunday, February 1, likely was the day after Langlos had been killed.

At the bank, Sullivan showed police why he figured the forger was an amateur. Langlos was right-handed, and his John T. Langlos signature reflected that on other checks. The signer in the market had slanted "John" like a lefty.

The check also had two folds, indicating it might have been in a wallet. Whoever forged check #163 apparently didn't realize how much money was in the account. It had a balance of $6,152.71. The other blank check that someone had taken from Langlos had a balance of $87.99.

"Nobody said criminals are smart," Westray said.

Boy's Market #33 on South Avalon was part of a statewide grocery chain. The assistant manager, Joe Jacobs, remembered that store employee Penny Hawkins had cashed the check at the courtesy booth. It was routine practice, and Jacobs was vague in his description.

At 6:55 P.M., Miller, Westray, and a police artist visited Hawkins at her home in Gardena. An angular-featured woman in her mid-twenties, Hawkins was cooperative but nervous.

"I definitely remember cashing that check," she said. "It was sometime last Sunday afternoon. I'd say between 2:00 and 4:00 P.M. Uh, is it true that the guy who the license belonged to is dead?"

"That's true," Miller replied. "Now, can you describe the person who cashed the check?"

"Well, as I remember, it was a white man . . . oh, forty-five to fifty-five years old. Wait a minute, probably forty to forty-five is closer. I think he was middle-aged . . . I can't be sure."

"You're doing fine," Miller encouraged. "How tall was he?"

"A couple inches taller than me. He was about five-six, five-seven. But he seemed to be slouching."

As Hawkins described the suspect, Tom Harrison used the police Identi-Kit to compile a composite drawing. He drew a round face at her direction.

"It was even rounder than that," Hawkins said. "He was chunky."

His hair was medium brown, possibly combed to the right side with a part on the left side. Hawkins couldn't recall if the guy had a mustache or wore glasses. Harrison showed her samples done several ways, but she remained unsure, especially about the glasses. The best she could do for a clothing description was the fact that the man had been dressed casually.

"He acted like he was nervous or something, like he had something to hide," Hawkins recalled. "He was strange, I know that. But he definitely showed a driver's license and he used the Mastercharge card that had a check guarantee on the back."

"If he was acting strange, why did you cash the check?"

"Store policy," Hawkins replied. "He had all the proper ID. That's all we can go on."

Miller could sense Hawkins's tension. Hawkins fidgeted in her chair, talked hurriedly, and apologized repeatedly for her uncertainties. Miller wasn't surprised. Four days ago, she had been a grocery clerk cashing a check for a customer. Now she was a potential key witness in a murder case. Talk about a strange twist. Miller figured it was time to give her the ultimate test.

"Could you identify him if you saw him again?"

A look of anguish rolled across Hawkins's smooth face. "Possibly. I mean, I think so."

The living room in the tiny two-bedroom bungalow fell silent for several seconds. Finally, Hawkins cut to the chase. "Do you think I'm going to have to identify him in person?" The thought of picking out a killer in a lineup terrified her.

"You'll do just fine," Miller tried to sound reassuring. "When we find this guy, hopefully we'll have other people who can identify him, too."

Armed with two sketches of the man—with and without glasses—the detectives rushed back to the Lakewood Center like two round-eyed kids at their first ballgame. The criminal had fouled up! And they couldn't wait to show those sketches around.

At the center, Felicia Perez eyed the sketches a few seconds and shrugged her shoulders. The head registered nurse of the swing shift, Perez knew just about everybody who came and went.

"They don't remind me of any patient," she said, handing the sketches to Miller.

"An employee?"

"No sir."

Miller couldn't hide his disappointment. Neither could Eric Lortimer, who had just returned from the funeral and joined them.

The administrator of the nursing facility looked at the sketches reluctantly. He grimaced. The new owners had changed the name to Lakewood Park Health Center to disassociate it from the mysterious deaths of the past.

Lortimer had hoped this investigation was just routine.

"Is this the man you believe robbed Mr. Langlos?" he asked.

"Robbed and possibly murdered him," Westray replied.

"Murder?" Lortimer nearly spit out the word. "I thought it's been ruled a natural death."

"We need to find the person who was in the room with him that weekend," Westray responded. "Maybe then we'll find out exactly what happened."

"I hope it's soon. No offense, but having police hang around here is bad for business."

"Crime isn't generally good for business," Westray replied sarcastically. "We're going to need a list of all employees and all visitors who were here January 31 and February 1."

"All right. I think there were some contractors here as well. They were working on the sprinkler system."

Miller handed him the sketch. It reminded him of Greg Wilson, a janitor on the graveyard shift.

"Miss Perez, take another look at this. Doesn't it look a little like Wilson?"

"Well, I hadn't noticed it before, but yeah, a little," she agreed.

Not exactly a positive ID, thought Miller. "When will he be in today?"

"He won't," answered Perez. "He only works weekends."

Miller and Westray were in no mood to wait. They were starved for suspects. And Wilson just joined a short list.

With a copy of Wilson's job application in hand, they drove into a hardscrabble neighborhood in south central Los Angeles. It was early evening, and the street was deserted except for the occasional stray dog.

Parked in front of the address on the application, the cops surveyed a wreck of a house. The bungalow was ill-kept, in need of paint and new shutters.

Westray nodded toward the clunker on the front lawn and noted, "Some people like trees and shrubs, some like '65 Fords."

They approached the front door cautiously, the howling of unseen animals getting louder. "Keep alert and stay behind me," Miller said.

"Gotcha."

A young, slender man in cutoff jeans and a USC T-shirt strolled to the door, a German shepherd at his heels.

"Greg Wilson?"

The man eyed the officers for a couple seconds. "Yeah, that's me."

The cops looked at each other. Miller eased his hand from his holster. Westray sighed and gently kicked a rock off the porch. Wilson had a full head of reddish-blond hair and was much younger and taller than the man who cashed the Langlos check.

Wilson's job also required that he patrol around the back of the building once an hour. He remembered passing by Langlos's office window early Sunday morning while taking rubbish out of the building. He failed to check the inside of the complex.

"The lights were out," he said. "And the window was closed."

Wilson studied the sketch that was supposed to be him. "Don't look like anybody I know," he said.

Another wasted trip.

The next day, Tom Lacey strode into the Downey police station. Lacey had gone over every detail of the morning he had found Langlos's body a hundred times. One detail still gnawed at him.

"I still can't figure out what happened to the keys," said Lacey.

"What keys?" The department's percolating coffee pot was the only sound in the room. Miller poured still another cup of coffee into a styrofoam cup. "Want some?"

Lacey shook his head and continued. "The keys to Dr. Langlos's office. The ones I normally used were in a drawer at the reception desk, but that morning they were gone, so I used another set."

"Did you ever find the other keys?"

"No."

"But the office was locked. Right?"

Lacey nodded.

"And the window was closed?"

"Uh-huh."

"Was it locked?"

"I didn't check to see if it was locked."

Lacey had recovered from the initial shock of finding his boss. But the long-term feelings of loss would remain for quite a long time. "Dr. Langlos was one of the nicest, gentlest men I've ever known." Miller nodded. He had heard that description from others but he still had to probe more.

"We didn't find a necktie in the office. What do you make of that?"

"It must have been stolen," Lacey responded. "I worked with him on and off for a year and a half, and I never saw him at work without a tie on. He was very professional about his appearance."

Miller frowned, sipped his coffee, and passed a piece of paper with some sketches on it across his desk. "Recognize him?"

For thirty seconds, Lacey stared at two drawings side by side on the paper. Each caricature was three inches wide and four inches high—identical, except one face had glasses.

Lacey's eyebrows went up. "This looks like Dr. Eugene Hartman. I've never seen him without glasses, but still, this sketch looks like him. He used to be an associate of Dr. Langlos. They worked together for about six months."

Lacey explained that Hartman didn't come around Lakewood anymore, because in August he had been reassigned to three rehab and convalescent hospitals in North Hollywood, Pasadena, and Reseda.

Lacey was barely out the door when Miller began feverishly thumbing through a stack of notes. Eugene Hartman. The widow had mentioned him. Something about a loan.

"Here it is," Miller muttered to himself. "Hartman borrowed two hundred dollars. He wanted five hundred. Doesn't seem like a reason for murder, but you never know."

Miller dialed the Langlos residence, hoping to get an immediate interview with the widow. Thad, one of Ruth's sons, answered. "I think you ought to wait awhile. We just returned from the cemetery." Miller agreed to come to her apartment Monday.

During the weekend, Miller and Westray staked out the Lakewood Health Center looking for anyone meeting the description of the check writer. They interviewed five employees, looking for new clues. Nothing.

In Encino, the cops met with the owner of a contracting company on Ventura Boulevard. Their crew had been scheduled to repair the center's sprinklers on Saturday but didn't go because the superintendent was ill. And they didn't work on Sundays.

At 2:00 A.M., Miller doused his corn flakes with milk. He couldn't sleep. Jack Langlos was on his mind. Between bites, Miller thumbed through a week's worth of notes spread across the kitchen table. Who have we forgotten to interview? Who? His eyes scanned pages of names of co-workers, friends, and others who had been contacted.

He stopped at a copy of the autopsy. "Immediate cause of death: Occlusive coronary artery disease due to arteriosclerosis."

He stared at the composite sketch. The man appeared to be smiling at him. Taunting him.

"What good is this drawing if we can't find the bastard," murmured Miller. He pushed the bowl away in disgust.

That stabbing feeling in the pit of his stomach struck again.

Chapter 5

Arrest at the Oakland Airport

Ruth feared there was a bomb in Jack's car.

Whoever had murdered her husband had been in his car. She was sure of it. Jack always parked behind the Lakewood Park Health Center in a spot reserved for him. Weekdays or weekends, Jack's habits didn't vary. However, police found the car in front of the building and told her she could pick it up once they had checked it out.

On the Monday morning after the funeral, Ruth went to claim the car with her son Jan and her friend Mary Wheeler. She demanded a bomb squad expert check out the car. The car itself was not damaged, but several things had been stolen, including a framed picture of the doctor's symphony.

"Jan and Mary, please take Jack's car home while I go in my car. I just can't touch the same wheel that Jack's murderer touched."

"My mother thinks the car might have been tampered with, so she wants me to drive it," Jan joked on the drive back. "I thought my mother loved me."

"I thought I was her best friend," laughed Mary.

At 3:45 that afternoon, detectives Miller and Westray came to the house and showed Ruth a sketch of a familiar face. "It looks," she paused, "kind of like Dr. Eugene Hartman," she looked questioningly at Miller.

"You're not the only person who thinks so," said Miller.

Ruth nodded, "I hesitated for a minute because I've only seen Hartman one time. We met in Hollywood at a business meeting. He seemed very nervous and left early."

"What was the relationship of your husband to Hartman? Were they together often?" Miller leaned forward.

She met his eyes. "Hartman and Jack were members of the Planned Living Council, a consortium of psychologists and health care workers who serviced several convalescent hospitals in the Los Angeles area. The head of the council, Dr. Harold Slater, had hired Hartman from a help wanted newspaper ad. Hartman was assigned to assist Jack at the Lakewood and later was reassigned to three other facilities."

"What can you tell us about him?"

Ruth tried to think. "There were occasional lunches, Hartman told Jack about his serious financial problems. He complained about his inability to get a lucky break and have the kind of life he thought he deserved. Hartman had hid from the landlady at an apartment in Pasadena and finally skipped out. He couldn't pay the rent."

"What about the loan you mentioned?" Miller mused.

"Dr. Slater had refused to loan Hartman any money, so he came to Jack. I suggested one hundred dollars, but Jack gave him two hundred dollars. He repaid us with a check that bounced."

"Did you ever get the money?" Miller pressed.

Ruth rubbed her aching forehead, "When I wanted to run the check through again, Jack wouldn't let me. 'Don't. I'm afraid to pressure Hartman,' he said without elaborating."

"Was your husband expecting to meet Hartman that Saturday?" Westray inquired.

"Not that I'm aware of. But Jack was expecting a large payment from Blue Shield that Saturday."

"Blue Shield?" Miller repeated quizzically.

"The psychologists received nearly all of their patient fees through Medicare (Blue Shield) and Medi-Cal (State of California)."

"Let me have the two-hundred-dollar check that had been returned," Miller said. Ruth passed it to him and he scrutinized it. Check #119 had been drawn on Hartman's account at the Security National Bank in Pasadena. It was dated December 21, 1975, and had been stamped "Non-Sufficient Funds" by the bank.

"I'd like to keep this check as possible evidence," said Miller.

She nodded her head. As Miller talked, Ruth began to wonder if Dr. Hartman was a suspect in Jack's murder.

"Could Jack have known he was in danger?" Ruth asked suddenly. "My husband had been unusually cautious in the last month. Suddenly, he developed this need to keep closing the curtains on our kitchen window that faced Sunset Boulevard. For years those curtains stayed open. But lately Jack said they should be drawn at night so nobody across the street could see us."

"Anything else?" Miller scratched his chin thoughtfully.

"Well, in the midst of Jack's security concerns, we had a mysterious fire in the garage under our apartment. It started at 4:30 A.M. the Monday before I left for Texas." The blaze had ignited in a trash can containing clothing, paint thinner, and leaves.

Before the detectives had time to comment, Ruth switched to another subject, telling them that Jack had carried rare stamps in his wallet as well as a Lincoln penny with the head stamped off center. But Miller and Westray wouldn't let her off the subject of Hartman.

"Do you know anyone we could contact about Hartman?"

She gave them some names of people who knew Hartman. One was Dr. Slater's bookkeeper, who lived in Hollywood.

"Do you know the last time your husband had contact with Hartman?" Miller asked, rising to leave.

"Jack had a luncheon engagement with Dr. Hartman about three days before he died. Dr. Hartman called and cancelled it. That's when Jack told him about the insurance payment coming Saturday."

For the next several hours, Ruth couldn't get Dr. Eugene Hartman out of her mind. Was he the one? Had he killed Jack? And, if so, for what purpose? Money? Hartman was a professional man. Why would he need money so desperately?

Nothing added up.

◆   ◆   ◆

Cruising toward Tinseltown, Westray was engrossed in a monologue. In his typical shoot-from-the-lip style, Westray fired away while Miller silently maneuvered the black and white patrol car along the freeway.

His second marriage was going to last forever.

When was the weather going to warm up?

The Lakers were going to win their third straight tonight. He had twenty-five dollars that said so.

Miller barely heard a word. He popped Rolaids into his mouth like popcorn, hoping to calm a nervous stomach. He had begun to believe Eugene Hartman was their man. But where was he? Was he even in California?

Westray studied his partner's serious face and frowned. Other officers called Westray "Wimp" in jest because of his rugged, no-nonsense treatment of lawbreakers. Of course, it was anything but no nonsense. For Westray, a day without a laugh was a bad day indeed. He was a perfect foil for a sober partner.

"Michael, you're as serious as a U-boat commander on a torpedo run. What's the matter?"

"Nothing, Wimp."

"Hey, whatever it is, it ain't no big deal," said Westray, slapping Miller on the leg.

A look of anguish came over Miller's face. He tightened his grip on the steering wheel.

"What's wrong?" Westray demanded.

"I can't stand another man touching me!" Miller was obviously shaken.

"What?" Westray was dumbfounded. After a few seconds of silence, Westray spoke in a serious tone he usually reserved for his kids when they were naughty.

"Michael, you're repressing homosexual tendencies. It's going to fuck you all up. Your hair will turn gray overnight. It's time for you to come out of the closet."

Westray reached over and grabbed Miller's leg with two hands. "Let go, you son of a bitch," Miller yelled. The police car swerved. Westray howled. Miller flashed him a dirty look and continued on his route to Franklin Street.

Dr. Slater's bookkeeper identified Hartman from the sketch from Boy's Market and also supplied the names of several other people who could identify Hartman.

On the way back to the police station, Miller was in a more talkative mood.

"Wimp, let's forget the whole thing about the leg. I just don't like to be touched by men, that's all."

"Yeah, okay," said Westray, already plotting how to keep the gag going.

A month later, a man wearing a bell hop uniform would embarrass Miller at the police station by singing to him in a falsetto voice. As the slightly built man plopped into the detective's lap, the other detectives roared. Miller didn't have to ask whose idea it was.

Arriving at police headquarters, Miller and Westray compared the handwriting on the check Hartman had written to Jack Langlos with the signature on the check forged at Boy's Market. There were enough similarities between the *Eugene C. Hartman* and *John T. Langlos* signatures to suggest they were written by the same person.

"It looks like a match. We've got to find Hartman," Miller declared.

Unknown to the Downey detectives, their prime suspect was in police custody at that very moment.

◆ ◆ ◆

On Sunday, February 8, two days after Jack Langlos's funeral, a tall, hunched-over man in a beige leisure suit approached Tim

Spencer, a Pacific Southwest Air Lines ticket agent at the Oakland Airport. It was 10:30 in the morning and traffic was light.

"I bought four discounted plane fares to San Diego at another airport with a MasterCharge. I want to upgrade the tickets." Spencer issued four new tickets and the man paid twenty-three dollars in cash, the difference between discounted and regular airfares.

On the back of the old tickets, the man wrote his name and address: Richard McKinley, 86 Desconso, San Diego.

Five minutes later, McKinley returned and pulled another ticket out of the front pocket of the multi-colored shirt he wore over a yellow T-shirt. "I want a refund for a thirty-two-dollar ticket I bought the day before."

This time his words aroused Spencer's suspicions. Slowly Spencer began writing out the refund check, then pausing, he said matter-of-factly, "By the way, could I see the new tickets I issued a few minutes ago?" He looked at McKinley. "I have to mark them as being purchased with a MasterCharge card," Spencer explained. "I forgot to do that, and without that marking the tickets could be exchanged for a full refund of the face value of $128."

"I'll get them," McKinley said and walked away. A minute later, he returned: "My wife changed her mind. She doesn't want a refund."

"Okay. Do you have the other four tickets? I still need to mark them."

"Unfortunately, I don't have them with me," McKinley responded with a slight smile.

By now, Spencer suspected the customer was trying to pull a scam. Ticket agents had been warned to watch for people trying to collect cash refunds on tickets paid for with charge cards.

"Can I see some identification, sir?"

"I don't have any on me."

"Sir, I'm not going to be able to return this ticket unless I see the other four tickets you upgraded."

McKinley shook his head and began walking away. Spencer contacted airport security. Two blue-uniformed men approached McKinley and asked for his ID. According to his temporary driver's license, the man's real name was Eugene Hartman. They arrested him.

At 7:55 A.M., Hartman gave a statement to Oakland police:

"I met a male caucasian, fifty-five years of age, five-nine, 165 pounds, by the name of Richard McKinley at the Burbank Airport. Mr. McKinley purchased a gin and tonic for me in the early afternoon after we became acquainted. He indicated to me that he was a salesman and that he needed some traveling money. He said he would buy some tickets—a group of them—on his credit card and sell them to me at a discount. I told him that I'd fly from Hollywood-Burbank Airport to San Diego and Hollywood-Burbank Airport to San Francisco. He purchased well over two hundred dollars worth of tickets on a MasterCharge card. I purchased the tickets from him for two hundred dollars in cash. I then drove to San Diego to visit my daughter and flew from San Diego to Oakland to visit my father on Saturday, February 7, 1976."

Hartman declined to admit in his written statement that he had signed for the tickets with the name Richard McKinley. He wanted to talk to a public defender first. But ten minutes after the statement was recorded, Hartman verbally admitted he had signed the back of the airline ticket *Richard McKinley.*

Unable to find any MasterCharge receipts or credit cards in Hartman's belongings, Oakland police had a corpus delecti problem. They couldn't prove Hartman committed a crime.

Six hours after his statement, Hartman was released.

• ◆ •

At about the same time, Miller and Westray made contact with Hartman's employer, Dr. Harold Slater, four hundred miles down the Pacific Coast.

Slater's wife answered the door and directed them to the patio. Seated in a lawn chair, Slater, a tall, gray-haired man whose business of treating patients with mental disabilities had been fruitful enough to earn him a healthy six-figure annual salary, now looked gaunt and strained.

"In August, I turned over much of the psychotherapy program to Jack Langlos." Slater's health was failing and retirement beckoned. "I worked off and on with Langlos for twenty years and trusted him to provide quality care for the patients."

"And Hartman?" Miller asked. "What about his background?"

Slater hunched forward in the chair. His voice was shaky. "He was a licensed psychologist." He paused and went on. "I didn't do any background checks; that didn't seem important. Jack Langlos was so easy-going he could work with just about anybody."

Miller and Westray's eyes met.

Watching them, Slater nodded, "Yeah, well, in a couple of months, I also knew I had made a mistake."

"In what way?" Miller asked.

"Hartman is a deadbeat," Slater told him. "He's been floating bad checks. In fact, Hartman recently stole my Cadillac." He frowned. "I notified the Pasadena police, but they haven't been able to locate Hartman."

Slater added, "I warned Langlos about that guy. Underneath the pretentious smile, Hartman was always jealous of Jack."

Chapter 6

One Hundred Ways to Disappear

Westray strode into the police station, nursing a large Coke from lunch.

"Hey, Wimp, you close on the 187?" said Patrol Officer Jim Steinhouse. Although only a rookie, Steinhouse dreamt of working with Westray on a big case. He had heard stories of how Westray dealt with scum. In Westray's beefy paws, a flashlight was like a brush to Picasso. No need to go toe to toe when a solid whack would suffice. Talk didn't gain the respect of street punks. Cold steel and aluminum did.

A 187. In police jargon, it was a badge of honor. The 187 penal code in the State of California dealt with the big crime: murder. For a cop who spent most of his time chasing down juvenile thugs, 187 had a nice ring.

"Kid, he has one leg in the big slammer already," Westray said. "He just don't know it yet."

Westray gazed intently at a handwritten message. "Sergeant Ron Mitchell, Fraud Detail, Oakland P.D., called. Eugene Hartman was released from their custody at 1400 hours yesterday.

Hartman had used a MasterCharge card belonging to Jack Langlos to buy tickets from Los Angeles Airport to San Francisco. He was arrested trying to make some type of fraud exchange on the tickets."

Westray fired the paper cup in the wastebasket with one hand and picked up the phone with the other. "Son of a bitch."

Sergeant Mitchell briefed Westray on the ticket exchange and Hartman's statement. "I was going to go for a warrant as soon as we got the credit cards or the receipts."

"Do you have an address on him up there?" Westray asked.

"I have a bunch of addresses, but he was extremely uncooperative. The guy's a clinical psychologist. I felt he was giving me a bunch of Freud as I was sitting there. At any rate, he indicates that when he is in the Los Angeles area he stays at the Monte Carlo Motel. I went through his wallet and found some other addresses. Let me give you one for one of his brothers, too. Supposedly this brother's a painting contractor in Salinas and Hartman stays with him when he's in Northern California. So Hartman says."

Westray jotted down three addresses and three phone numbers for Hartman. But he wasn't hopeful his suspect would be waiting to chat with police.

"Hartman did call me this morning and asked me for his temporary driver's license back," said Mitchell. "I refused to give it to him, because it's evidence."

"Do you think he'll call back?"

"I kind of doubt it."

"If he does come in, you can hold him for us for investigation of 187," Westray said.

"In your case, wasn't there some kind of theft of a wallet?" Mitchell asked.

"Yes, it's missing," said Westray. "But we don't know if it was stolen. We've got a forty-page investigation report on this already. His wallet didn't happen to be a green plaid wallet?"

"No. It was an old, dirty brown one. And there was no MasterCharge card either."

"Did you notice anything in the name of John Langlos?"

"I really wasn't looking for that. I figured I probably had a fraud, and I wanted to get as much future ID as possible for when I was able to prove it."

Mitchell provided the number for Hartman's Sears credit card that was found in the wallet.

Westray sighed, "We're not even sure he's a psychologist. If he was, he was working at a pretty menial level for a professional his age."

Mitchell shook his head. "I'm pretty sure he is, he had a license for the Board of Medical Examiners, State of California. He told me he had a masters degree in clinical psychology."

"Does he walk stoop-shouldered?"

"I didn't notice that. He has a receding hairline, beard, the whole bit."

"Did he wear glasses?"

"Yeah."

"All right. We're going to issue an all-points. If you run across him, we'd appreciate an arrest. We'll come right up and get him."

"Sure thing, we'll let you know."

Within hours, an all-points bulletin alerted Bay Area police agencies that Hartman was a murder suspect.

The next afternoon, Hartman was sitting patiently on a bench in a Greyhound bus depot in San Jose. The 1:45 bus to Salinas was going to be ten minutes late.

Leaning back with his eyes closed, Hartman appeared to be trying to relax. Perhaps he was dwelling on his life. The past few years had been meagre and penny-pinching. For someone so intelligent and talented to be constantly hounded by money problems was demeaning, especially while men like Jack Langlos seemed to have everything come so easily—an excellent job, an abundance of patients, a beautiful wife. Everything that Hartman himself had never had, everything that fate had denied him.

"Mr. Hartman? Mr. Eugene Hartman?"

The voice startled him. His eyes flashed open. He looked up to see two men in blue uniforms staring at him. "You're wanted for questioning in the death of Jack Langlos. Please come with us." Standing up, Hartman's expression was somewhere between a grimace and a grin. The two San Jose detectives carried Hartman's suitcase and garment bag as they escorted him out of the terminal.

Because they had no warrants for Hartman, San Jose police turned him over to the police in nearby Hayward. He was booked on suspicion of murder and fraud.

Miller and Downey Sergeant Fred Clinton didn't have far to go to get their suspect. Both were attending a police seminar on investigative techniques in San Jose when Steinhouse paged them.

On February 13, two weeks after the death of Jack Langlos, Miller could lay off the Rolaids. At 8:55 A.M., the two Downey cops moved Hartman from the Hayward police station. Hartman had agreed to fly with the officers from San Jose to Los Angeles. He would be interrogated in Downey.

Arriving there in handcuffs, flanked by the two policemen, Hartman was escorted down the hall to the interview room at the sparsely furnished Downey station. The bare walls surrounded a scarred wooden table and a few steel folding chairs. There was a tape recorder on the table. If suspects felt depressed in here, so be it. The room wasn't built for atmosphere.

Westray and Miller's background check had revealed that Eugene Hartman was a man with a troubled past. Born on August 10, 1928, Hartman had spent most of his life thirsting for success. Try as he might, he had not as yet quenched that thirst.

Hartman had spent two unremarkable years in the Army as a clerk typist and parachutist. He had held several teaching jobs but lost them all through firing or layoffs. His ventures into private practice in psychology never seemed to take off either. While others like Jack Langlos expanded their practices, Hartman fought to keep his from shrinking.

His personal life was no less disastrous. His first wife had committed suicide, and he was divorced from his second wife. He lived alone and hardly saw his daughter. If that wasn't bad enough, Hartman didn't measure up to the success of his brothers. One was a successful painting contractor in Salinas, the other an officer with Naval Intelligence in San Diego. He was a forty-seven-year-old black sheep, and he acted the part.

• ◆ •

Miller and Westray had learned that on February 1, with cash in his pocket and a charge card, Hartman went on a spending spree. He purchased three Pacific Southwest Air Lines tickets at the Long Beach Airport. The flights were one-way from L.A. to Oakland and San Diego at a total cost of $79.50. The bill was charged to Langlos's MasterCharge card, but a major blunder was nearly committed. The charge slip was first signed "Eug—," then the name "Jack" was written over it.

After cashing the one-hundred-dollar check at Boy's Market, Hartman bought three more flight tickets at Los Angeles Airport. This time he signed the slip "John T. Langlos."

Hartman then bought three PSA flight tickets at the Hollywood-Burbank Airport for thirty dollars apiece. The tickets were for one-way flights to Lake Tahoe. Hartman told the ticket agent he planned to use the tickets later in the week. Again, he used the Langlos MasterCharge card.

From there, Hartman swung by Zody's Department Store on North San Fernando Road in Burbank. In the jewelry department, he charged a new watch: a stylish Pultrom VIP digital model, gold with a black face. It cost $56.29 including tax.

Store employees later found the Langlos MasterCharge card along with the Langlos Saks Fifth Avenue card on the floor. The MasterCharge, with a January 31, 1976, expiration, was returned to the Langlos bank and the Saks card was sent to the Langlos home. Langlos's new MasterCharge, effective February 1, was still missing.

Before nightfall, Hartman made a last stop in Azusa, another community in the Los Angeles sprawl. Since mid-January, Hartman had been renting a room at the Monte Carlo Motel on East Arrow Highway. He made his last payment on the room on February 1 and left for San Diego.

For three weeks, Hartman had left no impression on the motel manager. He hadn't talked to the manager or anyone else. The only thing the manager knew was that Hartman lived in San Diego. At least that was the information Hartman supplied when checking in. Hartman's residence seemed to change with the weather.

Now they headed for the interrogation room. Walking up to Hartman, Miller read him his Miranda rights.

"I understand my rights," said Hartman smiling grimly. "I want to see a public defender."

"Do you want to make any phone calls?" asked Miller.

"Not right now," Hartman said, grinning again.

Fingerprinted and booked, Hartman was put in a cell. "All that goofy-looking shit does is grin," Westray told an officer in the booking area. The officer laughed. But Westray didn't mean the remark as a wisecrack. He was too angry to joke.

Miller's spirits were no better as he dialed the phone.

"Mrs. Langlos, we've arrested Hartman, but we're not sure we have the right person in jail," said Miller. "He's refusing to talk so far."

Another of Ruth's friends, Glenda Hillman, was with her, and Ruth told her the news. Glenda looked as though she had just heard tragic news.

"Let's get out of here fast!" Hillman declared. Without explanation, she rushed Ruth to the Miramar Hotel in Santa Monica. There she said, "Look, Ruth, if Jack's killer is still free, your life is in danger. And anyone around you is taking a big risk, too."

The thought plagued Ruth most of the night until she fell into a troubled sleep.

The next morning when Ruth awoke, she couldn't move. "I'm paralyzed," she cried out and dialed her doctor's number.

"Ruth, you can walk now," her doctor said in a stern voice over the phone. "Get out of bed and walk."

His order shocked Ruth into reality. She did as she was told, got up and walked. The doctor sent some medication over, but the best medicine came when Ruth called the Downey police department.

"There's no doubt anymore," Miller said. "We've got the right guy."

Hartman still wasn't talking, but his secrets were trickling out nevertheless.

"Wimp, look at this," said Miller. Going through Hartman's things, he pointed to four paperback books buried in Hartman's suitcase.

Westray picked up each one, scrutinized the cover, and read the title aloud.

"*One Hundred Ways to Disappear and Live Free.*"

"*The Paper Trip: Everything You Ever Wanted to Know about Disappearing but Couldn't Learn Until Now.*"

"*How to Beat the Bill Collector.*"

"*Credit.*"

"Wonder if he's read any books on committing the perfect murder," said Westray.

Miller searched for more goodies. He rifled through five cancelled checks on Hartman's account at Security Pacific National Bank. Included were seven service charge tickets for checks returned unpaid due to insufficient funds. The bank had requested an explanation.

"What a work of art this guy is," Miller said sarcastically.

Two letters wedged in Hartman's papers also interested them. One, dated January 15, 1976, written by Jack Langlos, requested Hartman contact him immediately. The other came from the Arcadia Police Department regarding a $79.91 check Hartman had given to Sav-on Drug Store. The letter warned Hartman that a criminal charge could be filed against him for writing a bad check. Hartman was asked to contact the police.

Westray pulled a multi-colored paisley tie from the suitcase. "Hey, maybe this is the missing tie," he said, holding it up.

After interviewing Hartman, Downey public defender Jim Smith gave police the proverbial good news and bad news: "Hartman will fill out the handwriting analysis cards like you want. But he won't talk about the case."

"Counselor, tell your client his jig's up," said Westray. By this time he was convinced they had the right man. He was beginning to think that it was not only Langlos's money Hartman had wanted, it was his identity, his respectability, his life.

Two days later, dark, craggy-featured Downey Lieutenant Rick Trombley picked at the soggy egg roll on his paper plate. Amid cartons of Chinese takeout were manilla folders marked "Case No. 76-1914, Langlos, John T." The suspected murderer remained sequestered 150 feet away.

Trombley had spend a few hours on the periphery of the Jack Langlos case, mostly doing background checks and interviews. He had seen enough to be smitten with the elegant widow. She was a classy, long-stemmed rose with blonde hair, a shapely figure, and red, luscious lips. She reminded Trombley of Faye Dunaway.

He telephoned her to come to the station house, then Trombley thumbed through a series of police interviews from earlier in the week. He perused the statement of a convalescent hospital administrator in North Hollywood between sips of hot tea. The woman said Hartman had been fired three months before for attempting to cash the check of a senile elderly patient. Hartman had conned the patient out of her check, the administrator said. Hartman had counseled patients there for two months before the incident.

"He sure wears out his welcome fast," Trombley murmured. The phone rang. Trombley picked it up.

"Mrs. Langlos is here to see you," said the cadet at the front desk.

Trombley didn't relish the meeting at all. He preferred beautiful women in the sack, not in the police station. During his twenty-five years on the force, Trombley had said his oath to uphold the law also included a pledge to screw every attractive woman he could. He was only half-kidding.

Fulfilling that pledge had cost him a couple marriages. Man was not made to be monogamous, he rationalized. But even Trombley realized the limits of good taste. Jack Langlos's widow was still grieving. She was off limits—for today anyway.

◆ ◆ ◆

Walking into the police station with her friend Laura Richter, Ruth was confused. She didn't understand why Lieutenant Trombley wanted to meet her this Sunday afternoon. He had been vague on the phone, something about more evidence in the case. Laura sat down while Ruth walked up to the front desk where a smooth-faced young cadet sat, and told him, "I'm here to see Lieutenant Trombley."

The cadet pointed down the hall. "First room," he said.

Slowly Ruth edged into the huge, dreary, windowless room filled with rows of empty desks. Few lights were on. Ruth shivered. It was eerie to see a police station without police. From the back of the room Trombley called, "I'm over here, Mrs. Langlos."

She walked toward him. Motioning Ruth to sit down, Trombley began to ask questions. He was much more aggressive in his questioning than Miller or Westray. For two hours without any breaks he grilled Ruth on numerous subjects. Many of his questions covered the same ground Miller and Westray had, but some made no sense to her.

"Have you seen this before, Mrs. Langlos?" he asked, pulling an ugly brown billfold from a bag behind the desk.

She shook her head. "No. My husband's billfold was green plaid with green trim on the outside."

Lieutenant Trombley held up a tie. "Seen this before?"

"No. I hate paisley."

"Do you know this woman?" He passed her a photograph.

Ruth studied the Polaroid for a minute. "I've never seen her before. Do you think she had something to do with Jack's death?"

Seemingly paying no attention to her question, Trombley rushed on. "What about these motel bills?" Trombley said. He slid a quarter-inch-thick pile of receipts across the desk.

Ruth started studying the bills, not knowing what she was really looking for.

"Why would Dr. Hartman have all these motel bills?" Trombley pressed.

"How would you expect me to know?" She was irritated. "I already told the police I only met Hartman one time."

"Where does Hartman live?"

"As far as I know, in Pasadena."

Hartman, Hartman, Hartman. Ruth felt she must have heard that name a hundred times before Trombley shut off the tape recorder. Her mouth was dry and she felt terribly tired.

Driving back home, Ruth recapped the meeting for Laura, who was silent most of the way.

When Laura turned the car into Ruth's street, Ruth looked at her questioningly. "Laura, if they want to know more about Hartman, why don't they contact his family, his friends, the people he worked with?"

Laura pulled into the driveway, turned off the motor, and turned toward her friend, "Ruth, I think you're a suspect."

"What!" Ruth said astonished. "You what?"

Laura bit her lip. "They're acting like they think you and Hartman could be lovers." She looked sadly at Ruth. "Maybe they think you were out of town to set up an alibi. Maybe they think there's some kind of conspiracy. I don't know. It's crazy."

Ruth was stunned. She had cooperated with the investigation every step of the way. Surely the police knew she loved Jack. "How could they suspect me? How?" She crumpled up in the car, lowered her head to her chest, and cried.

Chapter 7

Accepting a D.A.'s Dare

Miller and Westray had reached the end of the tunnel. Three bits of evidence matched nicely with their other findings bringing light.

The right middle fingerprint of Hartman matched a latent print lifted from the inside top of the wooden window frame in Dr. Langlos's office.

The Boy's Market clerk who had cashed the forged one-hundred-dollar check had identified Hartman's photograph in a lineup of six photographs.

And the coup de grace: a handwriting expert from the county crime lab had positively matched Hartman's writing with the forged signatures of Jack Langlos.

Miller and Westray had motive: money and envy. They had means: the window. They had evidence: bloody crime scene, forgeries, and a positive ID.

They also had a decent working relationship with Peter Thompson, a deputy district attorney for Los Angeles County. Thompson was the filing prosecutor for the Downey court. He didn't try the cases, but it was his job to separate the wheat from the chaff. Victories in court translated into smiles and fattened careers; losses translated into a career of hassling petty thieves and punks on a track headed nowhere.

Red-haired, stocky Thompson was no different than the other nine hundred deputy district attorneys in the world's second largest prosecutor's office. He liked to win. Still, Miller and Westray thought he was a reasonable guy—at least for a prosecutor.

"Gentlemen, it looks like we have theft, credit card fraud, and forgery here," said Thompson, ushering the Downey detectives into a spartan office at the court. The room barely had enough space for a desk, two file drawers, and chairs.

"And a 187," declared Westray.

"A homicide? We can't prove that," answered Thompson, fumbling for a file on his desk. "The coroner said Jack Langlos died a natural death from a heart attack."

"Bloodiest heart attack I've ever seen. Just look at those pictures of the death scene, Pete," said Westray.

"It doesn't matter what I think or what you think," Thompson said. "It's what we can prove to a jury. You know that."

"Pete, this guy was beaten up pretty bad and robbed," said Miller, figuring the deputy District Attorney was fishing for a compromise. "Maybe we go for second-degree and say he had a heart attack caused by a struggle. There've been convictions for attack-induced heart attacks."

"My theory is this guy—what's his name, Hartman—walked in on Langlos, saw him on the ground, and decided to take the credit cards and the wallet," Thompson said, running his fingers through his thinning hair.

"And the blood?" Westray asked sarcastically.

"The coroner didn't have a problem with that. The guy had a heart attack, became disoriented, and hit his head on the desk."

Westray couldn't believe his ears. The D.A.'s office actually was going to back off the murder charge.

"Yeah, Langlos came down on his head, then bounced off the wall a few times, sat in his chair, picked up the phone and dropped," declared Westray. He paused and his voice gathered

56

strength. "Then for good measure, he picked up the desk and plopped it on his head. I guess you're right, he was damned disoriented."

Thompson wasn't in the mood for Westray's sarcasm. "There's reasonable doubt here," he said curtly. "All the defense has to do is say he came in the room and found the guy dead on the floor. Or they're going to say Langlos gave Hartman the cards and the check before the heart attack. They'll portray Hartman as an educated man with no history of violence."

"That's a crock and you know it," said Westray, his voice rising. "There's a thin line between genius and ding-dong, and I think this guy crossed it long ago. Give us a filing for 187 and we'll get you a conviction."

"The answer is no."

"No?" Westray, whose IQ was 142, felt his intelligence was being questioned by the prosecutor's theories. Westray studied Thompson's determined face as he spoke. In his mid-thirties, Thompson aspired to head the D.A.'s district office in Norwalk, one of nine in the county. He wouldn't get there by filing cases that ended up in not guilty verdicts at taxpayers' expense.

This wasn't about justice; this was about winning, Westray thought. He thought the man across the desk from him in the impeccable dark gray suit was balking because he was concerned about his image in the prosecutor's office.

"Get me more evidence and we'll go for the 187," Thompson said. "Right now, we'll charge for forgery and grand theft."

"Pete, have you talked this over with Norwalk?" Miller asked, referring to Thompson's boss at the district office, Joe Schafer.

"It was brought up at a meeting yesterday," Thompson said. "The general consensus was that we don't have a case for murder with the way the coroner's report reads."

"Langlos was expecting a big check from Blue Shield that Saturday, Pete," Miller explained. "Hartman knew that and he was desperate for money."

"Mike, it's not enough," Thompson interrupted. "If we go to court, we're going to get our asses kicked."

On the short drive back to the station, Westray continued to fume.

"You know what he wants. He wants a signed confession, twelve witnesses, and a smoking gun."

"Mike, I'm disappointed too, but he's got a legitimate point," said Miller. "If we file now and Hartman's acquitted, there's double jeopardy; Hartman's home free. We've somehow got to find more evidence."

"Like I said, he won't be satisfied until we have a signed confession," Westray smirked. "And that guy Hartman hasn't said two words to us. He just grins like he knows how screwed up the system is."

"Calm down. Getting p.o.'d at Thompson isn't going to solve anything. We've still got to work with him."

"You think I'm upset?" Westray said. "Wait till Mrs. Langlos hears that her husband's suspected murderer won't be charged. You explain why, partner."

◆ ◆ ◆

Ruth thought there had been a cruel mistake. Hartman was charged with five crimes: forgery of a check at Boy's Market, two counts of forgery of a credit card sales slip at Zody's and Pacific Southwest Airlines, and two counts of grand theft. The first count was for stealing her husband's wallet containing at least $150, credit cards, two checks, a collector's coin, and rare stamps. The second was for using her husband's property to cheat and defraud the airlines.

Her husband's possessions had been taken from him. More important, so had his life. Yet there was no mention of that. Miller, Westray, Hernandez, and every cop who saw Jack's battered body in his office said it was a murder. Now, some deputy District Attorney who had never been there decided to overlook it, as though convicting Hartman for forgery and theft would make things square.

Ruth called Thompson. "Mr. Thompson, why did you drop the 187 P.C.?" Ruth said, getting right to the point.

"Mrs. Langlos, there's not enough evidence to proceed at this time," he said.

If Ruth could have reached through the phone lines and shook him, she would have. "I'm going to reopen this case."

"Mrs. Langlos, you're very upset."

"You better believe I'm upset. It had to be a homicide. My medical friends say there was too much bleeding for it to be a heart attack."

"The coroner says it was. Mrs. Langlos," he paused, "I've got a meeting now . . ."

"My husband was killed and you've got a meeting. Mr. Thompson, if you won't do your job, then I will. Go to your meeting. I'm going to reopen the case."

"I just dare you to!" said Thompson. No outsider would tell him what he would and wouldn't do. Not even a distraught widow.

A week later, on February 27, Ruth testified at a preliminary hearing. The courtroom at the Los Angeles County Municipal Court in Downey was smaller than she had envisioned. Everybody seemed closer together than they appeared on television.

Hartman never took his eyes off Ruth. When she took the stand, he continued to stare. But if he was trying to psyche her out, it didn't work. Ruth was prepared.

The day before, Ruth and Jan had visited attorney Todd Bolton, a former prosecutor, for tips on how to testify in a hostile environment. Ruth's biggest fear was that Hartman's attorney would intimidate her and then twist everything she said to suit his purpose.

"Mrs. Langlos, you don't have to answer a question with a yes or no," Bolton had said. "If you don't like the way they've asked a question, you ask them to please restate or rephrase it. Just say you can't answer the question the way it's been asked."

"And don't use words like *perhaps* or *maybe*. Be firm in what you say. Don't leave any doubt."

Bolton's words rang in Ruth's ears as she peered at a credit card slip. "No, that is not Jack's handwriting," she testified, emphasizing Jack's name. Ruth put her right hand up along the side of her face to block out Hartman.

"He never made a *T* that way, and he never made an *L* that way."

Ruth had no doubt that Eugene Hartman had murdered her husband and forged his signature. She was going to make sure that no one else doubted it either.

Hartman was arraigned on the charges. His bail was reduced from twenty thousand dollars to five thousand dollars. Hartman's brother, an official with U.S. Navy Intelligence, guaranteed his brother's appearance at trial.

Hartman was free on bond, with the help of his family. Meanwhile, Ruth's husband was dead. The police and prosecutors felt powerless. So did she. But she had to do something, find someone to help her.

♦ ◆ ♦

Keith Rogers looked more like a senior accountant than a private eye. In his mid-sixties, Rogers, a quiet, distinguished gentleman with neatly combed gray hair, wore well-tailored suits. At five-foot-ten and 160 pounds, Rogers was hardly an imposing physical specimen.

Ruth had met Rogers several years before when she was the director of the Loretta Young School in Pasadena. The school was filled with aspiring young models and actresses. A client had hired Rogers to find a Lee Remick lookalike for a commercial and Rogers hoped to do so at the school. Ruth couldn't help Rogers that day, but they had a nice chat.

Desperately needing an investigator, Ruth remembered his cool assurance. She had only met him once, but that was once more than anyone she would find in the yellow pages. She knew the knock on private detectives: big fees and little work. But she had to take a chance.

Fortunately, Keith Rogers also knew the knock on private detectives and was dedicated to upgrading the profession. He had founded his agency in 1947, written two books on investigations, and lectured around the world.

More importantly, Rogers had a wealth of good sources. One

week after the preliminary hearing, Ruth handed him an advance check of one thousand dollars with a simple order: "I want to know everything you can find out about Dr. Eugene Clarence Hartman."

Ruth couldn't stand being alone waiting for Hartman's trial, so she stayed with her son Jan's family in Texas. In mid-March, a letter from Rogers perked her spirits. A source was having dinner with the Downey chief of police and would try to get an update on the murder investigation.

"I will keep you informed. In the meantime, be quiet as a mouse," Rogers wrote in closing.

The mission wasn't accomplished. The chief was non-committal except to say the investigation was under control. Another closed door without a crevice of light exposed.

Meanwhile, in Norwalk, Joe Spelling, the deputy D.A., was losing control. Spelling knew the meeting wasn't going to go well as soon as Bruce Whiting strutted into his office whistling and carrying a box of jelly doughnuts.

As far as public defenders go, Whiting wasn't a bad guy in Spelling's book. Whiting took his role as watchdog seriously, but he was reasonable to deal with. At thirty years of age, Whiting, pleasingly plump and baby-faced, had settled into a comfortable niche in the public defender's office. He didn't aspire to the long hours and uncertainties of private practice. Regular hours meant more time to tee it up on the golf course.

At least he wasn't one of those bleeding-heart liberals that saw a police conspiracy behind every case. For that alone, Spelling was appreciative.

"I think Thompson overcharged this one," said Whiting, raspberry donut filling smudged on his upper lip. "You've got one case of forgery, if that."

"Your client is lucky we didn't go for murder," Spelling retorted, trying to wear his best poker face.

"C'mon, Joe, you know better than that. This guy Hartman is a college graduate with no priors. Didn't you read the coroner's report? We have a heart attack here."

Whiting's cockiness troubled Spelling. He leaned forward in

his chair, his face tightening.

Whiting smiled, "Listen, Joe, here's my client's story: He admits signing Dr. Langlos's signature to a check for a hundred dollars at Boy's Market, but he claims Langlos gave him the check as well as his ID because Langlos didn't want his wife to know about the transaction."

"Chrissakes, Bruce, is that the best he can do?" Spelling sputtered.

Whiting smiled again and licked his gooey fingers. "He says the doctor died the next day but he didn't find out until twelve days later. Hartman cashed the check and went to stay with his girlfriend in Azusa. Hartman says Langlos gave him another check to use to close out the account except for two hundred dollars. But he didn't go through with it."

"And why not?" Spelling was getting annoyed.

"He says he chickened out."

"Oh, chickened out. This client of yours has a vivid imagination. Maybe he should be a storyteller on kids' TV."

"He claims Langlos had a similar arrangement with another doctor," said Whiting, ignoring Spelling. "Hartman say Langlos was going to give him three hundred dollars for his share, because Langlos knew my client needed the money."

"Is that the end of the story?"

"My client is very willing to make restitution. He plans to check himself into the Veterans Administration Hospital in San Diego for depression. He's got multiple sclerosis, you know. He says he's contemplated suicide but didn't follow through because it would traumatize his daughter."

Spelling studied his adversary for a moment before continuing. He didn't want to go to trial if he could avoid it. His caseload was bulging with a rash of B&Es and aggravated assaults. He didn't want to waste too much time with forgeries and theft from a dead man.

"Okay, your client pleads guilty to forgery and grand theft and we go for a light sentence because it's his first time," Spelling deadpanned.

"Try one of these raspberry ones, Joe. They're great with a

cup of coffee."

Whiting smiled once again. *He's smiling too damn much,* Spelling thought.

"We'll plead guilty to forgery and you drop the rest. But no state prison time."

"Your client's story is a downright lie," Spelling fumed.

"Maybe and maybe not. Can you prove that Langlos didn't give him the check? The only reason my client is willing to plead guilty to anything is to avoid the negative publicity of a trial."

"I'll have to get approval for this," Spelling said, "but I can tell you right now we want this guy to spend some jail time for what he did."

◆ ◆ ◆

Keith Rogers's call woke Ruth from a nap. She hadn't been able to sleep through a night peacefully since Jack's death.

"Ruth, Hartman's trial is Tuesday morning."

"Why didn't the police or court contact me? They have my phone number and address here at Jan's house. I'm supposed to testify," Ruth said.

"That's strange. Maybe they think their case is so strong they don't need to put you on the stand. Anyway, when you arrive, we have some information to share with you about Hartman." Rogers paused for a couple seconds and added, "I think we have a bad boy here."

◆ ◆ ◆

On the day before the trial, one of Rogers's agents picked Ruth up at the airport and took her to the Los Angeles Hilton. She was too scared to stay at the apartment. She checked in as Janice Revere and met with the hotel's security manager.

At 8:20 A.M. the detective who escorted Ruth in noticed a man that resembled Hartman sitting in the courtroom. As Ruth approached the court bailiff to ask why she hadn't received a subpoena, Ruth stood face to face with the man.

It was Hartman. He had shaved, gotten a haircut, and dressed in a dark suit. He had changed his appearance dramatically, but she knew him immediately.

The hearing turned out to be a private, four-way conversation among the judge, two attorneys, and Hartman in the judge's chambers. Ruth found out she was plenty naïve. It was the first time she had heard of a plea bargain. She had expected Hartman to be convicted of all the charges.

When they emerged from the chambers, the judge read only one charge against Hartman: forgery.

Ruth looked at him in astonishment.

"You understand, Mr. Hartman, when you plead guilty you won't have a trial," the judge declared.

"Yes."

"You have waived your constitutional rights. Did you want to do that?"

"Yes."

"Is your plea freely and voluntarily given?"

"Yes."

On cue, Spelling took his turn. "Then Mr. Hartman, to Information Number A-439807, which charges you in Count 1 with forgery, a felony, in violation of Section 470 of the California Penal Code, to that crime, how do you plead?"

"Guilty," said Hartman matter-of-factly. The deal was done in less than a half-hour.

The crime was punishable by one to fourteen years in the state penitentiary, but part of the plea was a promise that Hartman's sentence would be a maximum of one year in the county jail.

Crestfallen, Ruth left the courtroom. Hartman was waiting for her in the hallway. He stared at Ruth and smirked. She didn't know whether to cry or yell. She was so confused at what had transpired.

The next day, more devastating news arrived. A deputy attorney general from the office of Attorney General Evelle Younger wrote to say they would not intervene in the murder probe as Ruth had requested.

The letter concluded: "In light of the coroner's report that Dr. Langlos died of a heart attack and the lack of evidence connecting Dr. Hartman to the death of your husband . . . the evidence is insufficient to warrant a homicide complaint against Dr. Hartman."

On May 4, it was almost a repeat performance in front of Judge Ralph Biggerstaff in Superior Court in Norwalk.

A frustrated Spelling made an objection. The probation report had recommended Hartman receive three years probation and credit for the jail time served.

"I would think that the defendant should have a felony sentence," Spelling reasoned. "I think he should be on probation for at least a period of five years and should be given substantial time in the county jail because, your honor, he somehow, someway from the deceased doctor's person or personal effects took the checks plus the credit cards. It seems to me that it was a well-thought-out, well-planned situation and not just a fluke. It just seems to me in all honesty because of what the crime had to take, he had to think it out and there is a loss to the victim."

Whiting predictably pled for leniency. "Your honor, Mr. Hartman is forty-seven years old. He has never been in jail before. He did thirty-four days in jail, and for him that was an extremely long time. The probation report concludes that the defendant was doing well in his career in Minnesota until he lost his job and suffered severe marital problems, and as the court knows, he is suffering from multiple sclerosis. The probation officer opines that this may have been the cause of the lack of judgment. I think we have to look at the man's entire life," Whiting concluded.

Judge Ralph Biggerstaff gave Hartman the benefit of the doubt. The sentence was relatively light: five years probation, no more jail time outside the thirty-four days served, a fine of fifteen hundred dollars, and five hundred dollars in attorney fees to be paid fifty dollars a month.

"He is to have no blank checks in his possession," the judge added. "He is not to have any bank account upon which he can write or draw a check."

Biggerstaff eyed the man before him. He had carefully thought out a warning.

"Now I want to advise you, Mr. Hartman, I am sentencing you on the basis of what you did, not on what the suspicions of the police department are. But I want to advise you that even though you have no record, you are a suspect, and if you get in any trouble, I will have no hesitancy in sending you to state prison. Do you understand that?"

"I understand that," Hartman said smiling.

◆ ◆ ◆

Ruth didn't understand a thing. The man who killed her husband was free. What about justice for all? Where was the justice for a decent, loving man like Jack Langlos?

Learning of Hartman's dark background didn't ease her mind. By pounding the pavement and plodding through court files, Rogers had produced a troubling portrait. Amazingly, Rogers had accumulated enough information for a fifty-four-page report. For a total cost of twenty-five hundred dollars, she had paid for a horror story.

Each page seemed to contain a new revelation:

• Hartman's checking account had a zero balance. The average balance during the three prior months was six dollars.

• Mt. San Antonio Junior College in California had filed a civil lawsuit in 1962 against Hartman to dismiss him as a teacher. It cited three reasons: immoral conduct, unprofessional conduct, and his being unfit for service. The complaint alleged that Hartman had sexual relations with Betty Childress, a married woman, and gave her capsules to abort the resulting pregnancy. He also was accused of impregnating another student. After a lengthy trial, the judge ruled Hartman could not be dismissed.

A year later, the college filed for a new trial. A different judge ruled there was sufficient cause to suspend Hartman from his teaching duties.

• Hartman's first wife, Barbara Jean Hartman, committed suicide on December 3, 1961. She had inhaled natural gas from an oven and died of asphyxia, according to the death certificate. Dr. Thomas Noguchi had performed the autopsy.

Barbara Jean Hartman's body was cremated. Sixteen days after his wife died, Eugene Hartman wed Betty Childress in Tlaxco, Mexico. The wedding occurred two days after Childress had gotten a divorce in Mexico.

Two weeks after the sentencing, Ruth had an appointment with Dr. Benjamin Crossman, a thanatologist at UCLA. Crossman headed a behavioral lab on life threatening behavior.

"Your safety could be in jeopardy, Mrs. Langlos," he said, "especially if you continue to pursue the investigation."

"I can't just walk away knowing Jack was murdered. I have to keep pushing the police and the D.A. or they'll forget about the case."

"Maybe you need a fresh start," the doctor said. "Have you considered moving to the East Coast? You could change your name. You'd be safe there."

Ruth raised her chin in that determined, defiant way she had had since a child. "My name and family heritage are an important part of me. I have no desire to disown my roots. I am willing to risk my life for justice."

Chapter 8

The Life of a P.K.

When Ruth Baker was born on an eighty-two-acre farm in Hollanburg, Ohio, about forty miles outside Dayton, her parents rejoiced. She was the girl her father, Reverend Jesse Baker, and his wife, Mella, had eagerly anticipated after having four boys. The town was barely big enough to earn mention on the local map. Her father was a school teacher and the minister of the Church of the Brethren.

From day one she was a P.K., a preacher's kid.

Every morning, the family gathered for worship. Her mother would put on a prayer veil and her father would read from the Bible. Then all the family members would kneel for prayer.

When she was ten, they moved to nearby West Manchester, a conservative small town nestled among a maze of similar communities. Their lives revolved around the church. On Sunday, it was Sunday school and services in the morning and evening. On Wednesday night, there was a prayer meeting. Nearly every week there was a church event: socials, council meetings, communion services, and the annual two-week revival meetings, as well as the weekly Ladies' Aid Society gathering, which Ruth attended with her mother.

Ruth's parents raised their daughter with help from the entire congregation. She never had a baby sitter; church members and relatives were always available. But most times, her parents took her to the church functions. Ruth was a regular at weddings, funerals, and visits to the sick.

From the very beginning, death was a real part of Ruth's life. She went to so many funerals that she became an official mourner of sorts. Ruth was so sensitive that she cried almost on cue. One time, the family members became hysterical during the service. So did Ruth.

As she sobbed, she murmured to herself: "I don't even know who died."

"Why are you crying so hard, Ruth?" a church regular asked her, snuggling Ruth in her arms.

"Because everybody else is."

Her father openly discussed death without reservations. He wasn't afraid of it. His only fear concerning funerals was his car.

An automobile is critical to a minister, but ministers always have money problems. So the Bakers always had a car with many years and plenty of miles on it. Whenever Ruth's father had to conduct a funeral, he would worry. A breakdown or flat tire would be critical in a funeral procession. Before every funeral he endlessly checked the old car, and Ruth's brothers would wash and wax it. Next to the Bible, the car was her father's most important possession.

He also was fond of poetry. He closed every graveside service and sermon with a poetry reading that would try to put death into perspective. As a little girl, Ruth heard his gentle voice recite Alfred Tennyson's "Crossing the Bar":

Sunset and evening star, and one clear call for me!
And may there be no moaning of the bar when I put out to sea. . .
For though from out our bourne of time and place the flood may bear
*   me far,*
I hope to see my Pilot face to face, when I have crossed the bar.

The first death Ruth remembers that touched her family was Annie Oakley's. The champion marksman was Ruth's great aunt on her mother's side of the family. Annie Oakley—her stage name—met her husband, Frank Butler, at a shooting match. They travelled with the Buffalo Bill Wild West Show for seventeen years.

When Annie did a command performance in London for Queen Victoria, Ruth's parents were very excited. They would tell people about her exploits and philosophy. The motto of Ruth's great aunt has stayed with her: "Aim at a high mark and you hit it. No, not the first time, nor the second, and maybe not the third. But keep on aiming and keep on shooting, for only practice will make you perfect. Finally you'll hit the bull's eye of success."

Ruth's mother visited Annie in a hospital in nearby Greenville, Ohio, shortly before she died. She told Ruth and her brothers that Annie was depressed and lonely. Her husband was very ill, too, and they had no children.

"It doesn't seem right for such a famous star to be so alone," Ruth's mother said sadly. Ruth was only seven years old and didn't understand. She had never met Annie.

Even though the news of her death came as no surprise, Ruth's mother was crushed. So was Annie's husband, who died eighteen days later.

Being around church services so much, Ruth's interest in music came naturally. She started piano lessons at age six and soon was playing at Sunday school. Before the age of twelve, Ruth was playing in church and singing with the choir.

At eighteen, Ruth married Waldo Emrick, a member of their church. The young couple sang duets for weddings, funerals, and special occasions. Her husband was a postal worker, and they lived most of their married years in Richmond, Indiana, where their three sons were born.

Ruth studied at the Gillum School of Music and continued to play the piano and organ every chance she got. An agent heard her playing at a Christmas party at a local hotel, and a new career was born. He gave Ruth the stage name Ruth Ames because he thought it would be easier for the public to remember. She was booked into clubs throughout Ohio, Indiana, and Kentucky. For six weeks at a time, she'd play the organ in a lounge during the dinner hour and into the night. Meanwhile, Ruth and Waldo had to hire a woman to watch their three sons.

Then the agent suggested she play a circuit of lounges across the country. Ruth knew the national exposure would enhance her career as an organist, but the extensive travel would keep her away from her family.

She decided to go home and raise her three sons. She gave up playing the organ professionally and never regretted it. To this day, she has a close bond with her sons.

Unfortunately, the relationship with her husband didn't fare so well. After about fifteen years of marriage, their arguments reached a critical point. They saw a counselor, but it didn't help. The counselor told Ruth she was having problems adjusting to her husband's contentment with his position at work. They were very different.

Ruth had been raised in a family of achievers. One brother was the superintendent of a school in Ohio, another the president of a book bindery company in California. Two of her brothers held master's degrees.

Ruth, too, was highly motivated and thirsted for new challenges. She performed in clubs, modeled, and attended the Patricia Stevens Finishing School. She also acted in civic theatre productions.

Her husband, likable but retiring, was satisfied with a simple life. Beautiful, intelligent, and extroverted, Ruth wanted much more from her life.

Ruth wanted a divorce, but that was a drastic decision for someone who was reared in the Church of the Brethren and as a minister's daughter to boot. She couldn't bear to put her parents through the trauma of knowing their only daughter strayed from God's word.

So she tried even harder to make the marriage succeed. Waldo took a job with the post office in Houston, and they sought more counseling. Ruth threw herself into caring for her children and work. She lectured and taught classes for the John Robert Powers Modeling School. She helped open two new schools in Texas.

In 1956, Ruth's father died, and her mother passed away two years later. They had served in church and school for forty-six years. Ruth knew they had a good life together, but she grieved their loss. A few years later her own marriage ended.

Soon afterward, her brother Paul called from Los Angeles with some startling news. "Sis, my wife left me," he said. "I need help. I wonder if you would come out and stay with us."

He had two children still living at home, eleven and sixteen years old. Ruth's sons were away at school, but the thought of being so far away from them seemed too big a sacrifice. Ruth's ex-husband preferred that she live out of the area. He encouraged her to go.

In December, Ruth flew to Los Angeles for a short visit. She was armed with a scrap book and portfolio of her experience with the Powers modeling school. She was hired to work with the Powers School in Pasadena, California.

Less then a month later she packed her belongings in her car and drove from Houston to L.A. to start a new life with her brother and his children. Before the year was over, her brother died after a massive heart attack. He was forty-seven.

Suddenly, Ruth had to spread her wings and start again. This time she was flying solo.

◆　◆　◆

Some things you never forget how to do: riding a bike, playing a musical instrument, driving a car. If you haven't done them in a while, you may be rusty, but you'll quickly catch on.

Being single again after twenty-three years of marriage wasn't quite like that. It was more like being expected to pilot a plane when you had only the experience of a passenger to go by. Ruth had been married more than half her life. Having wed a year out of high school, being plunged into the new dating scene was a foreign experience. Ruth trained young women to be poised and personable, but when it came to dating in a laid-back era, she felt awkward. She felt as though she had been born again in a strange unknown land.

So did Francois Toussaint. Born in Antwerp, Belgium, he had come to the United States two years before to see the land of milk and honey. His father was a renowned surgeon for whom a wing of the local hospital had been named. Toussaint had served in the Belgian Army and came to California to work in the shipping industry.

To say they met by chance would be a gross understatement. On a hot July night, Ruth wasn't particularly enthused about going to her first singles party. She went out of curiosity. Toussaint went because a coin came up heads.

His Porsche, brought over from Europe, was rebelling against its new environment. Instead of purring like a fine piece of machinery, it sputtered and choked. On one hand, the twenty-mile drive to the party in Los Angeles loomed as a risky proposition. On the other, he longed for friendships in a foreign country. Toussaint flipped the dime high into the air: "Heads I go, tails I stay," he decided.

That night, they danced as much as talked.

"I don't like to sit at parties," Toussaint said. A husky five-foot-eleven, Toussaint's blue eyes and thick French accent attracted Ruth. He was eight years her junior, but he guessed she was younger than he, a fact she attributed to a youthful attitude, a healthy diet, good genes, and knowing the art of make-up application.

Toussaint was so different from anyone Ruth had ever met, so polished and charming. He spoke four languages—French, Flemish, German, and English. He had been raised to treat women with the utmost respect.

"You dance so well." Ruth admired his effortless movements.

"You have natural grace, you just need practice," he said when Ruth knew he must be thinking she was a terrible dancer.

Within a few dates, they were friends and lovers. Because Toussaint's stay in America would be short, theirs would be a short but romantic relationship. Ruth had to keep reminding herself it would end soon to keep from falling in love.

After a year they parted amicably. Toussaint returned to his homeland and Ruth became immersed in her career.

Success begot success. She became the director of the Loretta Young Finishing School in Pasadena. Many of her students were models, some striving to become the Rose Parade queen.

As an instructor, she stressed the three Cs: don't condemn, criticize, or complain. And don't wear more than a size-ten dress.

When the Loretta Young School was sold, Ruth took a job with Max Factor of Hollywood. She worked with the cosmetics salesgirls in military exchange stores in South Carolina, Georgia, and Florida.

It was a prestigious assignment for a prestigious company. Ruth was among fifteen Max Factor beauty consultants working military bases and posts in the United States. But the travel was grueling—six months away from home at a time, two weeks at each exchange.

On vacation, Ruth was considering a move to another heavyweight in the field, Revlon, when a distinctive voice came over the phone line.

"Ruth, I'm back in California," said Toussaint. "I'm at the airport."

Part of her was ecstatic. That was the part which missed his companionship. But part of her was ambivalent. Toussaint was tied to his homeland and could return at any time. And Ruth had no desire to move to Belgium permanently.

Revlon was a more aggressive suitor. The company flew Ruth to New York and offered a very attractive package. Ruth would be one of five beauty consultants in the country for military exchanges. She would conduct training schools for Revlon cosmetics, lecture for clubs, and set up sales promotions. Basically, it was the same job she had at Max Factor except it offered more money and more time at home.

Revlon would give her a company car, a lavish expense account, and a big-league salary. Her five-state territory would be California, Arizona, Nevada, New Mexico, and Texas. Every Monday morning she would be flown out to her territory. On Friday she would fly home to La Jolla, California.

"That would be less travel than the other job," Toussaint said, sliding his chair closer to a table covered with a flowing red and white checkered cloth at La Mer, a seafood restaurant overlooking the ocean.

A young waitress said pertly, "Good evening, my name is Kate and I'll be your waitress this evening. We have several specials. Our . . . in clam sauce . . . a sixteen-ounce cut . . . our fresh catch of the day. . . . "

Ruth heard her voice but couldn't concentrate on food. "I'll have the special, whatever it is." She turned back to Toussaint. "Yes, there is less travel, but we'll only be able to see each other on weekends," she said, hoping for some reaction. What she really wanted was a chance to build a permanent relationship with him. For all his elusiveness, Toussaint treated Ruth as though she was special. He bought her presents, helped her with errands, and always was there when she need her spirits lifted.

"We'll just be friends," Toussaint said. They stared at each other in silence for a few seconds.

"Is that enough for you?" Ruth inquired softly.

"Ruth, who knows what the future will hold? I could be gone again in a year," he said, taking hold of her hand. "My brother has always wanted me to go into business with him. Is there something wrong with being friends?"

Ruth was disappointed but not heartbroken.

She said yes to Revlon.

◆ ◆ ◆

Like many military bases, Fort Huachuca was in the middle of nowhere.

Near the Mexico border in southern Arizona, military personnel had no choice but to stay close to their post. There wasn't a lot to do except admire the scenery.

About two miles from the complex, a small downtown had sprouted up. Mainly catering to the soldiers and wives, it had a restaurant, a show,and a bowling alley.

Ruth rented a room at the restaurant for a sales presentation.

After dinner, the manager rolled shut a sliding door for privacy.

Fifteen saleswomen from the military exchange store were present. They were wives of the Army personnel stationed there. Ruth had done this show so many times that she had to fight the impulse to sleepwalk through it. To generate enthusiasm for Revlon, she had to maintain her own enthusiasm. She demonstrated the uses of various beauty products and lectured on the attributes of a good salesperson.

Unknown to any of them, an uninvited guest lurked outside the room. He pulled open the door a crack to observe the presentation. He watched intently as women asked questions about lipstick shades, face creams, and skin lotions. The young man liked what he saw. He went back to the bar and ordered another whiskey sour.

At ten o'clock, Ruth finished lugging the final case of cosmetics into a rented Buick. The motel was only five minutes away, for which she was extremely thankful. She was bone tired and her morning flight back home was departing at 9:45.

Sighing, she slid into the driver's seat and slammed the door. Instantly, it opened and a strange face stared down at her.

"Hi, you did a good job in there," the man said with a smile. He was in his twenties, clean-shaven with a brush cut.

"I've been watching you all evening, honey, and I'm going to have you."

He jumped into the car and grabbed Ruth's dress. "Oh no, you're not," Ruth yelled, rolling toward the passenger door. She tried to scream for help, but two meaty hands wrapped around her throat. She grabbed his forearms and tugged. But the pressure intensified and she couldn't breathe.

Suddenly, he dropped his hands and with one motion ripped open the low neckline of Ruth's dress.

"Don't fight me, honey. You're going to enjoy this," he sneered, unzipping his pants. Lunging toward the driver's seat, Ruth bashed her knee on the corner of the air conditioner that protruded from the dashboard. Sharp pain shot through her leg.

"Help! Help! Help!" Ruth's screams pierced the still warm fall night. She pushed the door open but couldn't escape. Lying on her side, she felt his weight crushing down on her. He struck a crushing blow to the side of her head. As she tried to shimmy forward, her head jerked violently.

"Help!" Ruth's scream had become a moan. She braced for another blow—or worse.

Instead, the passenger door swung open and she heard the heavy pounding of feet on pavement.

"Are you all right?" a deep male voice asked. Ruth couldn't look up. Her head, back, and knee were throbbing.

The man, a customer leaving the restaurant, had heard her screams. She was shaking. Her knee was puffy and sore. But she was safe.

"Will you be all right?" he asked. "Should I call an ambulance?"

She shook her head, "No, no. I just want to go back to my room."

The restaurant manager took a description of the man and said he would call police and an ambulance. Ruth didn't wait. Later when she arrived home in La Jolla, she contacted friends at the post to learn if the incident had made the local paper.

It hadn't. It also had never been reported to the police. The manager feared the bad publicity would hurt business.

Meanwhile, Ruth's knee required surgery to repair damaged cartilage. She was on crutches for weeks and would never be able to do a job in which she had to stand for long periods of time.

Her career as a traveling beauty consultant was over.

Chapter 9

Beautiful Music Together

It was a beautiful, tranquil night on the Pacific Ocean.

The gentle lapping of waves. The salty breeze. The cool, wet feel of a sandy beach.

John and Sandra Whitehurst were hosting a lavish Christmas party for about thirty employees of C&I International. The company trained businesses in operational procedures, from setting up an office to counseling workers.

With offices in six cities across the country, C&I also designed and administered psychological tests for businesses that wanted to evaluate current and prospective employees. In addition to helping open new offices, Ruth assisted in preparing training manuals.

John Whitehurst had a luxurious waterfront home on Balboa Island befitting the president of a growing company. The sprawling, two-story home was tastefully furnished with the toys of the privileged: antiques, collector paintings, and an elaborate stereo system. A yacht was moored nearby.

After a dinner buffet that included lobster, crab, and steak, the guests were relaxing in clusters throughout the house.

Ruth sipped a sweetly sour strawberry daiquiri and admired the blue-green ocean through a floor-to-ceiling living room window. The soft sounds of Christmas music purred in the background. Christmas had always been an extra special time for her. Her father would always decorate the school room and their house. The kids would help him hang paper bells from the ceiling and decorate the tree with silvery tinsel and brightly colored ornaments. Then the children would watch wide-eyed as he hung the silver star. Tears rose in her eyes as memories surfaced.

"Mind if I sit down?"

She recognized the gentle voice before she looked up. It was Jack Langlos, the psychologist C&I used to organize the psychological tests. He had invited her to lunch the first time they met, but Ruth had had an appointment. *He's very nice and very professional,* she thought at the time. *And probably very married.*

"You look very nice tonight," he said. She smiled. They were both dressed for the occasion, Ruth in a red silk cocktail dress and he in a green wool blazer with black flannel slacks.

They discussed work for a couple of minutes. Then Ruth asked what he did in his spare time.

"I play the trumpet," he said, taking a sip from a dry gin martini.

"You may not believe this," Ruth said with a smile, "but I was first chair trumpet in my high school band."

"You're right," Jack laughed. "I don't believe you."

Ruth smiled again. She liked the craggy, mature face of this man, his easy-going, confident manner, and the way he laughed so easily.

She put three fingers on the back of his hand and proceeded to reproduce the fingerings of a trumpet's scale with all the chromatic variations. "C is open, D is one and three, E is one and two," Ruth said, moving her fingers like they were on the valves.

"F is one, and G is open," she concluded triumphantly.

"I bet you're a music teacher," he smiled.

"No, I played. Here's my embouchure," Ruth said, making a moue of her lips.

Ruth gently touched his lips with her finger. "I can tell you've been playing a lot. Your blisters are built up."

They talked into the wee hours of the mourning. About everything and anything.

Jack had been born and raised in Mt. Vernon, New York. His father died when he was five, and his mother died a year later. He was raised by an aunt and uncle. After getting a master's degree from the University of Miami in Florida, he headed west.

"Why did you decide to become a psychologist?"

"Well, you know, Ruth, people go into psychology so they can adjust to their maladjustment," he said with a twinkle in his eyes.

They both laughed. Ruth couldn't believe this handsome, witty man in his mid-forties had never married. But he was wed to his music and his career.

Jack roomed with jazz musician Ted Shafer in a modest apartment off Hollywood Boulevard in Hollywood. They were quite a pair.

Jack headed a five-piece Dixieland jazz band, "Thee Saints," that was an extension of his free-spirited personality. The band was showy, corny, and circus-like, wearing funny hats and doing magic tricks. In one part of the act, a band member would put a handkerchief on the floor and do a handstand while the music blared.

Shafer's group, the Jelly Roll Jazz Band, was more traditional. Jack didn't care—he played in that band, too. Langlos's ability to read music and versatility—he played the trumpet and the string bass—kept him in demand on the jazz circuit. He routinely practiced an hour or two a day on the trumpet with a mute so as not to disturb neighbors.

They performed for union scale or pocket change, but it didn't matter. Music was a lifestyle for the two bachelors. They played at USC and UCLA fraternity parties for several hundred college students. And they played on nights when the band outnumbered the audience. They played in elegant supper clubs in front of crowds that included celebrities like Patti Paige. And they played in crusty old lounges.

It didn't matter — lounges, fraternities, or parties — they

bopped, weaved, and wailed with all the verve and gusto they could coax from their instruments.

Jack was a clinical psychologist for Los Angeles County Hospital. Shafer repaired copiers. But those were jobs. Music was a mission.

A week after the company Christmas party, Jack Langlos invited Ruth to dinner. They would share a lot of dinners and music over the next year.

From the onset, Ruth knew their relationship could become permanent. Jack had "forever" written all over him. And she longed for that type of shared commitment. But she owed it to herself and Jack to settle matters with her European friend.

For seven years, Toussaint and she had been friends by his definition. In reality, they were lovers and confidants. They had two favorite spots to discuss important matters—the beach or a restaurant.

This conversation was more suitable for a restaurant.

On the Santa Monica pier, Moby's Dock stands like a sentry on the waterfront. Its lights provided a friendly beacon to boaters looking for a respite from sea life.

Here, from a booth overlooking miles of water, you can press against the glass and feel the majesty of a work of art. The picture is never the same.

"Francois, I've met a man and I think we could become serious about each other," Ruth said, studying his handsome face for a reaction. His gaze slowly turned from the ocean, settling on her. "Francois, if our relationship is going anywhere I need to know now."

"Ruth, I told you in the beginning that marriage wasn't in the picture."

"Why not? You say you love me."

"I do love you, but I think you can love someone and not be married to them."

Toussaint was being his same old noncommittal self. *Next he's going to show his practical side, stressing how his time in America was temporary,* she thought.

"It's the divorce, isn't it?" Ruth asked. Toussaint came from a strict Catholic family that didn't condone divorce. She could relate to that.

"Partly, yes," he said, looking down. "And you would not be happy in Belgium. Your sons are here and they are important to you."

"I wish we could have worked it out, Francois," Ruth said, her eyes beginning to moisten.

"Tell me about this man. Does he make you happy?"

Ruth's sudden smile lit up her face. "Very much so. We have a lot in common."

Toussaint looked at her for a long moment and said quietly, "Then everything will work out."

◆ ◆ ◆

Jack Langlos and Ruth were married that January at the Wee Kirk of the Heather Chapel in Las Vegas.

It wasn't the glamour, glitz, or gambling that attracted them. It was the music. They saw three shows, but the highlight was the performance of Louis Armstrong.

As usual, Jack knew somebody in the band at almost every lounge. During their courtship, they were dining at an elegant restaurant when a band member invited Jack to join in. It was the first time she'd heard him play the trumpet, and she was surprised. He was much better than she'd imagined.

"You're every bit as good as Al Hirt," she told him when he finished.

He just beamed. Jack was very reserved, the kind of man who said a lot with a few words.

His friend, Neil Hundley, liked to tell the story of how Jack avoided chores when they were living with four other guys fresh out of college in a two-story house in Hollywood Hills. Jack's uncanny insight in people was legendary among his friends and associates.

"Jack and I were supposed to split chores on a weekly basis, but Jack would skip his week," Hundley would say. "When I confronted him, Jack told me, 'You're compulsive, Hundley, I knew you'd do them.'"

Everybody would roar. But nobody laughed when Ted Shafer would explain why Jack was getting burned out as a county psychologist.

Jack would evaluate patients ready to be released from County Hospital, where he worked in the psychiatric ward. The discharge then would go to a judge for a decision. Most times, the judge would concur with Jack's expert opinion. However, one time the patient convinced the judge that he should be released over Jack's objections.

"He's just putting on a show of normalcy," Jack told the judge. It was in vain.

The patient killed his girlfriend the next day. That was one time Jack wished he had been wrong. He refused to discuss the case.

As Ruth found out months later, Jack didn't exchange nuptial vows without first analyzing their relationship. He had written down a list of Ruth's assets on a sheet of paper.

Ruth read it and smiled. "Plays organ. Enjoys Dixie trumpet. Socially (going out, visiting) compatible. Proud of public contacts. Business minded. Prods me business wise. Prods me socially. Has children for aging period. Sons are nice. Nice relatives in California. Keeps me from drinking. Loves me. Respects me. Thinks I'm a good psychologist. Thinks I'm a good musician. Will not stray. Sex oriented. Relationship highlights me socially. Effervescent on first meeting. Kindest, generous, most considerate. Do-it-now person. Keeps sex drive down. Extremely appreciative. Agreeable to everything. Won't talk if I get mad. A great companion."

If Ruth had done a list, she would have concentrated on the many interests they shared: photography, music, psychology, entertaining, attending church, reading, and baseball.

She never found a list of her faults, but she assumed the positives outweighed the negatives.

Despite their compatibility, their marriage had to survive one crisis. It came during the first year. One night, they were dining and had cocktails, Beef Wellington, and Chateau-Rothchild at a posh restaurant on Ventura Boulevard when she noticed that her usually meticulous husband was dropping bits of salad off his plate. Throughout the meal he acted strangely, almost out of it. His tie was loosened around the neck, and he looked off into the distance and said little.

"Darling, how did you like the restaurant last night?" Ruth asked the next morning.

"It was all right."

"What about the food?"

He looked at Ruth blankly.

"Do you remember what you ate?"

No answer.

"What did you think of the piano player?"

"The piano player?"

"Jack, I think you're drinking too much. You don't even remember where you were last night or what you ate."

"I was just tired, I guess."

At the beginning, Ruth had thought Jack was a social drinker. At parties or lounges, he would become more outgoing and talkative after a few drinks. Having a good sense of humor anyway, he became even funnier. Nobody minded. In fact, their friends said he needed to loosen up occasionally to escape the pressures of his job. And he seemed in control.

After only a few months of living together, she knew differently. The vodka and gin had slowly conquered his will power.

Her husband had an alcohol problem. He was never abusive, but he wasn't himself either.

She threatened to leave a couple of times. Instead she started attending Al-Anon sessions, where she learned that idle threats don't help an alcoholic. The alcoholic has to recognize and deal with the disease.

Then Jack's behavior became more erratic. Missed meals. Blackouts. Excuses.

One evening when he arrived home from work three hours late, he found Ruth packing.

"This is getting serious," Ruth declared. "I can't take watching you destroy yourself, and I am not going down the drain with you."

He stood speechless at the bedroom doorway.

"I won't lie anymore, Jack. When our families ask why we've split up, I'm going to tell them the truth."

He began to cry. "Honey, I know I need help. I have a problem."

Seeing him so helpless crushed Ruth. Be firm, she thought. As they hugged, he gently rested his head on her shoulder.

"Darling, I've seen a Dr. Pearson on TV advertise a program for veterans with drinking problems."

"Let's check it out," he whispered without hesitation.

On November 17, Ruth put her hand on the door knob as they headed for his first appointment. She stopped and turned to him. "Are you doing this for me, or are you doing it for yourself?"

"I'm the one who needs help," Jack said.

"Darling, I'll stick by you through this." For the first time, Jack had come to grips with his alcoholism. Ruth was euphoric.

They embraced, the warmth and strength of his body pressed tightly against Ruth, comforting her. They'd fight this thing together.

For two months, Jack went for counseling and treatment every morning at the VA Hospital in Los Angeles. He'd schedule appointments with clients in the afternoons and evenings. His boss never knew Jack was in a rehab program. He took his anti-abuse medication religiously. And he never had a drop of alcohol again.

As if fate had smiled, their fortunes started to multiply. Jack was hired to join the Planned Living Council, a group of psychologists who serviced several convalescent homes and hospitals.

They moved from Jack's crowded bachelor pad in North Hollywood to a wonderful two-bedroom apartment in Pacific Palisades. It had a large picture window that overlooked Sunset Boulevard. You could see the white-capped ocean.

They settled quickly into the good life. Their patio was like a second home. With a backdrop of flowers and greenery, they'd enjoy barbecued steaks, salads, and corn on the cob. Almost every weekend, it was off to the Will Rogers Beach. Another favorite spot was a secluded stretch near Malibu. They'd take a picnic lunch and sunbathe on a beach sandwiched between the water and the Santa Monica Mountains. It was breathtaking and relaxing at the same time.

Their romantic hideaway was a little motel in Carpenteria, a tiny community near Santa Barbara. The room had no telephone or television, but the ocean view was spectacular.

Bumping into celebrities at home was like encountering traffic jams. They were everywhere. They lived about four miles from Santa Monica in one direction and Malibu in the other. Beverly Hills and Hollywood were neighbors, too.

The city had about twenty-three thousand residents, including a healthy flock of people connected with the movie industry. Peter Graves was the honorary mayor of Palisades. To Ruth it seemed as though the official car of the area was the Mercedes.

Around town she'd see Ted Knight at the post office, Katherine Hepburn in a black convertible at the gas station, Eddie Arnold and Regis Philbin at a restaurant.

For a small-town girl from Ohio, it took some getting used to. When she was training with Max Factor, she had seen George Burns come into Max Factor to pick up a hairpiece that had been shampooed and styled, but celebrity sightings weren't that common at the time.

It was different now. Imagine going into the Pontiac repair shop and seeing Fred MacMurray having his station wagon serviced, or going to the beauty salon and watching Priscilla Presley getting her hair done. One time Ruth went to renew her driver's license and waited in line behind Walter Matthau and Mort Sahl.

Eventually, dropping names was like discussing the weather.

"Guess who I saw today? Efrem Zimbalist Jr."

"Yeah, where?"

"Near Santa Monica, making a movie."

"Oh yeah, I saw Peter Falk making a movie in town a couple days ago."

Their marriage never quit blossoming. Every day was like a new beginning.

Jack was easy to love. He rarely got upset about anything. Even their different religious affiliations—Jack was Catholic, Ruth was Presbyterian—became a shared experience. One Sunday they'd attend mass at Corpus Christi Catholic Church in the Palisades; the next Sunday, they'd go to services at the Hollywood Presbyterian Church.

Music was the glue that helped unite them. They'd spend hours playing together in the living room. Ruth played the Hammond organ just like in her lounge days, and Jack would accompany on the trumpet or string bass. They always ended with their favorite song: "I Can't Believe That You're in Love with Me."

In St. Louis, Jack played in the Ragtime Festival on a riverboat. He played in the Christmas Hollywood Boulevard Parade on Thanksgiving Eve. Afterwards, it was party time at the elegant Magic Castle in Hollywood. In Hollywood, Ruth sat in a recording studio tapping her feet to the music of a ragtime group Jack played with, The Dawn of the Century Ragtime Orchestra, directed by Dave Bourne. They recorded two albums and played sets at a theater with Eubie Blake.

Ruth didn't miss her beauty consulting career. She was too happy being the wife, friend, and partner of Jack Langlos.

The horizon seemed cloudless.

Chapter 10

A Grieving Pest

A ring rolled straight toward Ruth as if it had eyes.

Before it reached her outstretched hand, she noticed the three diamonds embedded in the white gold. It was Jack's wedding ring.

Ruth left it on the counter. She clutched herself as tears ran down her cheeks.

"You okay, ma'am?" asked the man behind the iron bars.

She longed to say the truth. No, she wasn't okay. For six months, she had repeatedly postponed picking up Jack's personal belongings. But she knew the time had come.

At the front gate, the guard's greeting fit in with the somber mood: "Are you from a mortuary?"

The Los Angeles coroner's office isn't an inviting kind of place. Its drab, plain motif reminds one of the operating room of a county hospital.

The first-floor room where people recover belongings of their loved ones was the most sterile place Ruth had ever encountered. Except for four folding chairs, the room was devoid of furniture. No pictures on the walls, no magazine racks or coffee tables.

A box of tissues sat on the counter, a telltale reminder of all the pain and sadness the room had seen. On the counter, a row of iron bars separated employee from the mourners. The precaution apparently protected the bearers of bad news from anyone who thought something had been stolen or misplaced.

When the man behind the bars ripped open the Jack Langlos envelope, the ring had dropped out.

"Everything's here," the man noted solemnly, comparing the contents to a checklist.

As he handed Jack's plastic-rimmed glasses to Ruth, she gasped. They still had dried blood and skin on them. The coroner's office hadn't bothered to clean them. She cried all the way home.

As soon as Ruth got to the apartment, she threw the glasses in the wastebasket. She couldn't stand the sight of them.

"Oh Jack, how you must have suffered," she murmured. "I can't stand to think you died like that."

Two days later, the ID technicians at the Downey police gave Ruth a large black plastic bag with things that had been confiscated from Jack's office.

Captain Sanders frowned when she told him about Jack's glasses.

"Are they still in the wastebasket?"

"No. They're gone with the trash," Ruth replied.

"Oh, that's too bad. They might have been a very good piece of evidence."

"Nobody told me to keep the glasses," Ruth said. She was angry at them and at herself. She changed the subject. "How are Westray and Miller doing?"

"Because we really want to solve this one, I've kept them on your husband's case longer than normal," said Sanders. "They're out of leads. I know they've had detectives from several other departments review the case file looking for anything they might have missed. But so far, nothing."

"Hartman is going to go scot-free, isn't he?"

"We're not giving up, Mrs. Langlos," said Sanders remorsefully. "I'm not taking Westray and Miller off the case till we cover every small lead." Sanders was the kind of boss cops liked working for. He hadn't forgotten the realities of the street or his fellow officers' feelings when he got on the management track. "Maybe, he'll slip up and tell somebody what he's done. How have you been doing? You look pretty tired."

Ruth sighed, "I feel like I'm on a treadmill. I just can't rest knowing Jack's killer is out there. He's got to pay for what he's done." She left clutching the plastic bag.

As if Ruth needed more reminders, the bag was filled with them—Jack's attache case, date book, dented silver pen, and papers. Inside was another package wrapped in brown paper and tied with a string. It contained a pinstriped shirt with three buttons ripped off, undershorts, and a blood-soaked maroon sports jacket.

Painful as it was, she kept the evidence this time.

◆ ◆ ◆

Ruth stood tall, squaring her chin, outside the Downey police station. She didn't trust anyone in the criminal justice system anymore. She figured any system that could conclude her husband had died of natural causes was corrupt, incompetent, or both.

So it was no wonder she was wary of Deputy District Attorney Joe Schafer, who was a shining example of the system she now distrusted. A Stanford graduate, he headed the Los Angeles County prosecutor's office in Norwalk, a few miles outside Downey.

Schafer was more of an administrator than an attorney. He analyzed cases; he didn't try them in a courtroom. It was said that he liked the feeling of power, the authority to make or break lives at a split second's notice. If Schafer wanted a case prosecuted, it was prosecuted.

In his early forties, rumor had it he longed to do business in the big house—the D.A.'s headquarters in downtown Los Angeles. It was an even-money bet he'd get there, too.

Subordinates quickly learned to adhere to Schafer's orders. The fastest way into his doghouse was to question his judgment. He was always right. At least he seemed to think so.

Ruth had become a regular visitor to his office in the Superior

Court complex, looking at documents, getting updates, and just letting the prosecutors know she wasn't going to leave them alone until they righted the wrong.

Often, her friends would accompany her for moral support. One day Ruth's son Chad agreed to come along during a visit. He had never met Schafer, and Ruth was anxious for his appraisal.

Schafer noticed them leafing through the court records and came by to exchange pleasantries. When Ruth had left the room for a minute, Schafer confided in Chad.

"There's something I think you should know," Schafer declared. "Your mother has been here ten to fifteen times since her husband died. She asks the same questions and we give her the same answers. She's making a pest of herself."

"What do you want me to do?"

"Tell her to stay home and get on with her life."

"I can't stop my mother. My mother is a determined woman. She's not going to back off until justice is served here."

"I've told her repeatedly that there's no case. The coroner says he died of natural causes."

When Chad told Ruth what Schafer had said, she wasn't angry.

"I must be getting to him," Ruth told Chad. "He wishes I were a feather and would float away. Well, I won't. As long as he refuses to do his job, I'm going to keep bugging him."

"Mom, he's pretty egotistical—not the kind of guy who's going to change his mind," said Chad, shaking his head.

Ruth met his eyes directly. "Well, we're going to have to force him to change it."

Two new documents in the case file had perked Ruth's attention. One was a letter to the court clerk from Hector Burke, Chief of Professional Standards for the State Commission for Teacher Preparation and Licensing. He wanted to know the results of the murder investigation involving Hartman, who was a certified teacher.

The other letter came from W. E. Rockefeller, a senior investigator for the State Department of Consumer Affairs. Because the agency had certified Hartman as a psychologist, Rockefeller also was inquiring about the disposition of the 187 P.C. complaint that led to Hartman's arrest.

But in each case there was no mention of the forgery or theft charges that could lead to revocation of Hartman's license. After a few phone calls Ruth found that the state agencies hadn't been aware of any other complaints. She made them aware.

Within a couple days, Rockefeller sent two special agents from the Attorney General's office to interview Ruth at her apartment. The A.G.'s office handled probes of improprieties of all professionals licensed or certified by the state. Ruth could tell from their faces and questions that they had no idea Hartman had been convicted of forgery. All they knew was that he had been a suspect in a murder case but had never been charged.

"Can we take these for a day and make some copies?" Jake Hansen, one of the investigators, asked after poring through the court and medical records she had amassed with the help of Keith Rogers.

"They're all public documents," Ruth said. "If you knew about the arrest, why didn't you find out about all the other things in his background?"

"It must have fallen through the cracks somehow," he said with a shrug.

Somehow, the cracks always seemed to help the criminal.

◆ ◆ ◆

The view from Ruth's apartment window hadn't changed. Below, traffic hummed along the winding roads. In the distance, the meeting of ocean and mountains provided a serene backdrop.

Still, it provided little respite. As she turned away to look around her, she realized once again it was no longer "their" apartment. It was her apartment. And nature's beauty couldn't cure her loneliness. Since Jack's death, she had lived out of a suitcase, staying with friends and family. When she returned home, she felt like a stranger in a strange place. She needed an emotional pillar to lean on. Slowly she walked over to the telephone and dialed. "Francois," Ruth said timidly into the receiver.

"Ruth?" The husky voice responded.

It had been over six years since Ruth had heard that accent. She really hadn't expected him to still be in California.

"Are you . . . married?" Ruth asked hesitantly.

"No," he laughed.

"Dating someone?"

"I just broke up with a school teacher."

"Jack, my husband was murdered," Ruth could feel the tension immediately.

"I don't like jokes, Ruth," he said sternly.

"I couldn't joke about something like that," Ruth declared, hurt by his remark. "He was killed in his office almost seven months ago."

"Ruth, I'm sorry," he said. Pausing, he added, "Would you like to see me again?"

"Well, if you can stand a person who cries a lot and looks terrible, I'd like to see you again."

That weekend, Toussaint took Ruth to Lion Country Safari and Malibu Beach. Ruth laughed and cried, sometimes at the same time.

Nothing had really changed in his life. He still made periodic visits to Belgium. He still didn't know where he wanted to settle. And he still cared for Ruth.

They'd be friends. Again, she would have someone to talk to, to help her. Ruth knew she was going to need all the help she could find to avenge Jack's death. Dr. Eugene Carpenter's autopsy report was her Waterloo. There would be no justice, she was convinced, until the flaws in that report were exposed.

To do so, Ruth was willing to get a second, third, and fourth medical opinion if necessary. No matter what the cost, she couldn't just get on with her life as deputy District Attorney Schafer wanted until Jack's killer was punished.

She talked to everyone she could, trying to get ideas on how the autopsy report could be overturned. One friend, Dr. Fisher, recommended that Dr. Weldon Walker be hired to study the autopsy results. Formerly of the world-renowned Walter Reed Hospital, Walker was a respected heart specialist whose opinion would carry weight.

Ruth called the doctor, now a member of a Los Angeles heart institute. "I want you to pull no punches in your evaluation of the autopsy, crime scene pictures, and police reports. If you think it's a professional exam, I want you to say so. And vice versa."

Dr. Walker's report, dated October 8, confirmed Ruth's deep dark suspicions: The coroner's office had made a tragic mistake.

"There is certainly evidence that John T. Langlos was robbed and great suspicion that he may have been the victim of foul play," Dr. Walker wrote in his report. "Relative to the autopsy report, this is considered to be an incomplete report in that there is no histopathology described at all."

His recommendation: An expert in cardiac pathology should review the findings with Dr. Thomas Noguchi, the coroner of Los Angeles County. If necessary, the body should be exhumed and re-examined for other possible causes of death, including toxic.

Walker concluded: "The superficial report of the cardiac pathology and the autopsy report would suggest a superficial autopsy."

"Amen," Ruth murmured as she read it. "Now I'm ready to fight."

Chapter 11

Confronting the Coroner to the Stars

It would have been easier getting a private audience with the Queen of England than a meeting with Dr. Thomas Noguchi.

Unless you were a celebrity or a member of the media, the world's most publicized coroner was a hard guy to corner. And even harder to figure out.

Born in Japan, Noguchi decided to become a medical examiner at the age of twelve after witnessing the importance of forensic pathology. His father, a painter turned physician, swabbed a patient's strep throat with iodine, a common practice in the days before penicillin. When the patient died suddenly, Noguchi's father was accused of malpractice and faced possible imprisonment.

He insisted upon an autopsy, which was rarely performed in Japan in the late 1930s. The autopsy uncovered the fact that death was caused by a reaction to the iodine and not asphyxiation. Noguchi's father was cleared.

In 1952, Noguchi came to California from the Nippon Medical School in Japan. Ten years later, he joined the Los Angeles coroner's office. He was a workhorse with limited fluency in

95

English, a doctor willing to do autopsies seven days a week at any time of the day or night.

Noguchi's star rose quickly. He was named Chief Medical Examiner/Coroner in 1967. The field of forensic pathology would never be the same.

By his own admission, Noguchi was two parts scientist, one part showman. In a field cloaked in secrecy, Noguchi's healthy ego longed for attention and recognition. He saw himself as Don Quixote with a scalpel. His flair for the dramatic surfaced with his first high-profile case—the death of Marilyn Monroe.

As he described it: "The body on Table 1 was covered with a white sheet. I pulled it back slowly and stopped. It was the first time in my young professional life that I had been affected by the sight of a decedent on an autopsy table. . . . No one, professional or not, Buddhist or not, could have been unaffected by the sight of the beautiful Marilyn Monroe, so untimely dead."

Fifteen months after appointing him coroner, the County Board of Supervisors fired him. His flamboyance and administrative flaws had become a political liability.

He was accused of praying in his office for Senator Robert Kennedy to die, dancing when he heard of a helicopter crash, and hoping a loaded jetliner would crash into a hotel near the airport—all so he could perform the autopsies and become famous. In a ten-page letter, county officials accused him of "exhibiting symptoms which indicate a need for psychiatric care." During a six-week Civil Service Commission hearing, he was psychoanalyzed by eighty witnesses.

The complaints centered on his administrative rather than medical ability. He was accused of ignoring routine cases because of an insatiable lust for publicity and bullying employees into running errands and acting as his personal chauffeur.

Noguchi spent more than $25,000 of his life savings and rallied the support of the Japanese-American community. The three-member commission cleared him of all misconduct and reinstated him with back pay. Noguchi blamed his firing on political backbiting and misunderstanding of his macabre sense of humor. He also accused the commission of bias because he was Japanese.

The publicity only seemed to enhance his mystique. At the time of Jack Langlos's death and subsequent investigation, the man dubbed "Coroner to the Stars" was a media fixture.

A television series modelled after him, "Quincy," was debuting with Jack Klugman portraying the inquisitive coroner. It lasted seven seasons.

Meanwhile, Noguchi had distanced himself from daily operations at the coroner's office. He traveled around the country testifying in criminal cases, speaking at various functions, and basically doing PR work for Thomas Noguchi.

Little wonder then that the widow of Jack Langlos wouldn't rate very high on Noguchi's priority list.

For months Ruth sought a meeting with him. She was told he was out of town, unavailable, in court, in a meeting, and so on. His subordinates shielded him well, but Ruth kept calling and let his office staff know she would keep calling until he met with her. It became a battle of wills. Noguchi gave in first.

On November 1, Ruth and her son Chad arrived in downtown Los Angeles for a 2:30 meeting with Noguchi. They lunched in Chinatown before heading to his office. Having Chad fly in from Denver to be with Ruth bolstered her confidence; he would carry the ball if she became too emotional. And he would be a witness to what was said.

Noguchi's office on the second floor was the antithesis of the spartan room where Ruth had picked up Jack's belongings. It resembled a plush salon in the Old West, with two huge desks, antique oriental carpeting, and a blue velvet sofa and chairs. There even was a complete kitchen behind the lavish office.

Adding a discordant note, on one wall a bank of security monitors revealed grisly scenes of the autopsy rooms below. If not for these, it would have been impossible to distinguish Noguchi's office from that of a head of state or business tycoon.

"What an incredible office," murmured Chad, as they were ushered to the sofa in front of a huge, ornately carved coffee table. Chad had been in ostentatious quarters before, but nothing like this.

It was a fitting atmosphere for a self-styled Renaissance man

with eclectic tastes. Noguchi had tried everything from scuba div-
ing to cooking and weaving. He didn't own a television set or
wear a watch. He truly marched to the beat of his own drummer.

On the other side of the coffee table, seated in a velvet wing
chair, Noguchi, wearing a dark blue suit and a perpetual smile,
acted like a charming host at a party. He was flanked by his chief
of staff and his top investigator.

Ruth quickly looked around, expecting to see Dr. Carpenter
but was disappointed. The coroner who had done Jack's autopsy
wasn't there. She tried to stay calm. If this meeting turned into a
shouting match, nothing would be accomplished. Nine months already had passed since the murder. Time was not on Ruth's side,
and she knew it.

"What brings you here today?" Noguchi's smile widened.

Ruth rose from the sofa and passed out copies of Dr. Walker's
medical report and Keith Rogers's investigative report. Ruth's
voice quivered at times, as she read aloud portions of the police report describing the blood in Jack's office and the condition in
which he was discovered.

At the mention of the gash on his head, Ruth had to pause.
Tears of anger filled her eyes.

"There is only internal bleeding with a heart attack," Ruth
said, gaining her composure. She looked directly into Noguchi's
eyes and with her own challenged him: "How do you account for
all the blood?"

The room turned pin-drop quiet. Noguchi studied the material briefly and ordered investigator Howard to photocopy the
reports.

"Mrs. Langlos, we need to check into this," Noguchi said
matter-of-factly with a strong Japanese accent.

Dr. Dean Wisely, the chief of staff for the pathologists, handed Chad an envelope with pictures taken at the death scene. Chad
gave Ruth three black and whites of Jack's office while he studied
the others. Ruth stared at the pictures in disbelief. Jack's office
had changed considerably. Two gray metal file drawers that had
stood against the back wall behind the desk were missing. Where
the four-drawer files had stood, the wall was bare except for three

large spots of blood. The front of the desk appeared to have been cracked.

Ruth had been in the office while attending a Christmas party less than two months before Jack died. Where had the files gone? she wondered. Jack never saw patients there, and the office was always locked. It was used only for completing reports and diagnosies, telephoning the relatives of patients, or contacting their physicians.

"After looking at these pictures, there is no doubt in my mind that Jack was murdered," Chad declared.

"Mrs. Langlos, it might help us if you looked at all the pictures," said Noguchi, ignoring Chad.

"No way will my mother look at those pictures," said Chad, throwing the manilla envelope on the table in Noguchi's direction. "To observe the graphic depictions of a killer's handiwork will serve no purpose but to further upset her," Chad added.

"I wish Dr. Carpenter was here," Ruth declared. "The top three buttons were ripped off my husband's shirt. How did he account for that?"

"The doctors discussed it at length," Wisely chipped in. "Your husband was the first coronary patient ever brought into the coroner's office with buttons torn off like that. We didn't come up with any definitive answers."

"Jack was *murdered*," Ruth emphasized.

Noguchi had been pensive for several minutes. But the word *murder* seemed to stir him. He turned his attention to Eugene Hartman and the facts of the case. He wasn't smiling anymore. He was asking lots of questions.

Why did Hartman need money? Where was Hartman from the time he left Jack's office until he was arrested in San Jose? Did Hartman know a lot about medications? What was the value of Jack's stamp collection?

"I have no idea why Hartman was always broke. He made a decent salary." The other inquiries Ruth answered patiently.

Howard asked, "Did Hartman take a polygraph test?"

"How can you test a pathological liar?" Ruth laughed sarcastically.

Noguchi ignored the interchange. "Where is your husband's necktie?" Noguchi asked.

What a stupid question, Ruth thought. "I don't know, and Jack never went to work without one. He was impeccable."

Noguchi started to rise. "As I said before, Mrs. Langlos, we need to check into this . . ."

Sensing another stonewall, Ruth interrupted: "Dr. Noguchi, I really think we should have a formal inquest."

He sat down, paused, and smiled.

"No, that might cause embarrassment to other agencies," Noguchi declared. "Mrs. Langlos, you have uncovered many discrepancies among the agencies, but I want professionals to decide this instead of a jury. I'll call an interagency meeting with my office, the Downey police, and the Prosecutor's Office. It'll be run my way."

Ruth didn't like the sound of his words *my way*. But at least the investigation would be reopened. Any hearing was welcome.

As Ruth and Chad drove back to Pacific Palisades, they agreed that despite Ruth's misgivings the one-hour meeting had seemed to go well.

"The truth will come out in the hearing," Chad said reassuringly. "In one of the pictures, it looked like Jack had been hit in the mouth."

"What did you think of Dr. Noguchi?" Ruth asked.

"He's a very charismatic guy," mused Chad, "but he doesn't seem to be too concerned with details. We'll have to make sure he follows through and holds that meeting."

Ruth brushed a few strands of blond hair away from her eyes. "I still wish Carpenter had been there. I'll bet he can't face us, knowing what he's done."

Chad frowned. "Mother, I don't think they want Carpenter near this case anymore."

But three weeks later, Carpenter again was a central figure in the case. To prepare for the interagency session, Noguchi ordered Carpenter to do histopathology on tissues taken from Jack Langlos's body. No microscop c testing had been done during the first autopsy.

Ruth immediately called Noguchi to voice her objections. "The coroner who didn't properly finish the autopsy in the first place is going to get a second chance. Why not have someone else on staff do it?"

Noguchi would not relent, but he did keep his promise to bring all the agencies together.

On December 7, ten people familiar with the case met at the coroner's office: Captain Sanders, Miller, and Westray of the Downey police; Schafer, Spelling, and investigator Fred Boyer of the D.A.'s office; and the medical examiner's team of Noguchi, Wisely, Howard, and Carpenter. Family members and attorneys were barred.

The result: A second autopsy would be performed on Jack Langlos.

But who would do it? After a few names were tossed out, Captain Sanders said forcefully, "Look, the only way you'll ever please Mrs. Langlos is to get a doctor who's never worked for L.A. County or Dr. Noguchi."

He was right. It was agreed that Ruth could hire a doctor of her choosing at her own cost to assist Dr. Carpenter in another autopsy. The county would pay Carpenter as well as the expenses for exhumation and the autopsy.

Hearing the news, Ruth shed tears of relief. One year after Jack's death, they were going to know once and for all how Jack was murdered.

Chapter 12

A Second Autopsy

Dr. Ervin Jindrich made a very favorable first impression. His azalea plant did not.

Ruth's search for a forensic pathologist to do a second autopsy had landed her in a cluttered office north of San Francisco. Elizabeth Aaron, a professor at the UCLA School of Medicine Ruth had called, recommended Jindrich as one of the best forensic pathologists in the country.

He had been awarded a fellowship in forensic pathology at the University of California School of Medicine three years before. Only eight fellowships had been given that year in the country.

Jindrich was the elected medical examiner of Marin County, home to some of California's wealthiest families. He had seemed friendly and encouraging on the telephone, but Ruth was apprehensive. She didn't think anybody liked having a meeting with a coroner. It was like sitting down and talking with a mortician: They performed a necessary service but one you'd just as soon avoid.

At the door to his office Jindrich greeted Ruth and her attractive blonde friend, Louise McCord. Ruth searched his face. A neatly trimmed goatee anchored strong, chiseled, masculine features. He led them to two chairs pulled in front of his desk. As Ruth sat down she noticed the desk was piled high with reports, consistent with a sign on the wall that read "Disaster Area."

Louise broke the ice without even intending to. On the corner of the desk, she spotted a potted azalea plant desperately in need of water and TLC.

"A coroner with a dead plant on his desk—not a good omen," murmured McCord. She paused and added, "You'd better hold a formal hearing for this plant."

Jindrich laughed heartily.

Ruth felt a sudden warm surge of affection for her friend. McCord, like several others, had supported Ruth from day one. They shared meals, thoughts, and tears throughout Ruth's ordeal. They would accompany her to meetings, attend court hearings, and ask her to spend the night in their homes when she seemed especially troubled. Their encouragement helped make a terrible time better. Ruth reached over and squeezed Louise's hand, thinking Louise had a heart bigger than San Francisco Bay. She had endured excruciating pain requiring three back surgeries. Maybe because of that, she couldn't bear to see anyone or anything uncared for. Once when she learned a greyhound had been mistreated at an Arizona racetrack, she quickly bought the dog. Her pet, "Bus," couldn't have found a more loving owner.

Ruth wasn't surprised when McCord noticed the limp plant. Nor was she surprised when Louise brought the doctor a new plant on a subsequent visit.

Ruth thought Jindrich's office and attire—open-neck sport-shirt and slacks—matched his reputation. He was said to be laid-back but hardworking. Most important, he was honest. Jindrich had testified on behalf of both prosecutors and defendants with equal vigor and effectiveness.

In California, Jindrich is in the minority. Only about one-third of the county coroners are medical doctors. The majority are sheriffs who hire doctors to perform autopsies and fill out death certificates.

Doctors generally don't aspire to be coroners for a simple reason—money. They can't earn six-figure salaries in the coroner's office. But Dr. Jindrich was different. He attended medical school at Northwestern University in Illinois and saw forensic pathology as a way to assist the criminal justice system.

Married with two children, Jindrich often was asked why he didn't go into the more lucrative forms of medical practice. "My job isn't stressful," was his standard answer. "Treating living patients can be stressful, because there's always the possibility you'll kill somebody."

Jindrich enjoyed being a pathologist. His office was in a sprawling county complex set in a shallow gulch overlooking Marin County. The 240,000 people of Marin have one of the highest per capita income averages in California. Its neighborhoods include stately mansions reflecting America's plenty. Many of Marin's residents work in neighboring San Francisco.

The complex that housed Jindrich and his seven-member staff was the last building designed by Frank Lloyd Wright, who died before he could see his creation completed. Punctuated by arches and glass, the complex opened its arms to natural light from all directions. Its cheery blue and gold color scheme welcomed visitors into various county departments.

But the building also has a dark history. A judge had been murdered in a highly publicized shootout at the courthouse in 1970. Activist Angela Davis was charged with murder and kidnapping in a conspiracy to free prisoners. She was later acquitted.

Some office workers complained that the complex was too spread out, requiring a hike between departments. For Jindrich, the building's sprawling layout was part of its charm, a respite from the crowded conditions in the Bay Area. Outside Jindrich's window, the sight of a beautiful garden offered escape during a taxing day. It sure beat a sea of pavement, Jindrich figured.

Except for their medical degrees, Ervin Jindrich and Thomas Noguchi, the Los Angeles County Coroner, had little in common. Jindrich was elected, Noguchi appointed by the County Board of Supervisors. Jindrich's office performed about three hundred and fifty autopsies a year, only a small fraction of the workload in Los Angeles County. Jindrich was quietly effective; Noguchi reveled in headlines.

They barely knew each other but had already clashed once at a medical conference. Upset at the high fees some coroners were charging for embalming, Jindrich pushed through a bill that stopped the practice. Embalming would be handled only by the funeral homes. Noguchi had vehemently opposed Jindrich.

Jindrich said little during the meeting. Instead, he pored over the police and medical reports Ruth had brought. His facial expressions spoke volumes. While reading the autopsy, he did a double take, re-read a portion, and glanced up, shaking his head. He stared at Ruth for a few moments, then began scanning the papers once more.

A couple minutes later, he looked up again. "There's something really wrong here," he said. "I'll take your case."

"They didn't do a complete autopsy, did they?" Ruth asked.

Jindrich grimaced. "The findings of the autopsy don't seem to support its conclusion." He paused then went on. "Maybe I can figure out what happened after I talk with the police and Dr. Carpenter."

"What do you charge for your services?" Ruth inquired. She was committed to pay almost any fee for peace of mind.

"How about fifty dollars, plus expenses," he replied.

Ruth flashed him an astonished look. "Are you sure that's all?" she blurted out.

Jindrich nodded. "This assignment isn't about money. I'm anxious to begin."

◆ ◆ ◆

Four hundred miles to the south, Wimp was on a roll.

"You think we don't know what you've been up to," Westray spit the words out. "You're gonna make a mistake sooner or later, kid, and then you'll be some Bubba's girlfriend behind bars. Is that what you want?"

Westray had backed an eighteen-year-old troublemaker against the fence in a hardscrabble neighborhood where the law took a back seat to street justice. Jeff Harden was at the crossroads. He had spent a year in a juvenile detention facility for breaking and entering. His rap sheet included a couple loitering and shoplifting charges. Westray and Miller had met a lot of Jeff Hardens, decent kids from broken homes who are vulnerable to the influence of thugs, pimps, and dealers.

Harden was a suspect in a wave of vandalism that had rolled through Downey's downtown, leaving shattered windows, slit tires, and a mass of angry citizens.

"You've got too much on the ball to ruin your life this way," Westray declared, eyeing Harden for some sign that his words were sinking in.

As he spoke, a small collie roamed through the yard sniffing for scraps. The pup calmly noted the commotion, edged closer, and heeded nature's call. Miller watched in astonishment as the puppy lifted its leg and nonchalantly peed on his partner's leg. Westray was so engrossed in making his point that he didn't feel a thing until the dog had almost finished its business.

"Get out of here! Scoot," he yelled. Miller tried to keep from laughing, but it wasn't easy. He walked back to the car to let Westray finish his talk with Harden.

"C'mon, Mr. Fire Hydrant, we've got work to do," laughed Miller.

"You saw that goddamn dog. Why didn't you warn me?" said Westray sheepishly.

"You want to file a complaint for malicious destruction of pant legs?" Miller deadpanned.

Westray started to laugh. "Okay, partner, you got me that time. But watch your back."

"Just tell the guys you got some information leaked on you," said Miller, unable to control his delight. The shoe finally was on the other foot. For a cop who had long been the brunt of West-ray's practical jokes, it felt mighty good to see his partner embarrassed.

"Tell you what, Wimp. I'll write up the reports on the vandal-ism while you slip into something more comfortable," Miller said.

"That way, maybe somebody will actually be able to read them."

Westray, who had the penmanship of a third-grader, continued to dab his pants with a handkerchief. "I don't suppose we can keep this our little secret?"

Miller looked at Westray and smiled a Cheshire grin.

"I didn't think so," he said.

The Downey detectives had been at their fun-loving best for days now. The reason: a break in the Jack Langlos case. Noguchi had finally agreed to a second autopsy. It was a major breakthrough. Without it, the prospects for bringing Hartman to trial were exhausted.

When Miller and Westray met Jindrich at the Downey police station they liked him. They could tell right away he wasn't like other bureaucrats as they watched him prepare for the second autopsy. Jindrich wasn't concerned about covering up for his fellow doctors in Los Angeles. He wasn't interested in making a tidy fee or getting a lot of public exposure for himself.

Jindrich was only concerned about two things: the victim and the truth. He listened intently as the Downey police traced the investigation from the moment they arrived at the Lakewood Park Health Center and found the body.

"By the way, how is Ruth doing? We haven't seen her for awhile," said Miller.

"She's having great difficulty adjusting to the death. But that's not uncommon," Jindrich replied. "In a sense, Jack Langlos is the man who wouldn't die. He's still alive for her, and I'm afraid he's going to stay alive until this is resolved. She really hasn't started the grieving process."

"We've done everything we could," said Westray. "I wish I could say the same for the coroner's office. We've gone over this case hundreds of times. We've had other investigators review the evidence. Everybody reached the same conclusion: Langlos was murdered."

Jindrich was only mildly surprised the Downey police had accepted a coroner's report they knew was wrong. Police, like the rest of the public, expect doctors to know what they're doing. The cops had been intimidated by the expertise attached to a medical diploma on the wall. Understandable, but unfortunate, Jindrich thought.

"The real mystery in this case is what's going on with the coroner," Miller shook his head.

"Hopefully, we'll find out tomorrow," said Jindrich.

He didn't want to reveal his suspicions until he had proof. A tragic mistake had been made, Jindrich felt. What else could explain the disparity between the findings of the police and the doctors?

The coroner's investigator at the scene said Jack Langlos was murdered. Police said it was a homicide. But it was a natural death, according to Doctors Noguchi and Carpenter.

Someone was wrong. Jindrich suspected the coroner had blown it, but he hadn't voiced that opinion to anyone. He knew the unwritten credo of the medical profession: Doctors don't criticize doctors, unless they want to be sued. Even the truth might not shield a doctor who pointed out the error of another physician. Jindrich knew that doctors could find themselves in costly litigation for damaging the reputation and earning capacity of a peer. So those in the medical profession don't take chances. If they feel another doctor is incompetent, they can report it to the State Board of Medical Quality Assurance.

Jindrich wasn't sure if he was dealing with incompetence in the Langlos case. Of course, he had clashed with Noguchi once on the issue of embalming, but other than that Jindrich didn't really know Noguchi except by reputation, and he didn't know Carpenter, the original coroner on the Langlos case, at all.

Carpenter had described the heart of Jack Langlos in the autopsy. The problem was, the heart he described wasn't that bad, and certainly not consistent with causing death. If the autopsy had revealed a ruptured heart from acute infarction, for example, Jindrich wouldn't have flown to Los Angeles. But he sensed Mrs. Langlos had been done an injustice. He just didn't know why.

On January 19, 1977, the casketed body of Jack Langlos was removed from an upper-level crypt at Forest Lawn Cemetery. Jindrich was among six people watching as the inner seal was broken behind the marble front. George Ward from the coroner's office and four representatives from the cemetery also attended.

At the coroner's office, Jack's trumpet was removed from the casket. The body was undressed, examined, and cleansed with soap and water. Photographs were taken at every step of the process. Finally, the body was stored in a refrigerated room.

The next morning, Miller had an opportunity to repay Westray big time for the siren in the locker and all the other times Miller had been the brunt of his partner's warped sense of humor.

Miller knew he would be tapped to attend the second autopsy of Jack Langlos because he was the senior detective on the case. But someone also had to fly to Fresno to pick up a grand theft suspect. Surreptitiously, Miller assigned himself to that task, leaving Westray for the autopsy watch. As the plane taxied on the runway, Miller leaned back in his seat, closed his eyes, and glowed in his victory.

◆ ◆ ◆

In the coroner's lab Jindrich wore gloves and a plastic apron, but he was there mostly to assist Dr. Carpenter in performing a second autopsy. Jindrich was skeptical they would learn much because second autopsies usually produce little new information. The purpose of a first autopsy is to establish the cause and manner of death; a second one is done on rare occasions to see if something was overlooked. For the second autopsy, the body is significantly decomposed and altered from having the organs already removed and put back.

Jindrich looked down at the body of Jack Langlos. It was fairly well preserved since it had been in a crypt only a year. There was no skull fracture, but it was impossible to determine the original characteristics of the wound because of an incision through it and the suturing.

While they methodically checked body parts, Jindrich and Carpenter chatted about the case. By reputation, Jindrich liked Carpenter. He was an old shoe, a general practitioner who had joined the coroner's office when he was already approaching retirement age. However, as Jindrich watched Carpenter, he realized Carpenter was much older than Jindrich had imagined and his actions were agonizingly slow and deliberate. But he was reasonable and easy to talk to, Jindrich decided.

The heart was retained in formalin. The coronary arteries showed minimal atherosclerotic change and were normal for a middle-aged man such as Jack Langlos. The myocardium was normal, too.

"I don't think the heart is consistent with causing death," said Jindrich as they studied the organ.

"I don't either," Carpenter agreed matter-of-factly.

Carpenter's cavalier answer surprised Jindrich. "Why did you put it down then?"

"Well, it's office policy."

"Office policy?" Jindrich repeated incredulously.

"Even before Dr. Noguchi came here, the staff was told never to sign out a case with an undetermined cause of death," Carpenter explained. "If you don't know what caused death, you go with the most significant finding you've got. The most significant finding I had here was coronary artery disease. So I called it a heart death."

"If no cause can be determined, it should be signed 'undetermined,'" Jindrich said tersely.

"I know, but that's not our policy."

So that's it, Jindrich thought. When in doubt, guess. Of course, make it an educated guess. He knew some coroners were reluctant to admit they didn't know why someone had died, but not in a case like this, where the circumstances pointed to homicide.

The two doctors continued their inventory like autoworkers on an assembly line. Since most of the cutting had already been completed, they concentrated on taking a close look at each organ.

Jindrich noted no damage to the hyoid bone or thyroid cartilage in the larynx, but both were extremely mobile. There had been an apparent hemorrhage in the left parotic gland in the neck. A section of the mid-tongue was missing, obviously taken for testing. The liver, lungs, and gall bladder were identified.

Also watching, clad in a cloth hospital gown, Westray pressed a handkerchief tightly around his nose. "Why aren't these guys wearing masks?" he whispered to a Downey lab technician. Westray didn't even breathe out of his nose if he could help it. The stench was suffocating.

"You see that powdery crap," Carpenter said, pointing. The body cavity was filled with a large amount of granular embalming material. Many of the organs were interspersed within this white substance.

"They use that to mummify the body," Carpenter explained. "If you breathe that powder and it gets in your lungs, it'll grow and kill you. That's the mummy's curse."

If it was a joke, Westray wasn't laughing. Westray had a dilemma. On one hand, he strained to hear what was being said by the two doctors. He hoped to pick up a new piece of evidence. On the other hand, the cop who supposedly feared nothing was terrified by the mummy's curse. He knew it wasn't rational, but he believed his life could be in jeopardy if he breathed in the powder. He didn't want to chance it.

"Where's the brain?" Jindrich's voice turned their attention back to the operating table.

"I usually cut it, retain what's needed, and place it in formalin. I put the rest of the brain in a plastic bag and leave it in here," Carpenter said, pointing to the body cavity.

There was no plastic bag. And no brain. "I don't know what happened to it," Carpenter admitted.

Using every bit of will power he could muster, Jindrich remained silent. It was clear to him now that the autopsy of Jack Langlos had been botched. What was worse, he couldn't repair the damage.

In looking at death scene photographs, he noticed the lividity of the victim's face. Jack Langlos could have been strangled. The facial discoloration hadn't even been described in the autopsy report. Or he could have died from a blow to the head even without a fracturing of the skull.

But Jindrich couldn't prove or disprove his theories now. The brain was lost! Without any description or microscopic sections of the brain, it was impossible to evaluate the possibility of death by strangulation or a blow to the head.

If so many things could go wrong in such an obvious homicide case as this, what about all the cases that weren't so obvious? How many times had this happened? Didn't anyone around here care about accuracy?

Jindrich shuddered. He fought back the temptation to pull off the apron and walk out. That wouldn't solve anything.

Jindrich saw other flaws in the autopsy procedures of Los Angeles County. No findings were dictated at the time of the autopsy. In his office Jindrich always used a dictaphone to record his impressions of what he observed during an autopsy. It only cost a little more, but it minimized the possibility of mistakes.

He shook his head, debating about what to do next. Some of the flaws were obvious. The autopsy report described a laceration on the top of the head on one page. On the next, it reported no external indication of injury to the head. It reported minimal tissue reaction and bleeding, but pictures showed blood splattered in various places.

Carpenter used a computerized autopsy format designed to speed up the process. The coroner only needed to list major findings that didn't conform with the form. If the abnormality wasn't that significant, it could be overlooked. The standardized form was convenient but not scientific. Jindrich preferred to list all his findings because there was less chance of making an error.

But Marin County wasn't Los Angeles County. Few places in the Unites States are. With an annual caseload of thousands of autopsies—more than most states—Los Angeles doctors couldn't afford the luxury of time.

About forty-five minutes into the autopsy, Dr. Noguchi stormed into the room, his silk paisley designer tie flapping.

Noticing Westray and the technician standing against a wall with noses covered, Noguchi veered in their direction.

"What are you doing? Take those handkerchiefs away. This is a healthy smell," said Noguchi, taking a deep breath.

Coroners are accustomed to the odor of death. Westray wasn't. He couldn't tell if Noguchi was serious or kidding. But he didn't move a muscle.

Noguchi smirked and joined the two doctors. Suddenly Noguchi began digging in the body cavity like a kid looking for treasure. His tie hanging into the skull cavity, he talked incessantly while his eyes darted with lightning speed from body part to body part. By the time he left the room fifteen minutes later, his shirt and tie were stained.

Westray couldn't believe what was happening. Lifting his handkerchief for a split second, Westray muttered: "That son of a bitch really gets into this."

At the table, the doctors discussed the next course of action. There would be a microscopic examination of tissues, an X-ray examination of the larynx, full-body X-rays, and toxicologic analysis of the partially decomposed and embalmed tissues.

Westray was shocked at what he was overhearing.

"So it's the department policy to avoid using undetermined as a cause of death," said Jindrich, making sure he hadn't misunderstood.

"Well, it's not in writing, but that's been the policy for many years," Carpenter replied.

"Does it happen often?"

"Yeah, I'd say ten percent of all our cases are undetermined. We just list the most likely cause and let it go at that."

"Any particular reason?"

"Well, for one thing the insurance companies don't always pay off if the cause of death is undetermined. The families would end up getting down on us. It can get to be quite a hassle. So sometimes we just rely on instincts."

"And in this case your instinct told you it was the heart," Jindrich said.

"Uh-huh."

Hearing Carpenter admit he wasn't sure how Jack Langlos died made the nausea he felt at the hour-long autopsy worthwhile for Westray. He couldn't wait to tell Miller.

But first Westray had to rid himself of the stench. At home, he took off his sport coat, shirt, and socks on the porch. Upstairs in the bathroom he dipped Q-tips in vinegar and cleaned his nose.

Then he showered, changed, got a polyethylene bag, went outside, and gingerly put his clothes inside. When he arrived at the cleaners, his buddy Al glanced up from behind the counter, picked up the smelly bag of clothes and drew back, saying: "What the hell happened here?"

◆ ◆ ◆

Jindrich didn't have to ask that question. Unfortunately, he knew. Now, as he sat with Carpenter and Noguchi in a meeting, the question that rolled around his mind was: How are these guys going to right the wrong?

Carpenter seemed uncomfortable. He sheepishly admitted that the cause of death on the Jack Langlos death certificate was probably wrong.

"It looks to me like it will be impossible to say with any certainty what caused Langlos's death," Jindrich said, looking at his notes.

As Dr. Wisely joined the meeting, Jindrich ticked off his concerns. Their autopsy had described a hemorrhage of the scalp, but no scalp tissue was shown on the tissue slides. The slides showed a hemorrhage of the tongue, but that wasn't described in the autopsy. "And, I suggest," he paused, then continued, his voice gathering force, "that the coroner's office search for the brain."

Jindrich waited for resistance. Instead, Noguchi smiled.

"We need to take another look at this case," he admitted. "I know I'm not convinced that the corner of the desk caused the wound on his head. The toxicology should have been performed prior to certifying a death under unusual circumstances. So should the microscopic examination."

Carpenter looked distinctly uncomfortable. "I don't remember taking a section of tongue. I assume there must have been a hemorrhage there that drew my attention," he said. "As for the brain, I don't know what happened."

"Dr. Wisely will review the slides, and then we'll make a determination," Noguchi said. "This needs to be resolved one way or the other. I'm curious, what do you think happened?"

Jindrich's jaw tightened. "Like you, I don't think that Langlos hit his head on the corner of the desk unless the desk was moved. There's no question he was sitting in that high backed chair while bleeding," said Jindrich.

He pointed to a photograph showing Langlos's blood-stained back. "Look, the blood had run down the chair the same distance as it had run down the back of his sport coat to the belt line. It's my guess he was being strangled while they struggled. The blood on the wall is consistent with his head going backwards and hitting the wall."

"That's plausible," Wisely said.

"Well, unless something new surfaces, my report will reflect the likelihood that Langlos died in a homicide," Jindrich continued. "Based on the evidence I've seen, I don't believe we can say it was caused by coronary artery disease."

"I'd have to agree, but I'd like to go over my notes again," Carpenter said quietly.

Noguchi's face was inscrutable as he nodded, but he stopped short of promising to let Carpenter change the death certificate. "I don't disagree with anything you've said, but I'd like to go over the entire file again."

"I'd like to test the clothes," Jindrich said.

"Of course," Noguchi agreed.

The half-hour get-together on the Langlos case was over.

"How about some lunch?" Noguchi cordially invited.

"I'd like to, but I've got a plane to catch," Jindrich lied. He wanted to keep this association as professional as possible.

"Oh yeah, one last thing," Jindrich said, pulling a copy of an autopsy from his brief case. "In researching this case, I came upon the autopsy you did on Barbara Jean Hartman. She was the first wife of the guy who was convicted of forging Langlos's name." He looked at Noguchi for a long moment. "I'd like you to take another look at it. Apparently the sheriff's department investigated it, but I couldn't find any report."

"That was sixteen years ago," said Noguchi. He glanced at the documents. They showed that Barbara Jean Hartman, age twenty-six, had been found on the floor with her nose near a gas jet on

December 3, 1961. The cause of death was determined to be as-phyxiation/inhalation of natural gas. It was ruled a suicide.

"I'll review this," said Noguchi matter-of-factly. "You think Hartman murdered Langlos?"

"The police are convinced of it," Jindrich answered and bid the others good-bye.

A short while later, as he boarded the plane for San Francisco, Jindrich felt self-conscious. He quickly shoved a duffel bag into the overhead compartment. Inside were the bloody clothes of Jack Langlos he was to have tested once he got home.

Jindrich sat down in the aisle seat he had been assigned, buckled up, and watched as the plane took off into an azure blue sky, climbing up above the clouds.

"What would I have said if airport security wanted to take a closer look?" The thought of having to explain made Jindrich nervous.

But he felt mighty good, too. As he had suspected, the autopsy of Jack Langlos had been a major foul-up. He wondered why the D.A.'s office hadn't pursued the case. They could have accepted the heart attack conclusion but said it wasn't natural. The excitement of the situation and the beating could have caused a heart attack, and any death that occurs during the commission of a felony is murder. There had been successful prosecutions along those lines.

It would have been cumbersome, Jindrich reasoned. But not unusual. The D.A. probably didn't want to antagonize the coroner's office by proceeding with the case and making the coroner look bad. After all, they probably had several other homicides pending that needed the coroner's testimony. Oh, those paybacks!

"Would you like something to drink, sir?" the perky red-haired stewardess asked.

"Pepsi, please," he responded.

Jindrich took a long gulp of the soda and started thumbing through a magazine, his mind elsewhere. He was confident that his input would convince Noguchi and Carpenter to right the wrong. They seemed willing to change the death certificate. That likely would reopen the case and lead to criminal charges for

Hartman.

He nodded to himself, thinking maybe then Jack Langlos would be able to rest in peace and his wife could get on with her life.

Chapter 13

Talk of a Scheme

It wasn't exactly the good life, but Eugene Hartman was getting by.

Considering the last fourteen months, that was no small achievement. Although he had not been jailed for the murder rap, he had spent thirty-four days in jail and lost his job. Not to mention a felony conviction.

For even the stout-hearted, that was a lot of emotional baggage to tote. But Hartman wasn't going to moan his life away. He just rebounded in another city.

Even Hartman must have wondered when the rebounding would stop. On the day before Hartman pleaded guilty to forgery, he had applied to Eric Lortimer for Langlos's job. He was familiar with the facility and the patients, but Lortimer, the administrator of the Lakewood Park Health Center, was overwhelmed by Hartman's gall. He coldly rejected the application.

With that rejection, and having few patients left, Hartman left town. San Diego seemed a logical refuge. A brother headed the Naval Intelligence Service nearby, the area was thriving, and Hartman had worked there as a psychologist prior to joining the team of psychologists near Los Angeles.

But he continued to wrestle with the financial demons that punctured his dreams. Hartman wasn't obsessed with money, but his lack of it was troubling nevertheless. People with less intelligence and skills were more successful. It seemed to wear on him.

Hartman had promised his probation officer that he would seek psychiatric help for depression at the Veterans Administration Hospital in San Diego. But he never did.

For several months, he tried unsuccessfully to sell hearing aids on commission. Desperate again for cash, Hartman turned to one area in which he felt comfortable: romance.

While not handsome, he had had his share of sexual conquests. He wasn't shy, and his cool sense of confidence and understanding of human nature helped him with women. At a party, Hartman wouldn't sulk if he was turned down for a dance. Instead, he'd simply try another partner. Ultimately, someone said yes.

So it was natural for Hartman to try to make money in the singles scene. Larry Laitner, an acquaintance he'd met at a party, had formed Single Scene America. With 420 members, the business made very little profit but showed potential. However, Laitner had grown tired of party planning and dating services and wanted out.

Hartman purchased the business for one dollar and became its executive director. The position didn't come with a salary, but it could prove to be a financial windfall. In the singles business one could find lonely people who had lost spouses through death or divorce. He'd counsel them for a fee and also help them ease back into the social scene for another fee.

But Hartman had underestimated the challenge. There were at least forty singles clubs in San Diego with thousands of members. Recruiting and maintaining active memberships was time-consuming and costly. When he hosted a singles party, Hartman usually would net about thirty dollars after paying for refreshments and invitations. Sometimes he'd lose money.

The sign on the door of Suite 5 at 3760 Fourth Avenue had revealed his mixed passions. It read:

Eugene C. Hartman, Clinical Psychologist
& All Singles Center.

But then Hartman had become president of another singles club,
The Vital Set. His financial interests were varied, but his income
remained modest.

Still, the cloud of disaster that shadowed him refused to leave.
On March 6, a fire had forced the closing of his office. It had reopened, but his name still hadn't been added to the door.

Hartman saw three patients here twice a week. The twenty-
five to fifty dollars a week he netted from the visits constituted
about a tenth of his income. The singles clubs continued only to
meet expenses.

The bulk of his income—$420 a month—came from a disabil-
ity pension through Social Security. Included was $120 monthly
for support of his seventeen-year-old daughter, who had moved in
with him in an apartment on Ninth Avenue.

At least once a month, Hartman's past loomed before him.
When his rent was due, Hartman had to pay with cash or a
money order. He wasn't allowed to write checks because of his
forgery conviction. And once a month he paid fifty dollars to the
public defender's office in Los Angeles County for his legal fees
and another twenty-five to the probation department for court
costs.

Of course, these were temporary problems that could be
resolved.

Then the state Department of Consumer Affairs moved to revoke his psychology license because of the forgery felony conviction. Now Hartman's face welled with anger as he sat in a small
courtroom in downtown San Diego. Sitting alone behind a table
with only a note pad and a pitcher of water, Hartman was defend-
ing himself before the state Psychology Examining Committee.

Across the aisle, blond, good-looking Deputy Attorney General Carlton Mittendorf radiated self-assurance. And why not?
One of the leading consumer advocates in the Attorney General's
office, Mittendorf took his job seriously. He enjoyed ridding the

state of professional shysters and incompetents. Well-briefed on Hartman by the police and Ruth Langlos, Mittendorf couldn't wait to get him on the witness stand.

Administrative Law Judge Jerome Schwimmer had some housekeeping to take care of first. As Hartman settled into the witness chair, the judge said, "Since you are representing yourself and have no one to put questions to you, you may testify in narrative fashion concerning any matters that you feel are relevant."

"Is it correct that you did plead guilty to the crime of forgery as set forth in Exhibit 3?" Schwimmer asked.

"Yes."

"And that you were placed on probation for five years with a requirement that you served the first thirty-four days in the county jail, pay a fine of fifteen hundred dollars, plus penalty assessment, make restitution, have no blank checks in your possession, and certain other terms and conditions of probation?"

Hartman smiled faintly. "That is all correct."

"Are you on probation at the present time?"

"I'm on probation at the present time," Hartman repeated.

"How often do you report to your probation officer?"

"Well, originally I was reporting every three months, and now I am just supposed to call him if I have difficulties."

"All right, sir. I'll try to make that the last interruption. You may proceed."

Hartman's opening statement would set the tone for the hearing. He had to convince the judge of two things: He was sorry for his offense, and it wouldn't happen again.

"The events leading up to my plea came under very severe and very unusual stress," Hartman began. "It's unlikely to be repeated. And in situations for which at that time I made a bad adjustment, the plea came about through advice of my counsel.

"The stresses that I'm talking about involved a dissolution of a marriage, a finding of multiple sclerosis illness, and very, very severe and threatening charges pending against me in court. These circumstances are extremely unusual. My adjustment to them was bad, and I have since made a better adjustment, and there is no likelihood there would be any repetition of any kind of situation related to the charges."

"Is there anything further that you wish to testify to?" the judge asked.

"May I make further testimony after I respond to the attorney general?"

"Surely. You will have the right to redirect examination or testimony. Let me ask you one question: Have you since the conviction been under psychiatric or psychological care, treatment, or therapy?"

"No, I have not."

Mittendorf nearly bolted from his seat at the chance for cross examination. Hartman's *mea culpas* hadn't impressed him. Mittendorf practiced the attorney's golden rule in the courtroom: Try not to ask a question you don't already know the answer to. He came out swinging.

"Mr. Hartman, have you made restitution to Mrs. Langlos as required by the probation?"

Hartman stared at some unknown spot on the wall and coolly replied, "No, I have not."

"What is the amount of restitution that you are required to pay to her?"

"I'm not sure exactly what the amount will be. I'm paying a fine. I'm paying for the public defender's cost."

"Is there any reason why you have not paid restitution to her as required by your probation officer—required by the order of the court?"

Hartman said tartly, "I'm prepared to pay one hundred dollars if that is the amount of restitution, but that's not to Mrs. Langlos. I am not aware of any restitution . . . "

In the second row, Ruth's friend Louise McCord nudged the attractive young brunette woman next to her and whispered: "He's lying. He's never made good on the bad check he gave Jack."

McCord and Dianne Warren, the niece of Ruth Langlos, were the only spectators in the courtroom. McCord was supposed to be jotting down notes, but her hands were shaking.

"You're going to have to do this," she said, handing Dianne a spiral notebook and pen. "I can't concentrate. This guy gives me the creeps."

"Who is the restitution to be paid to?" Mittendorf prodded.

Hartman scratched his head, then answered, "I think it was the Food Basket. It was to a market."

"The Boy's Market?" Mittendorf asked.

"The Boy's Market," Hartman echoed.

"You have not paid restitution in the amount of one hundred dollars to Boy's Market."

"That's correct," Hartman said dully.

Mittendorf nodded in satisfaction. "The guy is sorry but not sorry enough to make restitution," he murmured. Mittendorf picked up a piece of paper from the table, scanned it for a few seconds and headed into another area fertile with skeletons.

"Before sharing a practice with another psychologist in San Diego, where were you working?"

"I was in Minnesota. I was employed at Anoka-Ramsay Community College."

"When was this?"

"From 1967, I believe, until 1971."

Hartman had taught general psychology and the psychology of adjustment, two disciplines that served him well in his private life. Hartman also had a private practice. Prior to that, he had been a clinical psychologist at Cambridge State Hospital in Minnesota.

"Why did you leave your position at Anoka?"

"I was not a tenured teacher, and there was a drop in enrollment. I was laid off," Hartman said flatly.

"Prior to that, you came to Pomona, California. What year?"

"I came to work at Mt. San Antonio College, and that was in about 1957."

Hartman fidgeted in his seat, his face flushed. He seemed to know where Mittendorf was headed and resented it. For four years at Mt. San Antonio, Hartman had taught courses in general psychology, physiological psychology, and psychology of adjustment. He had worked part-time at a medical clinic and also at a hospital for the retarded.

But Mittendorf didn't care about Hartman's past.

"Mr. Hartman, was a lawsuit instituted against you at Mt. San Antonio to get you dismissed?"

"Yes."

"And what was the basis of that lawsuit?"

"The basis for the lawsuit?" Hartman said slowly. "I was a tenured teacher, and they charged immoral conduct."

"Was that a case brought in the Superior Court, or was it a disciplinary action in an administrative-type proceeding?"

"It was a court proceeding containing two court hearings, one in Los Angeles and one in Pomona." A pale ghost of a smile played around Hartman's lips.

"After the lawsuits, did you . . . were you terminated?"

"Yes."

"What kind of conduct were you alleged to have been involved in?"

"Well, there were two trials," Hartman explained, his eyes directed straight ahead. Then he looked at the prosecutor. "The first trial—it was alleged that I cohabited with an individual to whom I was not married. I won the case and I received back salary and reinstatement."

"And the second one?" Mittendorf stared back at him.

Hartman continued, chortling, "They brought up, if I remember, about five different allegations in that."

Mittendorf wasn't about to give up. "Similar charges for cohabitation?"

"Similar charges, right," Hartman said non-committally.

Mittendorf pressed on. "Were these five charges—did they involve five different people?"

"No. Let's see," Hartman paused. "There were three different people involved."

"Were these females?"

"Yes."

"Were they students of yo rs?"

"No."

"Were they students at the college who were not in your particular class?"

Hartman was moving around in his seat, seemingly unable to sit comfortably. "No."

"Now, as a result of the second action that was brought, were you then dismissed from your position?"

"Yes, I was."

Ruth's friend Louise and her niece looked at each other. "I wish Ruth could see this," whispered McCord.

"Hartman is really squirming up there," Warren wrote on a sheet of paper she passed to McCord.

"He has reason to," McCord said.

At Mittendorf's request, Hartman rattled off his professional background and qualifications. He had earned bachelor's and master's degrees from San Jose State University. He was one of the first psychologists to be licensed by the State of California.

After a year in graduate work at the University of Southern California, Hartman became a high school instructor. He taught history at Central High School in El Centro, California, for a year and taught English and social studies at Wilson and Huntington Park High Schools in the Los Angeles city school system. He stayed there for five years.

"Were you ever dismissed from any of those teaching positions?" inquired Mittendorf.

"No."

◆ ◆ ◆

During a break in the proceedings, Mittendorf walked out in the hall and noticed Louise McCord standing there.

"Where's Ruth?" Mittendorf asked with a smile.

"She didn't think it would be a good idea to come here," McCord said. "She's scared of Hartman. If he figures out that she tipped off the Attorney General's office about the forgery, well, she doesn't know what he'll do."

"She is staying at my house until this is over. It's only twenty minutes away," said Warren. "When do you think this will be finished?"

"This hearing will be done today," Mittendorf replied. "The

only witness is Hartman. Then the judge will review the case and make a ruling probably in a few weeks."

◆　◆　◆

After the break, Mittendorf zeroed in on Hartman's relationship with Jack Langlos. It was the meat of his case, and Mittendorf had prepared painstakingly.

"How long had you known Dr. John Langlos?"

"I had known him," Hartman was silent for a moment, as if mulling over the question, "let's see. The entire year I was working for Planned Living Council, Dr. Langlos was one of my supervisors, so I knew him about a year and a half."

Mittendorf's voice was chilly. "What kind of relationship did you have with him?"

"We were close friends."

Shaking his head, Mittendorf looked Hartman fully in the eye. "Did you ever attempt to borrow money from him?" Mittendorf asked accusingly.

"Yes," Hartman said quietly.

"For what reasons?"

Hartman looked sulky and defiant. "I borrowed money from him to defray expenses pending Medi-Cal payments that were delayed."

Mittendorf kept firing questions at him. "Were you in financial difficulty during these times?"

"Yes."

"Were you married at these times?"

"I was living by myself. I was not married."

"Did you have a family to support?"

"Yes."

"Did you work in the same building as Dr. Langlos in 1976, January and February?"

"I believe in January on occasion I was doing consulting work with Dr. Langlos at one of the hospitals where he was the chief psychologist."

"Now, how much money did Dr. Langlos loan you?"

"I guess, all told, on two separate occasions, three hundred dollars."

"Have you repaid that money to his estate or his family?"

Mittendorf read the contempt in Hartman's eyes as he kept pressing him. "I repaid that money to Dr. Langlos."

"How much money were you earning in your job at the time?"

"At the time on paper I was grossing two thousand a month. That was my accounts receivable."

"Were you arrested in Oakland on February 12, 1976?"

Hartman nodded his head. "Right."

"What was the reason?"

"Well, I was charged with about ten counts—burglary, fraud, illegal entry—I don't remember all the counts that were made."

"How did you obtain his MasterCharge card?"

Hartman shrugged. "He gave it to me."

"How did you obtain the checks?"

"He gave me the checks."

"When?"

"I don't know the exact date."

"How many days before you cashed them?" Mittendorf stared at Hartman. He could sense the uneasiness.

"Two."

"Two days before you actually went to Boy's Market?"

"Let's see. Sunday—no, it was four days."

"Four days before February 1?"

Hartman moistened his lips. "Right."

Mittendorf prompted. "Why did he give you the MasterCharge and his checks?"

A faint smile creased Hartman's face. "He stated that he wanted me to arrange for him to have some money. He wanted me to do him a favor and he would, in return, advance me some money."

"What favor did he want you to do?"

"He wanted me to write a check to clear out his bank account, his joint bank account. His bank account."

"Did he explain to you why he wanted you to do this?"

"Yeah. Because he didn't want his wife to know he was getting money."

The answer startled Judge Schwimmer, a quiet patriarch with steel not far below the surface. "Would you repeat that, sir?" the judge requested.

"He said he didn't want his wife to know he was getting money. He said that she was away in Texas and he needed the money for personal reasons without her knowledge."

Mittendorf's face flushed red with contempt. "When did he tell you this?" Mittendorf asked sharply.

"I don't know the exact date," Hartman answered dryly.

"What did he ask you to do then: Did he ask you to forge his name?"

"Yes."

Mittendorf took a deep breath. "Did you think that was wrong?"

"Yes," Hartman said apologetically.

"Did you do it?"

"I thought it was a peccadillo. I thought it was dumb."

"Why did you do it?"

"I really can't," Hartman paused, then blurted out, "I did it as a favor to him."

"It was against your better judgment?"

"Yes."

He's enjoying this, Mittendorf thought incredulously.

"You knew it was a crime?" he said sourly.

"No," Hartman insisted.

"You didn't know forgery was a crime," Mittendorf cut in, his voice harsh.

Hartman eyed him. "I didn't know that using somebody's credit card and his name with his permission was a crime."

Mittendorf's face tightened visibly. "Okay. Is that why you cashed the check at Boy's Market? Was that for Dr. Langlos or was that for your own personal use?"

Hartman mumbled. "The check I cashed at Boy's Market was for my own personal use."

"Did you do that with Dr. Langlos's permission?"

Hartman nodded. "Yes, I did."

Mittendorf's eyes impaled the other man. "He knew that you were going to cash a check for your own use for one hundred dollars?"

"Yes, right." Hartman gave an affirmative, dismal nod.

"Did he give you any cash on the four days before February 1?" Mittendorf pressed the witness.

"No," Hartman replied.

Mittendorf's questions and Hartman's answers came in staccato bursts. "Did he give you his billfold?"

"No."

"He gave you his license?"

"No."

"How many checks did he give you?"

"Two."

"What did you use the other one for?"

"I was going to use the other one for cashing a check to clear out his bank account—to get the money for him."

"How much money did he have in his bank account?"

"I don't remember. I think it was . . . he wanted eighteen hundred dollars."

"There was eighteen hundred?"

"I think that's what he told me it was."

Louise McCord couldn't believe what was happening. Ruth had told her Langlos had more than six thousand dollars in that account. "What a pathetic character," she whispered. McCord wanted to run to a phone immediately and let Ruth know what Hartman was saying about her husband, but she resisted the urge. Who knew what Hartman would claim next? And she knew Ruth would want a complete report.

"So, you wrote a check for eighteen hundred dollars to clear the account?" Mittendorf asked.

"No, I didn't."

"You intended to do that."

"That's correct."

"And you never got around to it?"

"Well, what I intended to do was to call Dr. Langlos and tell him I wasn't going to do that, and instead I went up to Hayward, California, to visit my parents."

"What happened to the check?"

"I don't know."

"Did you use that credit card to obtain money or buy goods?"

"Yes."

"Was that with Dr. Langlos's permission?"

"Yes, it was."

"Did you ask him if you could use his credit card?"

"He brought up the whole business, and then I brought up some things I needed to do."

"Well, what 'whole business' did he bring up?"

"The whole business of getting money that his wife wouldn't know he had."

"Did he explain how that was to happen?"

"Yes. I was going to cash this check at his bank account."

Unlike a criminal trial, the administrative law judge at a license hearing has the liberty of interrupting to question the witness himself. Schwimmer had been studying Hartman for a while, jotting down questions. Now Schwimmer sternly asked: "How was this to result in his wife not knowing any better than his cashing it directly? Did he explain that to you?"

"Because the check was," Hartman hesitated, then said, "the signature was not going to be his. It was going to be my writing his name."

Mittendorf shared the judge's skepticism. He wasn't about to let Hartman off the hook. "Did Dr. Langlos explain to you what would happen when the check would be recovered and his wife might look at the returned checks?" Mittendorf asked, raising his eyebrows and lifting his arms for effect.

"No, he didn't."

"Did you think about that?" Mittendorf's voice dripped with incredulity. "Did you think it would work?"

"No, I didn't."

"Did you care whether it would?"

"I decided not to do it."

"You did the one-hundred-dollar check."

"That's correct," Hartman said apologetically.

Once again Mittendorf moved in. "How about the Master-Charge? Now, you used that to buy some goods at Zody's."

"That's correct," Hartman nodded his head affirmatively.

"Was that for your own personal use?"

"Yes."

"You had the MasterCharge with his permission?"

"Yes."

"And he knew you were going to Zody's to purchase—"

Despite attempts to keep cool, Hartman was becoming flustered by Mittendorf's rapid-fire interrogation. He interrupted: "He didn't know I was going to Zody's. He knew I was going to buy certain quantities, certain amounts. He was going to give me five hundred dollars."

Mittendorf knew he had Hartman. He continued his siege, thrusting and parrying. "What was that for, the five hundred?"

"It was simply an advance on work I was doing in association with him. It was an advance, actually."

"It wasn't part of the deal, 'If you do this for me, I'll give you five hundred dollars as a gift?'"

"He would advance me five hundred, right."

"You had to pay it back to him?"

"No, I didn't have to pay it back to him." Hartman wiped the perspiration from his forehead. "I had to do a certain amount of work at his facility. That he would bill for himself."

"So you had to pay it back by working it out."

"Right."

"What did you buy at Zody's with his MasterCharge?"

"I bought a watch."

"Did he know you were going to do that?"

Hartman shrugged. "I don't think so."

Mittendorf's eyes impaled Hartman. "Where else did you use his MasterCharge?"

"I bought airline tickets with his MasterCharge. I purchased the tickets at three different airports. Hollywood-Burbank, LAX, and Long Beach."

Mittendorf raised his eyebrows. "Why did you go to three

different airports?"

"Because I couldn't purchase the tickets all in one airport."

"Why not?" Mittendorf asked blandly.

Hartman was ruffled. "Because I—I didn't know exactly what I was doing. I guess I could have done that. That's true. I guess I could have a large party going and purchase them all at once."

"Was there some reason that you thought you would get caught if you spent a large amount of money with somebody else's credit card?" Mittendorf said wryly.

"If I would be questioned, and I had no identification."

"You had his identification," Mittendorf scoffed.

"No, I didn't have his identification," Hartman replied, shaking his head.

"You had his driver's license at the time you cashed the check at Boy's Market," Mittendorf emphasized.

"I don't remember," Hartman said lamely.

"Did you read your probation report?" Mittendorf believed Hartman was improvising his story as they went along. Now, Hartman had been caught in an obvious lie.

"I never read my probation report," Hartman said dully.

Judge Schwimmer intervened: "You never read your probation report that you agreed to be received in evidence here?" He asked quizzically.

"I read a probation report which was not six pages," Hartman said, his voice barely audible, referring to the document Mittendorf was handing him.

Perturbed, the judge called a recess to let Hartman read what he had previously told his probation officer.

After the fifteen-minute break, Mittendorf was ready to deliver a knockout blow. He studied the witness in the charcoal-colored suit. From twenty-five feet away, Mittendorf could almost feel Hartman's anxiety. Hartman looked like a stranger at a family gathering. He avoided eye contact, fidgeted in his chair, and pawed nervously at his watch. *This guy's got to know his sworn testimony doesn't jibe with what he's told his probation officer,* Mittendorf figured. Mittendorf fingered the probation report in his hand, then he held it up as if to remind Hartman that the truth was at his fingertips.

His eyes shifted to Hartman's face. "There is some indication here in this report that you used the MasterCharge of Dr. Langlos as well as the doctor's driver's license number in cashing the check at Boy's Market. How did you obtain the driver's license?"

Hartman, edging forward in the wooden chair, tried to explain. "If I had—let's see. When I read that, I thought and thought over that and—okay. Dr. Langlos gave me the MasterCharge, two blank checks, and the driver's license personally."

Mittendorf smiled at the admission. Would Hartman have them believe that Langlos would give his driver's license away voluntarily?

Judge Schwimmer had his doubts, too. He asked: "Was Dr. Langlos using his automobile in connection with his practice?"

"Yes."

"Did his practice involve seeing patients outside the office?"

"Yes."

Mittendorf jumped in, hammering away at the improbability.

"As far as you know, Dr. Hartman, did Dr. Langlos drive to work every day from his residence to the office? Would that be his familiar routine?"

"That would be his familiar routine, yes," answered Hartman.

Mittendorf paused. He had made his point: Langlos used his car daily and wouldn't likely give his license away.

"Now," Mittendorf said, switching subjects, "did you tell Dr. Langlos you were going to use his card to buy tickets on Pacific Southwest Airlines?"

Hartman's face was emotionless. "I told him I was going to use his card to get three hundred dollars."

Mittendorf shook his head. "Well, was this part of the scheme to take the money out of the bank? How do those things relate?"

Hartman shrugged. "The scheme was that his wallet was going to be lost."

Mittendorf wasn't about to move away yet. "He was going to tell his wife or someone that his wallet was lost?"

Hartman nodded. "That's right."

"Did he give you anything else out of his wallet? Did he give you his wallet?" Mittendorf asked wryly.

Hartman grumbled in reply, "He gave me nothing else out of the wallet. He did not give me his wallet. He said he was going to lose it and report it stolen. He said he was going to tell his wife he lost it."

"Okay," Mittendorf said sharply. "Explain how this thing was going to work. He gave you those things. What was going to happen? What was the purpose of it?"

Hartman sighed. "I was supposed to use the credit card in different places, write his signature, and I was going to cash a check for one hundred dollars for myself and then cash the check at his bank for the money he wanted."

Mittendorf bit his lip and said, "The eighteen hundred dollars."

Hartman nodded again. "Right."

Mittendorf said sarcastically, "I take it the purpose of you going to various places and using the credit card was to show a different signature, which would substantiate his story that his wallet was lost and somebody else was using the MasterCharge. Was that your understanding?"

"Yes." Hartman sneered, "My understanding was he was going to tell his wife that he wanted to get the money and not let his wife know how he got it."

Mittendorf broke in. "And you knew at the time you used his MasterCharge that it was wrong."

Hartman beat a fast retreat. "No, I have used other people's credit cards before, and I have let other people use my credit cards. I did not know it was wrong."

Mittendorf couldn't disguise the contempt in his voice. "You thought it was perfectly legal to—"

Hartman interrupted. "Yes. This all started because I was working for him, doing some psychological evaluations, and he said I could do a favor for him, and he knew I needed money. We both were in sort of a tight financial situation because of serious delays in Medi-Cal payments."

Hartman was clearly irritated and restless. Mittendorf kept asking him over and over about the same things, trying to trick him into admitting the truth.

Ruth's niece and friend Louise were anything but restless. They watched mesmerized. For the first time since Langlos's death, Hartman was being forced to testify about the events leading up to that terrible weekend. When first charged, he had refused to discuss it with the Downey police or the prosecutor's office. Instead, he used the public defender as a shield. He invoked his legal rights and stayed mum.

Hartman's plea bargain had left numerous unanswered questions. Warren wrote feverishly, trying to capture every nugget of information. McCord, meanwhile, sat in stunned silence. Jack Langlos in a scheme? Why would he go to such extremes to get his own money? "How farfetched!" she stewed. And how convenient for Hartman to use this ploy since Langlos wasn't alive to defend himself.

Yet again Hartman was trying to explain the discrepancies in his account. According to his testimony, he was supposed to go to the bank that Monday and withdraw money for Langlos. They had conceived the plan on the prior Wednesday, when they worked together at the hospital. Hartman claimed it was the last time he saw Langlos alive.

But Mittendorf brought out that Hartman didn't go to the bank. Instead, he headed for the Oakland area to visit his parents in Hayward and work temporarily as a house painter in Salinas.

Why? Hartman said he had simply changed his mind. He didn't remember when.

"I decided to call him and tell him that I would write his name on the check and then he could cash it at the bank," said Hartman. "I called Dr. Langlos every day of that week—Thursday, Friday, Saturday, Sunday.

"During the day I tried to reach him at the hospital and I also called him at home."

Hartman said he tried two or three days after Sunday—February 2, 3, and 4—not knowing that Langlos was dead. He said he didn't learn of Langlos's death until he was arrested for the murder in San Jose.

"Dr. Langlos was found dead on Monday, February 2,"

declared Judge Schwimmer, reading the probation report. "Were you informed of that fact in response to any of your telephone calls?"

"No," Hartman snapped.

Judge Schwimmer wasn't about to be put off. "What were you told when you asked for Dr. Langlos?"

"I was told one time that they would buzz him, and another time they rang his office, but he was not there," Hartman replied.

Mittendorf stared at the probation report. He didn't believe Hartman and Langlos had had a scheme. In fact, he doubted most of Hartman's testimony. Mittendorf had chiseled at Hartman's credibility. Now it was time to use a sledgehammer.

Mittendorf's voice had a steel edge. "Mr. Hartman, let's go over this one more time. Why did you purchase nine airline tickets?"

Hartman, his face a mask, answered. "I purchased nine tickets to make up the three hundred dollars that I was going to get cash for. That was the money that was going to be advanced to me, and I also was using the credit card with his name to show it was used around."

"Why didn't you just go to a bank and use the credit card to get three hundred in cash?"

"Well, that might have been a better idea," Hartman conceded.

Disgusted, Mittendorf wasn't about to let go. "At the time of your arrest, did you make a statement that you had purchased the tickets at a discount from a credit card holder?"

"Yes," Hartman was growing visibly tired.

Mittendorf pressed his advantage harder now. "Was that true?"

"No."

"Why didn't you tell him the truth?"

"Well, because in essence that was the truth."

"Had you purchased the tickets at a discount?"

"No, they were purchased at full price."

"Had you purchased them from anyone other than the airline?" Mittendorf hammered away at Hartman.

"No."

"Was what you said true?"

"I had purchased some tickets at one time at a discount, right, from a credit card holder. Not at that time."

Exasperated, Mittendorf glanced at the judge and shrugged. Extracting the truth from all the double-talk took a careful ear and a lot of attention. They were playing mind games, and Mittendorf didn't like games. He liked being in control.

"Was what you told the interviewing police officer true?"

"No," Hartman mumbled.

"Why did you tell him an untruth?" Mittendorf asked gruffly.

"Because I wanted to get out of jail."

"Why would telling an untruth get you out of jail?" Mittendorf probed.

"Because he implied that it would. In fact, he even suggested it," Hartman said flatly.

"How did he do that?" Mittendorf grimaced.

"He said, 'I want to get you out of here today. There's just a few things I want to clear up, so let's clear these things up.' It was a very friendly conversation."

Hartman went on to explain that he had been arrested after trying to upgrade the airline tickets. He did so because the more expensive tickets could be redeemed for cash; the ones he originally charged could not.

"In any of these dealings, did you ever represent yourself to be Dr. Langlos?" inquired Mittendorf coldly.

"No," Hartman said curtly.

Mittendorf stared at him for a moment. Then he asked some questions about Hartman's multiple sclerosis and whether Hartman felt it affected his judgment. Mittendorf wanted to be sure Hartman didn't use his illness as a defense later.

Now Mittendorf stood eyeing the witness, a look of satisfaction on his face. He didn't feel the need for an involved closing statement. Hartman's testimony, riddled with inconsistencies, spoke more eloquently than he could.

Because he had been convicted of a felony, Hartman automatically would be stripped of his Medi-Cal provider number. By state law, he could no longer bill the state insurance for his psychology services.

To revoke his psychology license was a more drastic step. In effect, it would ignominiously cast him from the profession in which he had spent much of his life.

But Mittendorf felt in Hartman's case an even more drastic step was appropriate.

"A psychologist has the trust and the care of other people's mental health in their hands," Mittendorf forcefully declared. "To engage in these kinds of scheming activities as a license holder is the kind of activity which I think the public of the State of California needs protection against and particularly people who have mental problems. They are coming to you perhaps not armed with their best wits, and if someone is inclined to take advantage of them, this profession lends itself to that perhaps more than others."

Hartman sat slumped in the witness chair, obviously exhausted. If this round of probing wasn't bad enough, he also faced the possible loss of his teacher's license because of the forgery. That hearing was coming up in a few weeks.

Hartman's emotionless rebuttal took less than a minute. "Well, the only item that I have difficulty with—he's alleging that I took advantage of patients with this arrangement with Dr. Langlos. I don't see that this was the case at all."

Before leaving the courtroom, Warren and McCord thanked Mittendorf for his efforts on behalf of the Langlos family.

"What do you think the judge will do?" McCord asked.

"You want me to go out on a limb and make a prediction," Mittendorf said with a smile. "Well, I'd say the case against Hartman is strong. Actually, it's even stronger after today. His testimony was incriminating. I think the judge will revoke his license."

As he headed into an elevator, Mittendorf looked back and said: "Tell Ruth I'll let her know as soon as I'm notified of a decision." He winked. "I think she'll want to know."

It was the understatement of the day.

Chapter 14

"In Case I Disappear or Die"

For the first time since her husband had been killed, Ruth felt she was accomplishing something in his memory.

Hartman faced the prospect of losing his license to practice psychology. He still had his precious freedom, but his livelihood was in jeopardy.

Thanks to Drs. Jindrich and Walker, the coroner's office appeared ready to correct the autopsy. Once that occurred, Hartman would be brought to trial for murder.

Despite the progress, Ruth was deathly afraid. Her steely, determined exterior masked fragile, fear-ridden feelings. Hartman had to know she was determined to put him in prison. At the very least, he strongly suspected it.

Ruth had hired a private detective to investigate him. She had greased the wheels for his head-on collision with the state licensing board. And she had hired the doctors who were challenging the coroner's autopsy.

Hartman could see that the judicial system had sputtered, stalled, and stagnated. It was eager to move on to the other cases of the day. Jack Langlos was in the past. That only left Ruth in the way.

Lately Ruth had become frightened for her life. There had been an attempted break-in into her apartment. She was badly shaken by the incident. Ruth had found the lock on her sliding patio door had been tampered with. A locksmith told her someone had tried to pry it open. A new lock did not make her feel more secure.

She had refused to follow the advice of Dr. Crossman, a specialist in the study of life-threatening behavior at UCLA, to move away and assume a new name. Now she was about to sign a notarized statement to be given to authorities if she was killed.

With her son Jan seated at her side, Ruth picked up the two-page document handed to her by attorney Todd Bolton in his swanky L.A. office on Wilshire Boulevard. The padded leather chairs, plush carpet, and ornate wood decor reminded clients that their service would be first-rate. So would his fee, she knew.

Ruth didn't have a champagne budget, but Bolton, a senior partner in his firm, had come highly recommended by several friends. Ruth felt she needed someone good, not just a lawyer picked blindly out of the telephone directory, so she'd hired him.

Her hand trembled as she held and read the document.

I am making this statement because I have reason to believe that my life may be in danger. I base this statement and/or concern upon the following:

1. My husband, John T. Langlos, died under very mysterious circumstances on or about February 2, 1976. I believe that the cause of his death was a homicide perpetrated by one Eugene C. Hartman, a psychologist who had worked with my husband.

2. Dr. Hartman was arrested in Oakland, California, shortly after my husband's death, and at the time of his arrest one or more of my husband's credit cards were in his possession.

3. My husband told me before he died that he was afraid of Dr. Hartman, and we had a discussion over a

$200 check written by Dr. Hartman to my husband. This check was in payment of a loan made by my husband to Dr. Hartman. The check was presented for payment; however, it was returned by the bank because there were insufficient funds. I wanted to collect the monies from Dr. Hartman; however, my husband was afraid of Dr. Hartman and did not want to pressure him into paying this debt.

4. Dr. Hartman's first wife died under very mysterious circumstances on or about December 3, 1961.

5. Someone attempted to break into my apartment in Pacific Palisades on or about June 20, 1976. I reported this to the West Los Angeles Police Department.

In case I disappear or die under any circumstance whatsoever, in my opinion, a prime suspect and/or an individual who very probably might be associated with my death or disappearance would be Dr. Eugene C. Hartman.

I declare under penalty of perjury that the foregoing is true and correct.

With a determined sweep of the pen, Ruth signed the document.

"Hartman wouldn't dare kill me now," Ruth said with a nervous laugh. "And if he does, at least everybody will know who did it."

◆　◆　◆

She felt grimly satisfied as they drove home. It had been almost two months since the second autopsy, and Ruth had just been reminded that the battle was just beginning. Dr. Jindrich's nine-page, single-spaced report had soundly criticized the shoddiness of the first autopsy.

Then, the coup de grace arrived. Ruth scanned a copy of the letter from Dr. Jindrich to Dr. Noguchi. She read it and re-read it. Tears of joy and anger welled up.

Ruth savored the letter's contents, slowly absorbing every

phrase like a wine connoisseur tasting a vintage Beaujolais.

Dear Dr. Noguchi:

Having reviewed the records, investigative reports, and material evidence pertaining to the death of John Langlos (Your Case No. 76-01473), I have provided Mrs. Langlos with a detailed report of my findings and opinions. In essence, I have advised her that the medical cause of death has not been established, and the mode of death appears to be homicide. It is my opinion that the death certificate should be appended, the cause of death certified as "Undetermined," and the mode of death "Probable Homicide." At the least the mode could be stated as "Undetermined (Probable Homicide)" to indicate that the preponderance of evidence supports death at the hands of another.

In my report I informed Mrs. Langlos that although the cause of death has not been established, one would have to consider strangulation very seriously. The lividity of the face on post mortem photographs of Mr. Langlos (and not present on ante mortem photos in Mrs. Langlos's possession), the intra-oral hemorrhage, the missing necktie, and the absence of significant natural disease in the individual would all be consistent with such a cause of death. I also informed her that death could occur from a blow to the head without skull fracture, but that this possibility cannot be explored further due to absence of any description of the brain at the first autopsy, and of any brain tissue in formalin or at second autopsy.

I wish to express my sincere thanks for the cooperation and courtesy extended to me by you and your staff throughout my review of this most interesting case.

Very truly yours,
Ervin J. Jindrich, M.D.

A copy of the letter was in her handbag as she entered the lobby of the Tick Tock restaurant in Hollywood. It was one of the city's landmarks, a place to dine and watch people. The rack of lamb and the baked fish were superb, the service attentive, and the patrons included some of the movie industry's biggest film stars.

But Ruth didn't care about lamb or movie stars today. She had her mind focused on her luncheon with Deputy District Attorney Joe Schafer. She hoped it would jumpstart the criminal justice system to take action on the murder of her husband after more than a year of inertia.

Schafer had seemed interested when Ruth called to tell him about Jindrich's findings. He said he was bringing a friend who was interested in helping her.

Ruth was determined, at least outwardly, to try to mend fences with Schafer. They were going to have to work together and she wanted them to remain civil to each other.

Unfortunately, they had disliked each other from the onset. To Ruth, Schafer was the stereotypical paper-pushing bureaucrat. She had heard that he had joined the prosecutor's office to put criminals behind bars but through the years his goals had changed. People said his career had become more important than public service—and that he concentrated on the promotion track and avoided what would derail him.

According to the rumors, after a while, the line between public service and personal ambition had become blurry. The end result was an administrator who excelled at minimizing risks and maintaining the status quo. On the Langlos case, he had only met with Noguchi when forced to, and even then he was a half-hearted participant in the discussions.

In Ruth's eyes, Schafer was a fraud.

In his eyes, Ruth was a nagging pain.

She didn't care what he thought. Ruth set her jaw. She had been raised to respect authority, but she had also been raised to know the difference between right and wrong. As long as Schafer refused to prosecute her husband's killer, he'd have a determined, emotional widow with which to contend.

To her surprise, Schafer didn't bring another attorney, police officer, or administrator to lunch. He brought a writer.

Samuel Birdsong was a freelance writer and a published author. His first book, a true-crime paperback, had sold reasonably well in the national market. A cops-and-robbers gadfly, Birdsong hung around police stations developing sources and getting story ideas. Schafer met Birdsong while his office was prosecuting a serial rapist case. He liked the way Birdsong had portrayed him in a magazine profile of the case.

"Mrs. Langlos, I think Sam would be a good person for you to talk to. There might be a story here about the difficulty of coping with the sudden death of a spouse, especially since you think it was a homicide," said Schafer.

"Did you hear about Hartman's testimony at his license hearing?" Ruth said forcefully.

Schafer's blank stare spoke volumes.

"Well, Hartman had the gall to say Jack gave him his checks and the credit card. And his driver's license, too. Can you imagine that?"

"Frankly, that's not all that unusual," Schafer said coolly. Even away from the office, Schafer seemed guarded. His face and speech were toneless and unemotional. A wooden man, Ruth thought.

"I'd give a credit card to a friend," said Schafer.

"Okay," Birdsong laughed, holding out his hand.

"Jack wouldn't go around the block without his driver's license," Ruth said, her irritation surfacing.

"But Jack can't dispute what Hartman is claiming. So if Hartman says your husband gave him his driver's license and all the money in his bank account . . . Well, it may be improbable, but the burden is on the state to dispute it."

Birdsong, trying to change the subject, said, "It's been more than a year since your husband died. Do the police still consider this an open case?"

"They say it's murder, but they can't proceed because the coroner has ruled it a heart attack," she replied.

"Maybe you need to put more pressure on the coroner," said Birdsong. "I could study your case and possibly collaborate on a story. The publicity may help your cause."

Ruth looked at Schafer, seething.

"Your friend could help by charging Hartman. Dr. Jindrich was in on the second autopsy, and he says Jack most likely was strangled to death. Even the guy who did the first autopsy says Jack's heart wasn't in that bad a condition. How much more evidence do you need?" Ruth said without taking her eyes off Schafer.

For what seemed an eternity, nobody said a word. The gentle hum of chatter and laughter surrounded them. Schafer stabbed a french fry with his fork, and rolled it through a pool of ketchup.

Then he broke the silence: "Doctors don't agree on a lot of things, Mrs. Langlos. I still think your husband died of a heart attack. Hartman came in, saw the body, and decided to take advantage of the situation. Unless you or the police have some more evidence, you're going to have to accept that and get on with your life."

Ruth took a deep breath. "I've tried to give you more evidence, but I'm running out of money," Ruth said. "I've already spent twenty-five hundred dollars on a private detective."

Schafer interrupted: "I'd advise you not to spend another nickel on this case. It's a waste of time and money."

His pithy criticism stunned Ruth. She had heard that Schafer took draconian measures against employees who challenged his decision making. Transfers and impossible caseloads were common reminders of Schafer's vindictiveness. Once he determined that Jack had not been murdered, Ruth felt that she too was treated with acrimony. She had hoped that the license hearing and the second autopsy would have changed his outlook.

Ruth finished lunch hurriedly, barely speaking with Schafer. Birdsong, meanwhile, seemed sympathetic to her plight. His resume was impressive, but he wanted a five-hundred-dollar advance to help Ruth publicize her case.

"Your friend tells me not to spend another nickel. But I'll consider your offer," she said defiantly, rising to leave.

During the next few days her defiance turned to desperation.

A week later, seeking any new information that would add fuel to her quest, she went to a psychic—Kerry Ladue, the psychic used by several police departments when their tips ran dry.

Because of her religious beliefs, Ruth wasn't supposed to put any faith in psychics, fortune tellers, or anyone who claimed mystic powers. She convinced herself that she made the appointment to see Ladue solely out of curiosity. In reality, she was desperate for any shred of evidence or guidance. She didn't care where it came from.

Nervously she entered Ladue's office in Beverly Hills, which had oak paneled walls, beige velvet wingback chairs and a marble fireplace. This was no carnival act in a tent. Ladue's client list included police officials, movie stars, and corporate executives.

"My husband was found dead in his office and I know he was killed," Ruth said.

"And you want to know who killed him?" Ladue, an attractive brunette in her early thirties with round, brown eyes, replied.

Ruth nodded. "Well, I think I know that already, but I guess I just want to know if the murderer will ever be brought to justice."

Ladue rose from her chair and walked around the desk. She sat next to Ruth and closed her eyes for a moment.

"I see a cash register. Is money involved?"

"My husband's checks and credit cards were taken."

A furrow creased her forehead. "Swirling water. Something is being flushed away. I can't see. . . . Evidence. . . . Evidence has been flushed away."

"Jack's brain is missing." Ruth eagerly responded. "They looked for it at the second autopsy."

"That is making things difficult for you."

"Will I be able to get the man who murdered my husband convicted?"

"Yes, definitely," Ladue replied. "But I can't tell you when."

Even though she only partially believed in fortune telling, Ruth left the office rejuvenated and determined to spend her last nickel if necessary to attain her goal.

One month after receiving Jindrich's letter, Noguchi reconvened the interagency group that had approved the second autopsy. Downey's Captain Sanders, who had received a copy of the letter, notified Ruth of it. He was confident of good news.

For more than an hour, Ruth sat in the lobby of Noguchi's office with her attorney, Charles Simon, a partner of Bolton's. At one hundred dollars an hour, Simon, an imposing man, heavyset with a baritone voice that served him well in the courtroom, was expensive company.

"Remember, when we get in there, I'll do the talking," he reminded Ruth.

Ruth was happy to oblige. For weeks, she had been experiencing chest pains, but she didn't have time to be ill. She had to get the death certificate changed, but she knew it would only be the first step. Then there would be a long, agonizing trial.

When they finally were ushered in, the first thing Ruth noticed was the sullen faces of Miller and Westray. Noguchi smiled, motioned to a chair, and simply acknowledged: "Mrs. Langlos."

He looked at Schafer and continued: "There was no laceration of the tongue. It was a bruise."

Noguchi was wrapping up the meeting. Ruth couldn't tell what his decision was or whether he had even announced it yet.

"Ruth," Simon nudged her. "This isn't going well."

Why not? Ruth wondered. Carpenter had seemed so cooperative with Jindrich. She scanned the room. No Carpenter. She sighed heavily and forced herself to focus on what was being said. She had to get Noguchi to act, yet there now seemed no hope.

"There was no damage to the brain or skull," Noguchi was insisting.

"How do you know that, sir?" Simon interrupted. "It's my understanding that the brain has been lost."

Ruth's heart began pounding, her head ached. It wasn't some stranger they were talking about. They were discussing her husband. She simply couldn't bear to listen. She had to get away. She bolted from the room, a cauldron of emotions boiling over.

Suddenly, for no rational reason, a strange new fear crept over her. "Where's Jack's trumpet? I've got to find Jack's trumpet," she muttered. The trumpet had been taken from the casket before the second autopsy. She was afraid that it had disappeared mysteriously like Jack's brain.

Roaming the corridor, she was directed to investigator

147

Hiroto's office. He unlocked his desk and pulled out a clear body bag. Inside was a shiny trumpet with "For Mrs. Langlos" scrawled on a toe tag wrapped around the mouthpiece.

"Don't let anyone put their lips on it," Hiroto cautioned. "It has chemicals on it. It's not sterilized."

On the drive home, Ruth kept the trumpet on the seat next to her. At home, she carefully placed it in Jack's wardrobe in the closet of the den. As Ruth dialed Jindrich's number, she felt lightheaded, hysterical. She found herself laughing. She had paid an attorney five hundred dollars today to hear Noguchi reach the same decision he'd reached months ago. A costly déjà vu.

"Are you sure they're not going to change anything?" Jindrich asked incredulously.

"Noguchi isn't going to budge. He and Carpenter are standing behind the first autopsy "

"Carpenter isn't capable of playing hardball," Jindrich remarked. "He was willing to change the cause of death, but apparently it wasn't his option. Carpenter admitted he made a mistake."

"Then why won't they just change it?"

"I don't know, Ruth. I don't have the foggiest notion. Maybe they're afraid of a lawsuit."

"I don't want money. I want justice," she said, a steel edge to her voice.

"I don't know what to say," Jindrich sighed. "Something must have happened since I met with them."

"What can I do now?" Ruth asked agonized.

"Well, I would suggest you contact another forensic pathologist to review the case," Jindrich replied.

Ruth stiffened her resolve once again. "Can you recommend one whose opinion will be respected?"

"Dr. Ronald Kornblum."

"I'll call him." She took a deep breath and said decisively, "right now."

Chapter 15

A Brutal Attack in San Diego

Immersed in thought, Alfred Monheit strolled along 54th Street as the last vestiges of daylight began to fade from the San Diego skyline.

"Any spare change?" demanded a grimy-faced man in a ripped T-shirt and grease-stained slacks.

Monheit stared through the panhandler. The cinnamon scent of fresh pastry pierced the cool spring air. Monheit inhaled deeply, sighed, and turned into Aunt Emma's restaurant on 54th and El Cajon. It was 7:30 p.m., and the crowd at the popular coffee shop was at its peak.

At the counter, a husky man in a beige leisure suit with a snakeskin belt and a pink sport shirt was sipping a glass of Coke. He was reading the sports section of the evening newspaper.

"Hi, Gene," Monheit said with a smile.

The man looked up and responded listlessly. "Hi."

"Have you been waiting long?"

"Not really."

Al Monheit and Gene Hartman had met indirectly through a

newspaper ad for a singles group. Monheit had called the phone number in the ad, but the male voice at the other end asked what kind of woman he was looking to date.

"I'm not interested in dating," said Monheit, a frail-looking man with thin arms, pale skin, and thick glasses to compensate for his extreme nearsightedness. "I'm interested in meeting people."

Hartman referred Monheit to a singles group that met regularly on Morena Boulevard, where visitors paid $1.50 to mingle with other singles. Hartman was the host.

On first meeting Monheit, Hartman introduced himself as a "paid psychologist." Monheit figured, *That must be to distinguish himself from all the amateur psychologists around.* As time went on, Monheit and Hartman would see each other at various singles functions throughout San Diego.

Monheit loved the singles scene. But unlike thousands of unwed adults, he wasn't shopping for nuptials or sex. A lonely widower, Monheit only wanted friendship.

The rap sessions offered by the local singles club provided a natural forum for his conversational desires. Every Monday night, about fifteen single people gathered for a couple of hours at the home of Sandra Green to discuss a wide range of topics. Green, a celebrity of sorts, wrote a column on singles' issues for the *San Diego Tribune*.

Meeting new people was second nature to Monheit. He had owned a stamp and coin shop in the melting pot of New York City. Amid the theatres, restaurants, and peep shows of lower Manhattan, the short, genial Jewish entrepreneur wheeled and dealed for over thirty years. Monheit liked to banter with customers, and his friendliness helped ensure their return. Like Jack Langlos, he was a man to whom success seemed to come easily—the kind of success that had eluded Eugene Hartman for so long. Like Langlos, Monheit was the kind of man Hartman envied.

Selling the business and retiring to southern California had left him melancholy and homesick. But the move added precious years to the life of his ailing wife, Ethel. They settled into a spacious two-bedroom apartment and started to enjoy a more leisurely life. With their son at Yale, they were alone without a schedule to meet. They could rise when they wanted, hunt for antiques at their whim, and tour the state without a destination in mind.

After Ethel died, Monheit missed their lively exchanges about politics, religion, and current events. He even missed complaining to her when the weather turned unseasonably chilly.

At seventy-two, Monheit was old enough to be the father—in some cases the grandfather—of the singles at Green's house. Physically, he stuck out like a dandelion in a patch of sod.

But in other ways, Monheit blended in just fine. The other singles marvelled at his quick wit, intelligence, and perceptive outlook.

They weren't nearly as fond of Hartman. Although extremely intelligent, Hartman, they said, tried to control every conversation, always pressing to get in the last word. He seemed uptight in this kind of setting.

In the last month, as Hartman awaited the board's decision, he had become even more withdrawn. If the decision went against him he would never practice psychology or teach again.

Monheit was surprised when Hartman called early one day, offering to drive him to the singles rap at Green's home on Adelaide Avenue. They were only casual acquaintances, and Hartman hadn't shown any inclination to become closer before.

On the night of May 16, 1977, they left Aunt Emma's in silence, got into Hartman's white 1969 Ford, and headed off for the quick half-mile drive. When Hartman drove past Green's house without slowing down, the shadows of dusk were turning into darkness. Monheit questioned, "Why don't you stop here? They have parking," eyeing a vacant spot nearby.

Hartman stared straight ahead and didn't say a word. Instead, he made a left turn on 58th Street, then a right on El Cajon Boulevard.

"What . . . what's the matter?" Monheit stammered. "How come you don't park your car over here? There is plenty of room."

Instead of answering, Hartman pressed harder on the gas. A

few minutes later, he turned and looked at Monheit for the first time.

"This is a kidnapping, and I want you to put your hands on the top of the dashboard," he declared. Holding the wheel with his right hand, Hartman pointed a gun at Monheit with his left.

"Otherwise, I have to shoot you," Hartman said menacingly.

Monheit put his shaking hands on the dashboard. "What is this all about?"

"You have to give me twenty thousand dollars," Hartman sneered.

"Twenty thousand dollars?" Monheit protested. "I haven't got twenty thousand dollars."

Monheit's heart pounded. Hartman had borrowed money from him once before, but it was a small amount. Twenty thousand dollars? Could he be serious? Monheit eyed the .38-caliber revolver pointed at his head. Yes, Hartman was deadly serious.

Panic-stricken, Monheit lunged at Hartman, swinging his right fist with all his might. As Monheit grabbed the hand that held the gun, the car swerved to the left and then the right. Hartman, caught off guard, tried to fend off Monheit and drive at the same time.

While the men grappled for the gun, bullets suddenly began to drop out of the pistol. Monheit feverishly pushed cartridges under the seat until the car screeched to a halt. Before Monheit could try to escape, Hartman overpowered the older man and pushed him to the floor of the front seat. He pressed his right foot on Monheit's chest to keep him still. Fighting for breath, Monheit saw the revolver drop like a guillotine.

Thump. Thump. Thump.

The dull thuds of steel meeting flesh were interrupted only by Monheit's faint whimpers.

Thump. Thump. Thump.

The revolver hit its target with ugly precision. Blood flowed down his face onto his jacket.

"I'm going to knock you out yet," Hartman scowled.

"Enough . . . enough." Monheit's moan was barely audible.

"Do you want to be a good boy? Put your hands on the

dashboard."

Trembling, Monheit nodded.

Hartman calmly started driving again with the black handgun aimed at his passenger.

"I haven't got twenty thousand dollars, but I can give you five thousand," Monheit begged.

"All right," Hartman said coldly. "I'm going to put you in the trunk and drive all night long." He turned right on College Way. "In the morning you make out a voucher for five thousand dollars and go to your bank and draw it out: five thousand dollars."

The thought of spending the night in the stale confines of a trunk terrified Monheit. It was only eight o'clock. The bank wouldn't open for fourteen hours. Although shaken and light-headed, Monheit's eyes shifted from the latch on the front door to the steely glare of his captor. When Hartman glanced into his rear-view mirror, Monheit quickly tried to raise the door latch.

Too slow. Hartman reached across the seat and grabbed Monheit by the shirt. He violently yanked Monheit toward him like a rag doll.

Meanwhile, Duane Gribbin, a successful lawyer taking an evening drive, gently touched the accelerator of his red Porsche. Its engine purr was lost amid the blaring shouts of Mick Jagger on the stereo radio.

Gribbin attempted to pass a white Ford that had started to turn right into a Foodbasket store. Gribbin watched helplessly as the car stopped its turn then suddenly swerved back into Gribbin's lane. Before he could hit the horn, brake, or veer away, the sickening bang of aluminum crunching into metal and glass rang out in the night.

Hartman's Ford sideswiped the front end of the Porsche. The impact of the collision forced the Ford to fishtail down the street like the town drunk.

But the crash was only half of the horror for Gribbin—the driver of the Ford did not stop to assess the damage.

Gribbin followed the car, flashing his high-beams to get the driver's attention. But Hartman refused to stop. Instead, he kept driving for a hundred yards until he found himself trapped in a cul-de-sac on Estelle Street.

As he stopped, Monheit flipped open the door and crawled partly outside. "Help! Murder! Help! Murder!" Monheit hollered with his last spurt of strength.

Like a panther, Hartman sprung over Monheit's body, trying to pull him back in. Monheit struggled, kicking with his feet, but he couldn't overpower the stronger, younger man.

Hartman began to pummel him again with the gun. Monheit's will to resist was nearly gone.

Heidi Malone, a young housewife, had been relaxing on her front porch as one car, then another, came to screeching halts outside her home. When she walked toward the scene, she could see one man striking another and holding a hand over the victim's mouth.

So could Gribbin. He had parked near Hartman's car and crept from the rear along the driver's side of the vehicle. He saw a burly man reach inside the glove compartment. Fearing that the man had a weapon, Gribbin ran across the street for help.

San Diego Police Officer Greg Baxter was parked on a nearby side street in search of speeders when the call came over the radio. "Report of an accident and disturbance in the six hundred block of Estelle," the dispatcher said.

Within minutes, Baxter arrived on the scene to find a Porsche in the middle of the street and another vehicle in a driveway.

"Officer, a man is being beaten up in that car in the driveway," Gribbin yelled from the sidewalk.

As he approached, Baxter saw movement in the front seat. He shined his flashlight inside the car. Two men covered in blood squinted into the light.

"Help me. Help me. He's trying to kill me," cried the gray-haired man.

Baxter opened the driver's door, his right hand poised to draw his pistol. "Step outside. Now!" ordered Baxter, pointing his flashlight at Hartman.

Slowly, Hartman crept out. Baxter handcuffed him and quickly panned the vehicle. He observed a bloodstained front seat, a .38 handgun on the dash to the left of the steering wheel, and several loose .38 cartridges on the floorboard.

Baxter checked the blood-stained weapon. It was empty. A box of forty-seven rounds of ammunition was in the glove box.

Monheit faded in and out of consciousness. When Monheit groggily opened his eyes, he saw a woman's face. "It's alright now. It's alright now," Heather Cook repeated softly. "You're safe now."

Monheit noticed the uniform. San Diego Police.

"He's got a gun," Monheit blurted out.

"Where?"

"He has got a gun. I don't know where. The bullets I pushed underneath the seat here."

Seconds later, an ambulance took Monheit to the emergency room of the Villa View Hospital. He had received eleven wounds on top of his head, two on the forehead, and two on the chin.

But he was alive.

The District Attorney's office had no lack of willing witnesses against Hartman. The gun was registered to Hartman's girlfriend in La Jolla: Kimberly Elston.

Investigator Richard Boyd found that even Hartman's family and friends didn't seem shocked at his behavior. They told Boyd that Hartman was a manic depressive.

Gary Hartman suggested that a friend of his brother's, Kevin Arless, knew him as well as anyone.

When Boyd reached Arless by phone, he did not hear another ringing endorsement of Eugene Hartman.

"He was a former office tenant," Arless said. "And I know Gene socially."

"Is he still renting from you?"

"No, he was behind in his rent, and then he wrote me a bad check," explained Arless. "Gene always tried to be the big spender type. Because of that, he was in serious financial difficulty."

"How did Hartman and Monheit know each other?"

"They belonged to some of the same singles clubs. They had been talking about starting a singles business with Monheit being the financial backer. But it never got beyond the talking stage. I don't think they had any problems because of that."

"What do you think of Hartman?"

"He's a nice guy," said Arless, adding, "but he definitely needs psychiatric help. He's self-destructive and has a hard time getting along with people."

"In what way?"

"He just turns people off."

Two weeks after the beating, Alfred Monheit was released from the hospital in time to testify at Hartman's preliminary examination. The charges: assault with intent to commit murder, kidnapping, assault with a deadly weapon, armed robbery, hit and run, and operating an unregistered vehicle.

The hour-long testimony of Monheit, Gribbin, and Baxter was lucid, consistent, and damaging to Hartman. For San Diego Municipal Court Judge T. Bruce Iredale, the decision whether to bind over Hartman for trial was a no-brainer. His young daughter watched the proceedings, wiping tears from her eyes.

Iredale had one question about the evidence: Was it strong enough to show Hartman intended to murder Monheit?

"I think there has been ample testimony that the defendant did, indeed, have a weapon in his hand and that he struck the victim over the head with that weapon at least eight to ten times," said deputy District Attorney John Estevez.

Iredale nodded. "Right. I think there is no question, but there was an assault with a deadly weapon, which is one of your charges, and I think there is no question that there was a forceful kidnapping here, but was the assault with intent to commit murder? That's the issue under Count One."

Estevez replied sternly, "I think there has been ample testimony to the effect that the defendant was trying to render the victim unconscious, and I think that it could be construed as an attempt to commit murder."

"I would concede to the court that there are no statements that directly show the defendant wanted to commit murder that night, but I think there is sufficient cause to believe that the force utilized against the victim—that is eight to ten times—was sufficient to be construed as an attempt to commit murder."

Hartman's young, earnest public defender, Eli Wagner, knew

the importance of getting this charge dismissed. If convicted of kidnapping and assault with intent to commit murder, his client could spend most of the rest of his life in a state prison.

He leaned forward now and said dutifully, "I would suggest, your Honor, that the contrary is shown. I mean, if we accept the testimony of the complaining witness, the statement made by my client—attributed to my client—was 'I'm going to put you in the trunk, and tomorrow we're going to go down to the bank and get . . .' something."

Iredale interrupted Wagner. "He wanted him alive."

Wagner nodded. "Yes."

Iredale's gaze shifted to Hartman and back again to his defender. "The only thing I made notes on were things that could happen if certain things did not happen. For instance, he said, 'I will have to shoot you, unless you give me the twenty thousand dollars.' Well, he wasn't using the gun in the sense of shooting anyone. He was using it as a bludgeoning instrument, you might say, rather than shooting.

"If he had shot it, that would be closer to intent to murder. Also, during the process of hitting him with the gun, he said, 'I'm going to have to knock you unconscious if you don't cooperate.' That is not to say that he had in mind 'I'm going to knock you until you're dead.' There is a difference, plus, as you just pointed out, he wanted his use the next day for the withdrawing of five thousand dollars, which wouldn't have worked very well if he had a dead body."

Iredale dropped the charge but ordered Hartman to stand trial on the other charges. He set bond at twenty-five thousand dollars.

"I have heard the evidence in this case, and there is a lot more than meets the eye here that I've not heard," concluded Iredale. "Certainly, force and violence was used on a very elderly man that could very well have done more serious damage than it did."

"The defendant can be thankful that a murder charge or attempted murder charge was not made out. It falls short of that in my mind, but nevertheless, we were on the way that evening."

News of the Monheit beating rocked the Downey police station with sudden, devastating force.

"It wouldn't have happened if we had gotten him for murder the first time," sighed a stonefaced Miller.

"We did everything we could," said Westray. "I hope those damn doctors feel good now."

Even though they had been ordered off the Langlos case months before, Miller and Westray never quit thinking or talking about it. That wasn't unusual, for dedicated cops, unsolved crimes don't disappear merely because the case file is accumulating dust.

Miller and Westray desperately wanted to finish their unfinished business.

"Look at this, Wimp," Miller said disgustedly. He flipped a section of the *Los Angeles Times* at his partner. From the front of the Metro section, Thomas Noguchi's smiling face stared at the reader.

"If publicity was money, this guy would own General Motors," Westray moaned.

"Monheit might be the key," Miller replied.

"The key to what?"

"Opening Noguchi's eyes. The similarities are obvious."

On a yellow notepad, Miller wrote the word *gun* in big, bold letters. He smiled, shook his head, and tilted back in his chair.

"Langlos didn't hit his head on the desk. He was clobbered with a gun," Miller declared.

"Well, I'm glad you're coming around. If you remember, partner, I never bought that head-on-the-desk theory."

Miller acted as though he hadn't heard his partner. He rattled off a series of comparisons, striking the desk with his forefinger to emphasize every point.

"Monheit was hit with a gun. The wound on Langlos's head could have been caused by the butt of a gun."

"Monheit had loaned Hartman money. So had Langlos."

"Hartman lost control when Monheit resisted giving him more money. Langlos's death was brutal, likely at the hands of someone who went berserk."

"Monheit owned a stamp and coin store. Langlos was a stamp and coin collector."

"Monheit was an easy-going guy, the kind Hartman thought

he could intimidate. So was Langlos."

Westray interrupted Miller's roll.

"One major difference," said Westray coyly. "Monheit lived to identify his attacker."

For the second time in sixteen months Hartman avoided trial by plea bargaining. On August 9, he pleaded guilty to assault with a deadly weapon and possession of a firearm by a convicted felon. His sentence: six years to life in prison. In exchange, the kidnapping and other counts were dismissed.

But the crime broke the conditions of Hartman's parole for the forgery conviction. Almost five months after the attack on Monheit, Hartman returned to Los Angeles for an October 13 hearing on his parole violation. Hartman seemed bewildered as he shuffled into the nearly empty courtroom of L.A. Superior Court Judge William Munnell. His short stay in the Chino State Prison had left him looking haggard and depressed.

"Mr. Hartman, do you have a lawyer?" asked Munnell.

Hartman mumbled, "Yes. . . . No."

Munnell noticed a public defender standing next to Hartman. He ignored the defendant's confusion.

"Do you have the money to hire an attorney?"

Hartman shrugged. "No, I do not."

"Very well, the public defender is appointed."

It didn't matter. With no defense for his actions, Hartman simply waived his right to an evidentiary hearing. Munnell ruled that Hartman should be transferred to Vacaville, a state mental hospital within the California Department of Corrections. Among the hospital's notorious residents: Charles Manson.

Munnell's voice had a direct no-nonsense quality. "You have had some training in psychiatric matters?"

Hartman nodded dully. "Yes."

Munnell went on. "You must recognize, and I am sure you do, you have some psychiatric problems. Your educational background is impressive. I don't know what's happened to you. It may be they can assist you at the hospital within Vacaville, although the result of your activities in recent years has indicated that you do constitute a danger to society, for whatever reason. I am sure you agree that's true."

Hartman slumped down in his chair. "Yes," he admitted tonelessly.

Chapter 16

Hitting Rock Bottom

"Did you hear what your friend did?" Mittendorf began, his voice low and serious on the phone.

Ruth knew immediately he meant Hartman. For weeks she had been checking with Mittendorf's office for a verdict on Hartman's psychology and teaching licenses.

Now, the time had arrived. Out of habit, she geared for the worst.

"Please don't tell me they ruled that Hartman can still practice psychology."

"No, Hartman has been charged with trying to kill an old guy in San Diego," Mittendorf replied.

"*What!*" Ruth screamed.

"It's all over the papers here," Mittendorf said. "Listen to this: 'A forty-eight-year-old San Diego man was being held in county jail on multiple felony charges in connection with the alleged beating and attempted extortion of twenty thousand dollars from a seventy-two-year-old acquaintance.

"'The victim, Alfred Monheit, was recovering at Villa View Hospital from head cuts and bruises received in the incident.

Police said the suspect, Eugene C. Hartman, identified himself as a psychologist to officers.'"

Ruth felt numb. As Mittendorf continued to read the newspaper account, she didn't know whether to cry or cheer.

"I guess Hartman can forget about his psychology license now," she said limply.

"He'll never get to keep the license, but that's the least of his worries," Mittendorf observed.

Hartman's attack on Monheit gave Ruth little satisfaction. She could have said, "I told you so," but what good was that? A gentle, innocent man had almost lost his life just as Jack had.

In fact, Hartman's conviction made her feel even more helpless. After nearly sixteen costly months of imploring the system to do its job, Jack's death was still ruled a natural one.

Ruth's quest for justice had left her broke, angry, and depressed. That quest had been spread in many directions since the second autopsy.

Attorney Bolton, who had a talent for smelling money, convinced Ruth to file a claim against the County of Los Angeles and Dr. Noguchi. This was a notice of their intent to sue the county if it didn't change the autopsy.

The claim was sent to the County Board of Supervisors. It alleged that the coroner's failure to do a complete autopsy, including the loss of body parts, had prevented Ruth from collecting twenty thousand dollars in death benefits. It also sought the fourteen thousand Ruth had paid in fees for attorneys, investigators, and pathologists. And, for good measure, the claim sought $1.5 million for severe mental anguish and $5 million in punitive damages.

The purpose of filing such a claim was to alert county officials to the problem so they would try to avert litigation. It didn't work.

Wallace Murray, a chief county investigator, wrote in response: "Investigation of this matter fails to indicate any liability on the part of the County of Los Angeles, its officers, agents or employees. No further action will therefore be taken on this matter."

In effect, the county was saying, "See you in court."

Unable to afford Bolton's fees any longer, Ruth switched to a civil attorney recommended by friends. In his early thirties, John Leigh was a younger, much less established attorney than Bolton, but she hoped for more personalized attention at costs more in line with her limited finances.

At their first meeting, she observed that Leigh, a handsome, curly-haired barrister, spoke with a pronounced stutter. In a profession of smooth talkers, a stutter might seem like a major handicap, but it didn't seem to bother Leigh. Ruth immediately admired him for that.

The county's rejection of Ruth's claim was one of the main items on the agenda when they first met in his small office on Sunset Boulevard in Hollywood.

"Mrs. Langlos, you have s-s-six months to file a court action," Leigh said.

"Will a lawsuit force Dr. Noguchi to correct the autopsy?"

"It d-d-depends on the s-s-settlement. Dr. Noguchi might c-c-countersue for damages to his reputation."

"I can't handle a legal fight with the county or Dr. Noguchi. I'm almost out of money."

"I think we can prove negligence on the corner's o-o-office," said Leigh. "That w-w-would be worth a lot of money to you."

"This isn't about money. This is about justice. I just want them to do what's right."

"T-t-they're not going to admit a m-m-mistake, Mrs. Langlos. You may not care about the money, b-b-but they do."

Leigh seemed surprised, even shocked. On one hand, Ruth Langlos was standing toe to toe with the county bureaucracy, trying to get her husband's killer brought to trial. On the other, she was reluctant to go to court with the prospects of making a tidy sum for her troubles.

She could have told him the reason was simple: A lawsuit could take years to settle and would not guarantee the autopsy would be changed, which was all she really cared about.

To accomplish her purpose, Ruth was more interested in meeting Alfred Monheit.

◆ ◆ ◆

A few weeks after Hartman's hearing, she visited Monheit at his apartment in San Diego.

He was waiting at the street when Ruth pulled up. He asked if she'd mind if two of his neighbors sat in on their chat. Ruth sensed he was afraid to be alone with a stranger. Who could blame him?

Inside the apartment Ruth passed out some photographs of Jack Langlos at the crime scene, and they compared notes for a couple minutes when Monheit rose from a chair and sat down on the sofa next to her.

"I don't know how I could have been taken in by Hartman," he said bitterly. "I knew he wasn't the easiest guy to get along with, but we never had any problems. I considered him a friend."

"How are you feeling?"

"Not well. I've been having dizzy spells and headaches all the time. The doctors don't know how to stop them."

"My husband was hit on the head, too." Ruth said softly.

One of Monheit's neighbors, Jerry Ditmer, suddenly cried out: "Al, look at these photos. The gash on her husband's head looks like the ones you received."

Monheit looked at the color picture showing a closeup of the Half-moon-shaped gash on Jack Langlos's head. He gasped and stared at Ruth, tears forming in his eyes.

"I'm afraid I haven't been his only victim," Monheit said. "Fortunately for both of us, he's in prison."

"But for how long?"

"It won't be long enough to suit me. I don't feel sorry for him a bit, but it was kind of sad to watch his seventeen-year-old daughter at the trial. She had to see her dad led away in handcuffs."

"I would love to see him led away in handcuffs," Ruth said earnestly.

She and Monheit resolved to stay in touch and trade any information they learned about their mutual nemesis. Monheit's health was never the same. His headaches became more frequent. Within three years, he was dead.

In the criminal justice system, he was just another statistic.

That system wasn't even vigilant enough to prosecute his attacker without Ruth forcing the issue. It was her phone call to Deputy D.A. Schafer's office that led to Hartman's hearing for violating his probation and ultimately the order that he undergo psychiatric treatment. Schafer said it was an "oversight" that Hartman hadn't been tried before her call.

Dr. Jindrich had made an oversight of another kind. When Ruth received his $167.76 bill for expenses in flying to Los Angeles for the second autopsy, it included $51 for airfare, $35.68 for auto rental and $58.13 for a room at the Holiday Inn. It did not include the paltry $50 fee he quoted for his services. Helping Ruth right the wrong was enough for him. She sent him the extra $50 anyway, never forgetting that gesture of kindness.

Unfortunately, Ruth had now come to the conclusion that the Schafers and Noguchis outnumbered the Jindrichs and Westrays. That knowledge was suffocating.

She could think of little else. Her life was a shambles. She knew she needed more help. To combat the feelings of utter hopelessness, she had been in crisis therapy at St. John's Hospital in Santa Monica for more than a year.

She saw Dr. Kevin Rottermal twice a week and also attended a group session weekly, but battles with the District Attorney's Office and Dr. Noguchi had taken their toll. It was David verses Goliath, and Goliath had inflicted a lot of damage.

The apartment that Ruth and Jack had lived in, once a love nest, had become a prison—her prison. Now she unplugged the telephone, pulled the curtains shut, and stopped going to the market or post office. She was finally, totally, irrevocably alone.

On November 16, she glanced in the refrigerator. Empty. The cupboards were barren except for a package of noodles. She cooked them, added salt, and watched TV.

The next day, she began to cry during her session with Dr. Rottermal as she had many times before. Only this time, she couldn't stop.

She was escorted to Xavier, a large building across from the main entrance to St. John's. It was the hospital's mental health section. The doctor wouldn't let her move her car, get a tooth-brush, or pack some clothes. She was taken to a locked floor. The hollow sound of the closing door hit her like a slap in the face. She had lost her freedom!

The nurse took everything—Ruth's clothes, Ruth's purse, Ruth's shoes. "Why are you checking my heels?" Ruth asked, tug-ging at the hospital gown.

"I'm looking for grass."

"I walked on the sidewalk."

She studied Ruth for a few seconds and laughed. "I'm looking for marijuana, honey," she said.

"Oh."

"People like to hide drugs in their heels."

Ruth was now in the psychiatric ward. The bathroom had a shiny square of metal for a mirror. At meal time, they ate with plastic spoons and forks for security purposes. They could walk down the hall and into a room for recreation and dining. Period.

Ruth soon realized she was under close observation. When her friend Francois Toussaint came to visit and get a list of things she wanted from home, an orderly sat with them. He wanted to make sure nothing was handed to Ruth.

◆ ◆ ◆

"Dear, wake up." The nurse gently prodded on Ruth's first night.

Ruth looked up at a blurry image.

"Where are your glasses, dear?"

"Under my pillow."

"You won't need them while you sleep."

"I need them to see my watch when I check the time."

"I'm sorry, but you can't have any glass in your room."

Patient's rooms were checked every hour during the night.

There was a good reason for all the caution and secrecy. Al-most all the patients were very ill and very strange.

How strange? It seemed as though only Hilda Marker knew. Marker, a fellow patient and the ward gossip, was a frumpy-looking woman in her mid-forties. She did little to enhance her appearance. Her dishwater-blond hair was dirty and disheveled, badly in need of a brushing. Her strikingly blue eyes were sunken, underscored by deep circles that stood out against her pale complexion. She wore a loose-fitting cotton shift and sandals.

Marker was not an unattractive woman. She just needed a makeover. Ruth pictured her with a light coating of lipstick, blush, and eyeliner, a new hairdo, earrings, a stylish dress, and dental work to close her gap toothed smile. Hilda Marker had possibilities.

She was friendly and took an immediate liking to Ruth. Why, Ruth couldn't figure out. Maybe she always befriended the new kid on the block. On Ruth's first afternoon in the recreation lounge, Marker became like a tour guide, pointing out the scenery along the way.

Of course, she never told Ruth why she was there.

"See that young man," Marker nodded toward the corner of the room. "A drug user. He's a rich kid from Beverly Hills. Wait till you see how his parents dress."

"Oh, watch for her," Marker rolled her eyes in the direction of a young woman seated near the door. "She's a lesbian. I've already had to tell her I'm not interested."

"Why is she in here?"

"Don't know. But be careful around her."

Suddenly, a loud laugh filled the room. A scruffy, dark-haired man about forty was guffawing uncontrollably while watching TV. He said something to those around him, pointed at the screen, and started laughing again.

"He's in outer space," Marker said matter-of-factly. "I kind of figured that when I saw the feather in his hair." Ruth laughed. It made her feel a little better.

"Wish you could meet Colleen," whispered Marker, "but she can't come out of her room for a while."

"Is she sick?"

"Oh yes," Marker nodded. "She cut her wrists yesterday trying to commit suicide."

While Marker described everyone's idiosyncracies, she passed by a nun who was sitting alone near the television. The nun was blotting her eyes as though she had been crying.

"Is she really a nun?" Ruth asked. The woman was dressed in a habit, but on this hospital floor Ruth figured nothing was certain.

"Sister Mary?" Marker smiled. "You should see all the nuns and priests who come to visit her. All she ever does is cry, especially at meal times. It's enough to ruin your appetite."

◆ ◆ ◆

Why am I here? Ruth wondered. At five-foot-six, she had once weighed 130 to 135 pounds. Now her weight was dropping precipitously. She was diagnosed as suffering reactive depression. The doctors said she was possibly suicidal and non-functional.

Worse, Ruth knew what they said about her was true. She had hit rock bottom. She didn't even have boots to pull herself up by the boot straps. She had lost the man she loved and didn't care what happened to her.

To pass time, she had found some playing cards but couldn't find anyone who was coherent enough to play. She was about to give up when a patient who had been a school teacher, Julie Allen, volunteered. Julie had been there only a few days and had been very quiet. Marker didn't have the lowdown on her.

As Ruth shuffled the cards, a woman in a gray business suit came up and introduced herself. Mary Brenneman was a soft-spoken woman in her mid-forties. Her smile and gentleness exuded hope and warmth. Brenneman was the psychiatrist assigned to Ruth.

In a small, sparsely furnished room, Brenneman asked Ruth about her childhood, her first marriage, her marriage to Jack, and her struggles after his death. Almost immediately, Ruth liked this empathetic woman who had been a pediatrician before making a career change. She seemed to care about Ruth's problems.

In discussing Jack's death, Ruth tried to stifle the tears waiting to gush from her eyes. Brenneman softly held her hand, smiled, and in a soothing voice said, "Go ahead, Ruth. There's nothing wrong with tears. You've been through a lot of pain."

Brenneman was a strong believer in dream therapy and had been trained in the Jungian method. Handing Ruth her card, she said, "Ruth, I want you to try to remember your dreams. Go to the nurse's station and ask for a pencil and paper and write them down. I'm going to get you moved to another floor tomorrow. You'll be happier there."

That night, Toussaint came to visit Ruth. He kissed her gently on the lips and handed her a suitcase. The security guard and nurse's aide in the visiting room dumped everything on a table and searched the contents.

"Is this necessary?" Toussaint asked.

"Hospital regulations," replied the guard as he rummaged through a case of toiletries.

"Francois, I have the nicest doctor," Ruth said, showing him the business card she had given her.

Underneath Brenneman's name, it read: "Dreams are the key to your unconscious. Tap your unlimited reservoir of creativity. Discover yourself through your dreams with emphasis on Jungian Symbols."

"She wants me to tell her about my dreams," Ruth said. "We'll have a lot to talk about. I have a lot of different dreams."

"A lot of nightmares, you mean," said Toussaint.

Ruth was moved to what they called the medical floor the next morning. Patients there were being tested for their tolerance to various kinds of medication. After a complete examination, including a treadmill test, she was put on Tofranil for reactive depression.

Her new roommate was a teenage girl who had run away from home and became involved with a man who later dumped her. She was extremely depressed.

The elevator on the floor was locked, but the patients still had a good deal of freedom. Their schedules were full each day. There were group sessions, arts and crafts, and a game room with a pool table, a TV, and a piano. As Ruth warmed to the more friendly atmosphere, she began playing the piano, reading poetry, and even participating in sing-a-longs.

The daily reminder of their shared trauma occurred in group therapy, when they gathered in a circle around a group leader and described their various experiences that had brought them to the hospital.

At her first session, Ruth sat in awed silence as a series of heart-rending tales were told.

One woman had been robbed while working at a dry cleaners. The thief injured her neck and she was facing delicate surgery. Another young woman, a bank teller, had witnessed the shooting of a guard during a robbery. She had been ordered to lie face down on the floor and figured she would be shot, too.

An elderly man told the group he had recently lost his wife. "I was her shadow," he admitted. "I'm totally lost."

A ballet instructor talked about taking an overdose of sleeping pills in a suicide attempt. A well-dressed woman from Bel Air told them she had worked to put her husband through law school and then he had left her. A nurse described her breakdown after a divorce. Her ex-husband seldom came to see their child. Meanwhile, she felt the pressure of working full-time at a hospital and then running a household.

A doctor from Long Beach grappled with the same type of reactive depression that had sapped Ruth's strength. While he was attending a medical conference, his wife had been shot to death in her bed by a robber.

When it was Ruth's turn to speak, she described her happy life with Jack. As she told of his mysterious death, she began to cry and shake. The women on each side of her gripped her arms protectively. Slowly, others started to cry, too. That was the end of Ruth's story for the day.

But the story picked up that night in a dream. She was at the cemetery with an armful of red roses and greenery. She tried to cover Jack's grave. She tossed in all the flowers one by one, but she couldn't completely cover it. She looked around desperately for more flowers. She couldn't find any. It was hopeless.

Ruth sat up in bed in a cold sweat. The dream was vivid and recurring. Dr. Brenneman said it was a sign that Ruth hadn't finished her grieving.

Dr. Brenneman also interpreted Ruth's other dreams. In one, Ruth was in a crowded church covered with dust and cobwebs. It meant, according to Dr. Brenneman, Ruth's spiritual life wasn't in order, her faith had been shaken by Jack's murder. In another dream, Ruth kept seeing two empty egg cartons. "Eggs are a symbol of life," Dr. Brenneman explained, "and you see your life as completely empty."

After twelve days in the hospital, the doctors pronounced Ruth ready to tackle the outside world. But Toussaint wasn't so sure.

"Ruth, I think maybe you should come and live with me for a while," he said one night.

"In that bachelor pad of yours?" Ruth laughed. Then realizing he was serious, she added, "No, I couldn't leave my apartment."

"How will you take care of yourself? Ruth, it's been almost two years now," he declared. "It's time for you to leave. You've got to move on."

"Francois, I'm not going to give up trying to bring Jack's killer to trial."

"If that's what you must do, I won't discourage you."

"You don't mind sharing an apartment with a widow who cries a lot?"

"You know I don't."

"It'll just be for a while, until I can get my life straightened out."

"Of course. We'll just be friends," Toussaint smiled.

"Friends."

They hugged tightly.

Chapter 17

Blowout in Superior Court

Ruth had never thought browsing in a religious bookstore could be cathartic, but a friend who was a Seventh Day Adventist, watching her suffer and wanting to help, had suggested that Ruth send Hartman a book on finding God as a gesture of forgiveness.

After two years of agonizing grief and frustration over bureaucratic stonewalling, Ruth was ready to try anything to find a little peace of mind.

"What kind of books do you have for someone who isn't a Christian?" she asked the plump, grey-haired woman behind the counter of a religious bookstore.

"Did you have something particular in mind?"

"Well, I need something appropriate for a guy police say is a murderer," she said matter-of-factly.

The woman eyed Ruth with suspicion. "Is this so-called murderer in jail?"

"Yes, but not for murder," she replied. Noticing the confusion on the sales clerk's face, she added, "It's a very long story."

The woman pointed Ruth toward a row of shelves in the

front of the store and recommended six books. Tomes on born-again Christianity were as common here as romance novels in drug stores. Ruth bought all of them and shipped them one at a time to the prison. Inside each book, she painstakingly wrote: "Dr. Hartman, may God save your soul. Ruth Langlos."

Only the last book was returned because Hartman had been transferred to another site.

After Ruth shipped the books, she felt better. She was not sure why, but she felt better. Still, though she sincerely hoped God would save Hartman's soul in the next world, she wanted him tried for her husband's murder in this one. And evidence of that murder continued to mount. Almost every investigator and forensic pathologist who examined the case ruled that the death did not occur naturally.

Ruth got in touch with Dr. Ronald Kornblum, the doctor Jindrich had suggested review the case. Kornblum, the coroner of Ventura County, California, had a resume that commanded respect. Formerly the deputy chief medical examiner for the State of Maryland, Kornblum was on the Board of Directors of the National Association of Medical Examiners. During his career, Kornblum had performed about six thousand autopsies and reviewed seven hundred autopsy reports from agencies around the country.

For a $250 fee, he agreed to investigate all the records and draw his own conclusions. Without specifically criticizing the L.A. coroner's office, Kornblum's two-page report reiterated previous findings.

"Photographs of the face show bluish-red discoloration, however, I am unable to make out any petechial hemorrhages. . . . Although the flushing of the face is suggestive of asphyxia, the evidence is inconclusive."

Kornblum figured that the desk probably had been moved after Jack Langlos was dead. The blood on the wall, baseboard, and floor suggested "that the head was bumped against the wall and is highly inconsistent with thrashing movements during a heart attack."

"The overall conclusion based on the evidence from the scene indicates a struggle and is inconsistent with a natural death."

In his review of the autopsy report itself, Kornblum opined that "the cause of death is not established by the original autopsy or by the exhumation. . . . The degree of heart disease is insufficient to explain the death and is not an uncommon finding in an individual of Dr. Langlos's age. Although asphyxia must also be considered as a possible cause of death, the evidence from the scene and both autopsies is inconclusive."

Kornblum's final conclusion mirrored that of Jindrich: "The only reasonable conclusion to draw at this point is that the cause of death is undetermined and that the manner of death is probably homicide."

Ruth should have been ecstatic, but by now her cynicism was harder than a petrified rock. Kornblum's conclusions seemed to her like a rerun—nothing was changing.

Nevertheless, she continued fighting with the aid of attorney Leigh. She was starting to collect some money to fuel her conflict with Noguchi.

Based on an investigation by the Attorney General's office, The State of California awarded her $10,000 plus interest—a total of $11,353.73—under a state law that compensated the victims of violent crimes. The State Board of Control, which was the agency that handled the claims of victims or their families, ruled that Jack indeed had been a crime victim.

In a desert of futility, this payment was her oasis. It was no small victory considering the fact that Ruth had less than a one percent chance of success. At the time, only seven states—California, New York, Minnesota, Hawaii, Illinios, Maryland, and North Dakota—gave crime victims a cash award. Only 3,500 of 400,000 victims had received compensation.

Two months later, Occidental Life Insurance also concluded that Jack did not die naturally. After a thorough probe, it paid the double-indemnity benefits of fifteen thousand dollars on Jack's life insurance policy.

Occidental sought the opinion of Dr. Richard Myers, a forensic pathologist who had reviewed cases for many police agencies, including Scotland Yard. In a three-page letter to the supervisor of Occidental's Group Life Benefits Department, Myers spelled out the obvious:

"In this instance, the first autopsy examination was somewhat less than ideal," Myers wrote, "and a second autopsy after nearly a year of burial is considerably less satisfactory that the initial examination on a recently dead body. It must be accepted in this instance that a definitive or unequivocal cause of death has not been established after two postmortem examinations."

Like Jindrich and Kornblum, he pointed out that physical evidence and findings at the death scene also are important in reconstructing events that led to death. In the case of Jack's death, Myers said the evidence was not like that found in cases where "the individual literally drops dead and may suffer agonal or actually postmortem injuries from falling and striking objects such as furniture."

According to Myers, there was a reasonable assumption—homicide.

"Thank you for asking me to review this extremely interesting, if not entirely satisfactory, and puzzling case," Myers concluded in his letter.

They say God works in mysterious ways and doesn't give us more than we can handle. Ruth believed that. Without her newfound money, she would not have been able to continue the fight. She had already spent their life savings on doctors, lawyers, and investigators.

And on people willing to take advantage of the situation. For example, she had paid fifteen hundred dollars to Samuel Birdsong, deputy D.A. Schafer's friend, to publicize her plight. He had done virtually nothing but advise her who to contact at various newspapers and television stations.

Yet she couldn't give up and wouldn't let all the dead ends defeat her. As she fought on, Ruth decided to learn as much as possible about her nemesis, Dr. Noguchi. She didn't care what it cost. While doing research at the UCLA library, she was told that some articles about Noguchi were missing. So she traveled to New York City to continue the research. At the New York Times library, she uncovered articles about Noguchi's strange behavior. "Obviously, he needs care," said L.A. County Supervisor, Warren

Dorn, in one story.

Ruth stayed with Jack's relatives in Connecticut. It was a costly way to gather information, but learning what made Noguchi tick helped her immeasurably. She now knew she wasn't the only one who'd had trouble with him.

Yet, in Jack's case, she knew he held all the cards.

"Let me see if I've got this right," Ruth said, fire burning in her eyes. Leigh fidgeted behind his desk, anticipating Ruth's wrath. "The pathologists I've hired say Jack probably was murdered. The police say it's definitely homicide. Then the State of California says Jack was the victim of a violent crime. Now the life insurance company agrees. And we know how fond life insurance companies are of paying double indemnity." Ruth paused for a breath. But only a breath. "After all this, the suspect is in prison for almost beating another man to death. And on the other side, we've got a coroner who refutes all this evidence, and we have to take his word for it. Sorry, I can't . . . and I won't."

"It's very d-d-difficult to force a coroner to change a death certificate if he doesn't want to," said Leigh.

"What about a formal inquest? Let's get this out of the hands of the bureaucrats and have a jury decide."

"That would take a lot of time, especially if Noguchi fights it like I think he would. It would be quicker to p-p-petition the court for immediate action."

"What are our chances?"

"Well, Noguchi has never been forced to change a cause of death to the best of my knowledge. So . . . " his voice trailed off.

"So he's going to do it for the first time!" Ruth exclaimed. "Maybe in the future his staff will be more precise in their work."

On April 14, the schedule posted outside the courtroom of Los Angeles Superior Court Judge George Dell featured the case *Langlos v. Noguchi*. Dell was known as the "hot potato judge" because of the plethora of high-profile cases he'd handled. For him, a writ of mandate hearing was like a day off.

An impressive array of legal paperwork had been filed for both sides.

Besides the statements of Drs. Jindrich and Kornblum, Leigh

argued that Dr. Noguchi had not done his legal duty in determining how Ruth's husband died. According to the law, the cause of death appearing on a death certificate signed by the coroner shall conform with facts ascertained from an inquiry, autopsy, and other scientific findings. In this case, it didn't. Dr. Carpenter had simply followed a practice of utilizing coronary artery disease when he couldn't determine another cause.

Leigh maintained that the coroner's office had abused its discretion. He requested the death certificate be amended to show homicide as the cause of death.

The Los Angeles County attorneys representing Noguchi simply categorized the issue as a disagreement among medical experts. They used written statements of Drs. Carpenter and Noguchi to buttress their contention. Neither attended the court session.

Dr. Carpenter agreed that the circumstances of Jack Langlos's death were suspicious. For a man of his experience, that was a mouthful. He had been a physician since 1940.

According to Carpenter, Langlos's coronary arteries were seventy percent closed. Although no tissue damage was found, he said the most common cause of death of heart attack victims is ventricular fibrillation, a cardiac arrest that doesn't leave morbid alteration of the heart.

"No injury caused Mr. Langlos's death," he steadfastly maintained. "Perhaps he was confused by chest pains, struck his head, or struck his head and became confused, got chest pains, and staggered and stumbled, wiping blood onto objects. The fact that his head came to rest beneath and against the desk is as compatible, or more so, with confused crawling as with struggle. The man isn't dead, he's dying. It takes time to develop pulmonary edema from heart failure or terminal convulsions."

Carpenter said he would amend the death certificate if there were proof of a confrontation between Langlos and Hartman. "The police must first put him in the room. Sophistry, even in expert hands, cannot."

In his statement, Dr. Noguchi offered this version: "Drs. Jindrich and Kornblum have concluded the position of the body, the blood stains, and the disarray of the desk area indicate a physical struggle and hence criminal activity."

"I feel such evidence is consistent with the action of a man experiencing a fatal heart attack. The evidence supports a finding that Mr. Langlos had a coronary, tore his shirt open in an attempt to breathe, fell and hit his head on the desk as he was falling, thrashed or crawled around on the floor for a short period of time, and then died."

Having read the documents, Judge Dell was irritated. There didn't seem to be a case here. He wondered whether this might be an attempt to change a death certificate to get insurance money.

"My goodness," he said, alternating looks at the file and Leigh, who was standing in front of him. "Well, this is an interesting matter. As I understand it, the only basis on which the court could grant this kind of a writ is if there is a determination that the respondent's assessment of cause of death was arbitrary and capricious and entirely unsupported by any evidence. Is that really the state of the record, Mr. Leigh?"

Leigh, his voice gathering force, answered, "It's stricter than that, your honor. It's not merely a showing of capriciousness or arbitrariness. Well, the c-c-county coroner is mandated by state law that the cause of death must be in conformity with the facts. The county coroner hasn't done his job merely because he assigns a cause of death or he thinks that such a cause may be the cause of death. I think that the language used by the deputy county coroner, Dr. Carpenter—your honor, I assume, read this part of the doctor's declarations where he—"

Dell's irritation seemed to be turning into a slow boil. He didn't see the merits of the case, and now the attorney was making comments about whether he had done his homework.

"You may assume that I have read everything in this file," Dell said sternly, raising a manilla folder. Glaring at Leigh, Dell added, "And I see no merit in the petition at all, counsel."

"But, your Honor," Leigh pleaded, "the point I'm making is that when the deputy county coroner makes a statement, 'We're not really sure of the c-c-cause of death and it's the policy of this d-d-department, when we're not sure of the cause of death, to assign heart attack,' then that's hardly following state law."

"It's not the whole story either," Dell declared. "You've just stated a part of what the coroner has said. What you want me to do is assess this as a homicide, even though your experts aren't sure that it's homicide."

Leigh, getting a bit irritated himself, replied: "Well, my experts aren't sure because at the original a-a-autopsy the brain was not retained, nor was the tongue or sections taken from the brain."

"Does it make any difference why they're not sure, Mr. Leigh?"

"Because these sections would have definitely stated whether or not strangulation was the cause of d-d-death, or a blow to the head."

Ruth could see Dell didn't buy it. Shaking his head in disgust, Dell said, "But does that have to do with whether or not the coroner is performing his duty in a proper manner and using his discretion in assessing the cause of death? On the basis that the coroner did not conform to the standard that you think is appropriate, you are thereby assuming that if he had performed those duties, that there would be additional evidence present from which your experts maybe could assign the cause of death as a homicide with more certainty than they do. Based on that assumption, you feel I should grant a writ of mandate to compel the death certificate to set forth a new cause of death, namely homicide. Doesn't that seem to lack something by way of a chain of logic, Mr. Leigh?"

"Not really, your Honor. What would be more helpful in this case is a c-c-continuance, perhaps, of six weeks allowing me to take depositions—"

"Well, I'm just going to deny your motion, your application for the writ," interrupted Dell. "If you want to renew it, be my guest."

Deputy county counsel Joshua Murray smiled. He hadn't said a word except to introduce himself, and he had won the case.

Dell continued his scolding. "You really haven't presented a case, and I don't see any reason why, when you haven't presented a case, I ought to simply continue it because you want to take depositions. I don't think this is the right remedy."

"Your Honor—"

"Really, I don't know what's behind the ice flow here, but I'm sure there's an iceberg pushing its nose up somewhere along the line and that maybe buried a few fathoms down is a lawsuit against an insurance company on a double indemnity."

"Mr. Murray is nodding his head. Maybe that's what it's all about. But you just really haven't established there's been a dereliction of the discretionary duty. I certainly don't foreclose you coming in with something further."

Judge Dell denied the writ but agreed to amend his ruling if Leigh could come back with more evidence.

Dell scoffed at the likelihood. "I just don't see anything here."

Leigh was fuming as he and Ruth left the courthouse fifteen minutes later. Not only had they lost—they had been humiliated.

"Ruth, it doesn't make s-s-sense to bring this case back here. The judge had his mind made up before we argued the case."

"Why didn't you tell him that we don't need a writ of mandate for insurance money?" Ruth said. "Occidental has already approved double indemnity."

"I couldn't get a word in edgewise. The judge was really steamed for some reason. He believes the law gives c-c-county officials wide latitude in doing their jobs."

"Even when they're covering up the truth?"

Leigh shrugged his shoulders.

Sitting in the courtroom further convinced Ruth that the only way she would get a fair hearing on the facts was in front of common citizens. Logic didn't seem to work on bureaucrats, prosecutors, and judges. Ruth longed to state her case before her peers.

Three months later, she took the first step in doing just that. She requested a grand jury investigation.

In a two-page letter to the legal advisor for the grand jury in Los Angeles County, she summarized the case and showed the need to scrutinize deficiencies in the coroner's office.

"Errors in certification by the Medical Examiner can have many adverse effects on families and on society," Ruth wrote. "I do not know how common errors are within the medical examiner's office, but this case demonstrates their reluctance to admit an error when one is made."

In October, the grand jury said no to Ruth. Ernest Goodman, chairman of the criminal complaints committee, responded: "The committee had determined that there is insufficient evidence to bring criminal charges in the death of your husband."

He said the grand jury had no jurisdiction in the matter of the death certificate.

Three weeks before Christmas, nearly three years after his death, Ruth and her family buried Jack Langlos for the last time. They moved him from Forest Lawn to the newly opened Riverside National Veterans Cemetery. On a Tuesday morning, Reverend Ralph Osborne of Hollywood Presbyterian Church read the 139th Psalm. Ruth was presented with the American flag that had covered the casket.

Her darling Jack was at rest, but the cause of his death still remained unresolved. After three years of fighting for justice, Ruth had three options: press on, give it up, or call Ron.

She had met Ron on a college campus while receiving therapy. He had heard of her plight through a mutual friend and had asked to meet Ruth in a nearby park. A respected teacher, he had been published many times and seemed to be well connected with influential people in the Los Angeles area. Ruth figured he might know how to convince the grand jury to reconsider.

"Ruth, I think you're going to have to pressure Hartman to confess," Ron said.

"How am I going to do that? He won't talk to the Downey Police, and I'm scared of him."

"You don't deal with his type of talk," Ron said, rising from the park bench. He motioned for Ruth to follow him down an evergreen tree-lined path.

They walked twenty yards in silence. The pungent smell of grilling chicken filled their nostrils. Ron walked slowly, deep in thought.

"This guy has taken away the man you loved, Ruth. I can have his legs broken for $250."

"Are you serious?" Ruth cried out.

"For $750, you can have him blown away," Ron declared. "It's best to have it done while he's in prison."

"You're not kidding, are you?" she said, staring at him. They had stopped near a group of kids playing a game of tag. The children's happy squeals punctuated the beautiful sunny California afternoon.

"Ruth, consider it. That may be the only way he'll be punished for what he did."

"No way, Ron. I have to look at myself in the morning. God would never forgive me. I would be no better than any other murderer."

"I understand," he said, gazing at her sadly. "If you change your mind, you know how to reach me."

In Ruth's darkest moments, she thought about Ron's offer, but she never changed her mind. She would not commit a crime in order to avenge Jack's death, but she would not give up, either. She would use every legal means to pursue Hartman and bring him to trial for Jack's murder, even if it took the rest of her life.

Chapter 18

An Unlikely Team

Lying in bed, Ruth felt very, very guilty. Francois Toussaint's head gently touched her arm as she stared blankly at the ceiling.

Jack had been dead for more than three years. But her conscience ached.

"Francois, I don't like living this way," she said softly, turning to face him.

Toussaint's eyes were closed. He didn't move. Ruth rolled away, figuring he was asleep.

A few seconds later he said, "We're not cheating on anyone, Ruth." He looked at her. "We're not committing adultery."

"That's true. But we're living like man and wife."

"I'm not hurting anyone by being with you," he replied. "And you're not hurting anyone by being with me."

Good old practical Toussaint. He had never misled her.

His apartment in Huntington Beach was about fifty miles from the place Jack and Ruth had shared. It offered a panoramic view of tree-lined streets in a quiet California neighborhood. On a clear day, you could see the Pacific Ocean and Catalina Island from the balcony. On most mornings, gazing out the glass sliding doors was like looking at a beautiful landscape painting in an art gallery. The azure blues and kelly greens of Mother Nature were exhilarating.

After Ruth was released from the hospital, she had planned to spend a couple of weeks there. But weeks had turned to months, and then to a year and a half. Now three years had passed.

Sometimes, it felt so right. But some nights Ruth stayed awake for hours thinking about their relationship and her Christian beliefs. She would look at Toussaint snuggled beside her in deep sleep, and mixed emotions would attack her from within.

Marriage had been a taboo subject with Toussaint. One of Ruth's cardinal rules is: Don't be afraid to ask anybody anything. All they can answer is yes or no. A lot of people don't get answers because they're afraid to ask questions. Ruth had broken her own rule by not asking Toussaint about the reasons for his aversion to marriage. He was close-mouthed about the subject, and she suspected one of the reasons was his strict, conservative Catholic upbringing. Toussaint was raised in an environment opposed to divorce. Marrying a divorced woman wouldn't set well with his parents and family.

On this spring night, Ruth tried to get him to talk.

"We shouldn't be living together," she said.

"Why not? Does a piece of paper make it right?"

"In this country, that's how it's done."

"Ruth, you're fighting to bring Jack's killer to trial," Toussaint said, turning toward her, "and I know you aren't going to give up. But if we were married, I couldn't go along with it. I couldn't have my wife spending all her time working on a case involving her deceased husband."

"I know it's been tough on you," Ruth answered. "I don't know if I could put up with you talking about your wife all the time, if the roles were reversed."

He patted her hand. "I want you to win your case. And you will."

She sighed heavily. "I wish I was as sure as you are. My only chance is to get a formal inquest. But Noguchi will probably block that. He's a powerful man."

"Patience et longueur de temps sont plus que force et que rage," Toussaint replied.

"What?"

"Patience et longueur de temps sont plus que force et que rage," he repeated. "Patience and length of time are greater than strength and rage."

"Meaning?"

"Be patient, Ruth. Your cause is just and you will triumph over those more powerful."

"You're very special," Ruth said, kissing him lightly on the cheek. "You really are, you know."

"I'm glad that damn dime came up heads," Toussaint said, recalling their fateful meeting.

They embraced, laughing.

The preacher's daughter and the European shipping manager had become an unlikely team. Toussaint was a silent partner in Ruth's fight against the judicial system. He helped write letters to authorities, gave advice, and provided stability in Ruth's life.

In many ways, they were opposites. Toussaint didn't like to see a woman in slacks, Ruth liked to wear slacks. He didn't enjoy going to movies or clubs with live music, Ruth lit up like a Christmas tree anytime live music played. He was a private person, Ruth was outgoing and assertive.

But the relationship worked. They went out to dinner often because eating out was a luxury to Francois. In Belgium, people dine out only on special occasions because the cost is many times higher than in America. On weekends, they'd walk on the beach or take long trips around California with Francois taking plenty of pictures. The trips would help Ruth unwind from working on Jack's case during the week.

Unfortunately, nothing seemed to be working in her ongoing fight to get a new autopsy. Unable to get any California officials to authorize a formal hearing on Jack's autopsy, Ruth turned to Washington, D.C., and the military.

She requested a review of the case by Dr. Hugh McAllister, a cardiovascular pathologist with the Armed Forces Institute of Pathology. Included with her request were two packages of documents, microscopic slides, and pictures.

A month later, the packages were returned unopened. A letter from a military attorney explained that pathologists at the institute were prohibited from reviewing cases or acting as expert witnesses. McAllister's services were only available for career military personnel. Another door slammed shut.

For every door that closed, however, another opened. This time it opened on the campus of Stanford University in Palo Alto, California. Dr. Margaret Billingham, a professor of pathology, is one of about thirty cardiac pathologists in the United States. She received her medical training in England. In 1968, she was a member of Dr. Norman Shumway's team which performed the first successful heart transplant in the country. Her forty-five-page single-spaced resume includes noted writings, lectures, and research about the heart.

The field of forensic pathology is extremely specialized. It includes the study of changes caused by disease or injury in body tissues, fluids, or secretion applied to situations that have a legal connotation. It is pathology in the service of justice. At last count, there were only 824 forensic pathologists in the United States. Dr. Noguchi already had discarded the opinion of three of them—Drs. Jindrich, Kornblum, and Myers.

Could anyone convince him of his office's error? Ruth's friend, Louise McCord, suggested Ruth let Billingham study the case. She was, after all, one of the world's foremost heart authorities, and her opinion would carry a lot of weight.

Billingham, a dark-haired, soft-spoken woman, agreed to study the case, but insisted that she do so for no fee. She looked at police reports, Dr. Carpenter's autopsy, ten glass slides of tissue sections, and twenty Kodachrome slides. She also studied the conclusions of Drs. Jindrich, Walker, and Kornblum.

In Billingham's office, Ruth's heart pounded as she sat across the desk from the doctor, waiting for her verdict.

"Mrs. Langlos, there is no evidence here to indicate that your husband died of heart disease," Billingham said matter-of-factly.

Ruth could feel the tension releasing from her neck muscles. Billingham's diagnosis meant a lot to Ruth. It confirmed beyond any doubt that her cause was just.

"Doctor, you don't know how happy you've made me."

"Well, Mrs. Langlos, I must admit I thought you had exaggerated," Billingham said. "I figured it would be a straightforward decision in favor of the coroner. But you seemed sincere and upset, so I decided to take a look."

"Several things stood out," she continued, looking at her notes. "Even if your husband had a heart attack, the heart stops beating or flutters for a little bit . . . it's not able to pump blood. You get very little blood, but there was blood all around the death scene and on his clothes. That's not going to happen if the heart has stopped."

"What was the condition of Jack's heart?"

"From a pathological viewpoint, like many middle-aged men, he did have some evidence of coronary disease," Billingham said. "But it wasn't obtrusive. No vessels were blocked . . . they were reduced in diameter in some places but not enough to cause a heart attack."

"Then how is it that the coroner's office persists in saying it was a heart attack?"

Billingham shrugged her shoulders. "How they reached that conclusion," she paused, and her voice conveyed exasperation, "well, it's very strange. By our standards, it was not a good autopsy. A section of tongue was mislabeled, the brain was missing. Let's just say it wasn't a very good job."

"Would you testify to that, Doctor?"

"Certainly." Billingham nodded vigorously.

On the thirty-mile drive to Ruth's niece's home in Oakland, Ruth cried a lot. For the first time, she realized how long Jack must have suffered. With the amount of blood that came from the head wound, he could have lived in agonizing pain as many as fifteen to twenty minutes. Armed with Dr. Billingham's report, she renewed her efforts to get a formal inquest.

In July 1980, more than four years after Jack Langlos's death, Downey Captain Frank Sanders requested the formal inquest on behalf of the police department. From day one, Miller and Westray had smelled murder. Only the death certificate had stopped the prosecutor from acting.

The evidence disputing that autopsy report had grown to prodigious proportions. Five highly respected doctors had ruled the death a probable homicide. The State of California and Occidental Life Insurance had concurred.

Finally, there was the coup de grace. In her report, Dr. Billingham concluded: "There is no evidence from the histopathology available that the patient died of heart disease, myocardial infarction, or that he had significant coronary artery disease."

State law mandated that the coroner hold an inquest if requested by police, the district attorney, or the attorney general. Four months later, one of Dr. Noguchi's subordinates promised Captain Sanders that an inquest would be scheduled.

"Be patient," the spokesman for Noguchi advised. It turned out to be another stalling tactic that lasted over two years.

Meanwhile, Ruth filed a lawsuit against the Lakewood Park Health Center under the Wrongful Death Act. Ruth alleged that the center had been negligent in failing to provide a safe environment. The Center, she said, had not conducted security patrols around Jack's office area that weekend.

Attorney Leigh referred Ruth to another lawyer, Walter Ritz, who specialized in such cases. About a week before the trial, a settlement conference was held at the Norwalk Superior Court.

Ritz emerged from a meeting with the center's attorneys with a noncommittal look. They escorted Ruth into the judge's chambers.

"They've made an offer, Mrs. Langlos," he said. "Ten thousand dollars."

"Ten thousand dollars," Ruth frowned. "They're not serious."

"Mrs. Langlos, I think you should seriously consider their offer," the judge replied. "If you go to trial, they're going to point out that the coroner ruled your husband died of heart disease."

"But the coroner made a mistake."

"The burden of proof is on us," said Ritz.

"All right, we'll prove it," Ruth replied defiantly.

"There's no guarantees at trial. The ten thousand is guaranteed," Ritz pointed out.

"Well, ten thousand dollars is an insult. I won't starve. My sons will help me if it comes to that."

"You want to reject the ten thousand then?"

"Tell them we're going to court. I'd rather take a chance at losing than accept ten thousand dollars."

The next day Ritz and the opposing attorney met again with the judge.

"They've upped the offer," Ritz said sheepishly, "to sixty-five thousand dollars."

Ruth smiled. "Guess they didn't have as much faith in that coroner's report as you thought."

Ruth's share of the settlement was $40,765.42. Ritz and Leigh made over $24,000, or about eight times what they would have if Ruth had agreed to the original settlement he advised. The money ensured that Ruth would be able to continue her fight with Noguchi. But Ruth's joy was soon shattered.

Hartman was again a free man. He had been paroled more than a year ahead of his scheduled release date. Ruth's fears and anguish tortured her once more, especially at night.

"Doctor, I'm really scared," Ruth admitted to her psychiatrist, Mary Brenneman. Since they had met at the hospital, Ruth had been seeing her once a week.

"Scared that you won't be able to prove that Jack was murdered?" asked Brenneman.

"No, I'm scared that Hartman will come after me. I see him in my dreams."

"What else do you see?"

"One night I dreamt about music and Christmas. Everybody was caroling."

"Go on."

"One night Jack was wrapped in white and I could only see part of his face. My son Jan was there, and I asked, 'Should we bring him back to life?' Jan replied, 'Mother, I don't think we should, because we don't know the condition of his brain.' Then last night I dreamt I was trying to rescue a big white fish."

"In my opinion," Dr. Brenneman said thoughtfully, "many of your dreams are spiritual, Ruth. Christmas is a spiritual time, and your father was a minister. The fish represents Christ." She paused and changed the subject. "How are your sons doing?"

"They're fine," Ruth sighed. "Sometimes I wish I could spend more time with them. But they're in three different states, so that makes it kind of hard."

Brenneman looked at Ruth searchingly. "Have you been indecisive about things lately?"

"Oh, yes," Ruth laughed. "I saw a beautiful brass eagle at the store. It's about three feet wide and cost three hundred dollars. I don't know if I should buy it."

Brenneman smiled. "An eagle is a symbol of sovereign power. That eagle represents a part of your soul. That's you. Why don't you buy it?"

On the way home, Ruth did. Not because she was feeling powerful—quite the opposite—but she hoped seeing the object at home would inspire her and perhaps change her luck. However, during the next few weeks she still felt powerless and her ill fortune seemed to continue. Dr. Noguchi continued to ignore the Downey police request for a formal inquest. Without a hearing, the death certificate would stand.

Ruth's funding had been replenished, but she was out of options. She needed a miracle, or something close to it.

Chapter 19

Finally, a Formal Inquest

Death had been a nice living for the Coroner to the Stars.

Over the past few years, Dr. Thomas Noguchi's autopsies of Marilyn Monroe, Robert Kennedy, Janis Joplin, John Belushi, and others provided him a stage for his own bid for stardom. Many said that the flamboyant doctor craved attention and milked every ounce of publicity with energy that would make a press agent envious.

The mounting success of the "Quincy" television series only enhanced his charismatic image.

For Ruth, time was passing as success eluded her. It had been six years that Ruth had been trying to convince officials at every level of government that the common citizen wasn't being served by Noguchi.

"Unless you're a movie star, don't die in L.A. County," Ruth warned repeatedly. "An ordinary guy like Jack Langlos doesn't stand a chance. Noguchi can't get his picture on the front page or his face on television with the Langlos case."

In early 1982, Ruth's concerns about Noguchi became public knowledge when the minor miracle for which she'd been praying occurred.

The County Board of Supervisors launched an investigation into allegations that Thomas Noguchi had mismanaged his office and mishandled celebrity deaths. He was accused of creating a litany of horrors in the nation's second largest coroner's office.

Among the charges: Noguchi ran a sloppy operation in which bodies were looted and evidence lost and damaged; used county time and resources to do consulting work, and sensationalized the alcohol-related deaths of celebrities Natalie Wood and William Holden.

As Noguchi fought for his $69,341-a-year job, the media had a feeding frenzy. Charges and countercharges filled the news reports. Dr. Noguchi was headline news again, but this time he wasn't smiling.

Noguchi's problems opened a window of opportunity for Ruth. She sent a blizzard of letters to nearly every government official she could think of, detailing the background of her husband's case.

"I am sending this letter to you in connection with the current investigation you are conducting in the highly questionable behavior of Dr. Thomas T. Noguchi," she wrote to Charles Norris, chief of management services for the county. Copies of the February 22 letter went to Attorney General George Deukmejian, County Supervisor Mike Antonovich, and others involved in the Noguchi probe.

In less than a month, media reports of the Jack Langlos case added an intriguing element to the ongoing story. Reporter Patty Ecker of the Los Angeles CBS affiliate did a feature on the case for the six o'clock news.

The incongruity of a man dying of a heart attack in a blood splattered office made for riveting television. So did Ecker's interview of Downey Captain Sanders.

On camera, Ecker asked, "Captain, is there any doubt in your mind that Dr. Langlos's death was a homicide?"

Sanders replied decisively, "Not in my mind, or the investigators'."

The extensive media coverage of Jack Langlos's death prompted other people to inform the supervisors of other cases where the L.A. coroner's office had misplaced body parts and organs of their loved ones.

One week after the CBS report aired, Supervisor Antonovich proposed a resolution directing the coroner to immediately institute a policy of keeping all body parts together with the decedent. It passed.

Waiting for a break in the case, Ruth moved to Denver in an attempt to ease back into the workforce. She became a housemother at a three-quarter house, a mental health facility for those who had left a halfway house but needed more counseling before they rejoined society.

At first, Ruth enjoyed the experience. On Friday nights, she was responsible for coordinating recreational activities. On Sundays, she drove the single men and women to a nearby church where they had a service for singles.

While in Denver, Ruth received a brown manilla envelope that Francois had forwarded.

> Dear Mrs. Langlos:
> This is to inform you that Attorney General Deukmejian has directed the Division of Law Enforcement to conduct an investigation relative to the death certificate of your late husband.
> William Anthony, Division Director

Ruth felt jubilant. Justice was within reach. On another front, the County Board of Supervisors had suspended Noguchi pending the outcome of its investigation.

Everything seemed to be going better. Ruth even thought her job could turn into something more permanent. At work Ruth met Sarah Smythe. Only twenty-two years old, the young woman was trying to win her personal war with drugs. Although shy and withdrawn, Smythe opened up to Ruth. They talked about

Sarah's father and the distance that had been wedged between them. They discussed how she missed her mother, who had been killed in a car crash, and they talked about how bright her future could be drug-free.

One Sunday morning, Ruth knocked on Sarah's room, adjoining Ruth's. No answer. Ruth thought nothing of it until she returned from church to see the flashing lights of police cars and emergency vehicles surrounding the house. They wouldn't let Ruth inside but told her that a girl had hanged herself in her room. It was Sarah Smythe.

Another untimely death of someone she cared for was almost more than Ruth could bear. She immediately resigned and returned to Huntington Beach. Luckily, it was just in time for some long-overdue good news.

In a letter dated April 21, Ruth was informed that a formal inquest into Jack's death would be held. It came from Judge Carlos Teran, chief of the inquest division of the coroner's office. As Ruth scanned the contents, she smiled. Ironically, the name at the top of the stationery was Thomas T. Noguchi.

That letterhead required a change six days later. The Board of Supervisors formally demoted Noguchi to autopsy physician, citing mismanagement of his office. He vowed to fight for his job and already had started raising money for his legal fund with a gala testimonial that attracted more than 650 supporters, including comedian Flip Wilson.

The next month, on the morning of May 27, 1982, Judge Teran eyed the nine jurors seated in Room 303 on the ninth floor of the Criminal Courts Building in downtown Los Angeles. The formal inquest into Jack's death was about to begin.

The judge's voice was strong and clear. "Ladies and gentlemen of the jury, you are not here to determine the guilt or innocence of any person. Our sole function is to determine the cause and mode of death. There are four possible verdicts that our government code lays out as to what you may bring in.

"One is that it was a natural death by natural means caused by natural events, and it may be a heart attack or any disease of the body that is a natural result, resulting in death.

"The second of the possible verdicts is suicide.

"The third is an accidental death through some unforeseen, unintended act or event. An accident can result in the death of a person.

"The fourth is that it was not an accident and not any of the prior ones, but death at the hands of another person. You need not bring in the name of that person. Those are the four possible verdicts."

As Dectective Westray testified, Ruth scanned the courtroom, desperately searching for Drs. Jindrich and Billingham. Their testimony would be critical. Before the inquest, Teran had requested in writing a list of the people Ruth thought should testify. Drs. Jindrich and Billingham were at the top of the list.

Ruth's heart skipped a beat. They were not in the courtroom.

At 11:10, during the morning recess, Ruth approached Teran. "Where are Dr. Jindrich and Dr. Billingham? They're supposed to testify."

"We had to take them off the witness list," Teran said. "County regulations don't permit us to pay to bring in somebody who's over 150 miles from L.A."

"Pay?" Ruth asked astonished.

"You know, expenses like mileage, motel rooms . . . "

"But their reports are very important to this case," Ruth said angrily. "I would have paid their expenses if you had informed me that the county wouldn't pay to have them testify. Dr. Jindrich is the one who—"

Teran interrupted her. "I'm sorry, Mrs. Langlos, I thought you knew they weren't going to testify," Teran apologized.

Fortunately, Ruth had come prepared. Wherever Ruth went these days, her files went, too. With the aid of a mobile luggage carrier, she had brought reams of paperwork into the courtroom.

"Could you at least read their reports into the record?" Ruth asked, rifling through files.

"Yes, I can do that."

That afternoon Westray and Miller testified to their finding at the death scene, including the buttons ripped off Jack's shirt, the wound on his head, and the blood on the wall. Jack's assistant,

Tom Lacey, testified to finding Jack in the morning.

Dominic Hernandez, the coroner's investigator at the scene, was a key witness because of his link to the coroner's office.

"What investigation did you make of the body?" Teran asked.

"Primarily it was the trauma that was apparent at the time. The desk had been partially removed from on top of the decedent's face," Hernandez responded, his head down. "I noted the laceration and as Detective Miller cited before, we made a copy of the corner of the desk, and we matched this to a laceration on the top of the decedent's head, which gave us the fact that the trauma was probably sustained from the corner of the desk."

Teran wasn't about to stop there. He pressed now. "Well, the officer mentioned something about the corner of the desk having some evidence. What did you find?"

Hernandez looked up. "There was blood on the corner of the desk."

Teran quickened the pace. "What did you conclude from that?"

Hernandez replied, "That apparently he had struck his head on the desk or been forced against the desk."

Quickly Teran asked, "Where on his head was the laceration?"

Hernandez said, "The laceration was toward the back of the head. It was a V shape or a 45-degree angle pointing forward."

Meeting the witness's eyes, Teran asked forcefully, "How would a laceration on the top of the head be possible on the corner of a desk?"

Hernandez met his gaze and said firmly, "I'm not an expert on this particular type of trauma, but it would appear to me from my past experience that the decedent had to be forced probably head-down so that his face was pointing inward toward his body, toward his chest, so that the laceration could have been taken from the desk in this particular fashion."

Teran nodded affirmatively. "Because if a man were falling, it would seem to me it would be more to his forehead. Would it not?"

Hernandez answered softly, "Yes, sir."

"And this was not that kind of a wound?" Teran asked searchingly.

Hernandez shook his head. "No, sir. It was too far back for a fall of that nature."

Teran asked, "But would it be possible, if he fell in the right way, to get a laceration by falling?"

Hernandez hesitated a moment then acknowledged, "Yes, it is possible."

"What other evidence do you have to present to the jury?" Teran said curtly.

Hernandez took a deep breath then replied, "Other than that laceration, the fact that his wallet was missing and his rear pocket appeared to be turned inside out, the missing clothes articles and the buttons, of course, that were lying on the floor denoted some type of struggle had taken place."

Teran asked, "Did you at that time make any report as to your conclusions that it was an accident or that it was a possible homicide?"

Hernandez's voice gained strength. "I carried the case right from the beginning as a homicide. It was processed all the time as a homicide." After a few more questions, Hernandez stepped down.

Ruth felt that the next witness, Dr. Ronald Kornblum, had a possible conflict of interest. He had replaced Noguchi as the acting coroner of Los Angeles County. Now he was in a position to offer damaging testimony against his own department based on his previous analysis of the case.

How did he handle it? According to reports on Channel 2, the CBS affiliate in Los Angeles, Kornblum modified his stance, softening his position against the department he now headed. Still, his testimony contradicted Dr. Carpenter's autopsy findings.

Kornblum said: "Dr. Langlos does have heart disease, but not of the type— . . . he did not have acute coronary occlusion or a myocardial infarction, which often happens at or near death. In my opinion it was not of a severe enough nature to call it occlusive coronary artery disease.

"I had a meeting with Dr. Noguchi after I had gone over the

material and explained my findings to him."

"What was his position?" Teran inquired.

Kornblum hesitated a moment then went on. "It is hard to say. I explained the situation to him. He listened, and I'm not really sure that he made any decision at the time."

When it was her turn, Ruth's testimony was much less confining than it would have been at a criminal trial. She was given latitude to express her opinions occasionally. And she did.

"Had your husband lent any money to Hartman?" Teran asked.

Ruth nodded vigorously. "Oh yes, two hundred dollars, but he paid us with a bad check."

"That's what we heard, but I wanted you to verify that."

Ruth's face was animated. "That's right. So it's my guess—I am assuming now—that Hartman came in and asked for more money and my husband refused because he paid him with a bad check. Why give him any more money?"

It felt good to Ruth to be able to say what was on her mind without an attorney objecting every two seconds.

Teran, like others before him, was fascinated with the missing necktie and the torn buttons on Jack's shirt.

"Did your husband always wear a necktie?"

Ruth couldn't suppress a smile. "Always. He was impeccable in his dressing. He was very neat."

"You do not feel he would have removed his tie that day?"

"Oh, no." She shook her head. "The tie is still missing. Who knows where it is?"

"As to the buttons on his shirt, did you know of any buttons missing before he went to work that day?"

"Oh, no. My, no. At least I can sew buttons on."

After lunch, it was Dr. Carpenter's turn. Ruth watched him closely. He did not look well. Clad in a wrinkled blue suit, he shuffled to the witness stand at a snail's pace.

Teran asked, "What were your conclusions as to the cause of death?"

Carpenter's voice was barely audible. "This was a suspicious case when it came into the coroner's office, and we considered it as a possible homicide from the beginning. But we found no evidence of homicide. We found a laceration on the head which did not in fact kill the individual. The man did have an enlarged heart with coronary artery disease, and in the absence of any other evidence we determined the cause of death to be occlusive coronary artery disease.

"It is not a satisfactory diagnosis because it is still suspicious circumstances, but that's what the evidence states."

"Since we are laymen," Teran said dryly, "would you explain what you mean by the coronary problems he had as recited on the death certificate."

"Arteriosclerosis is a general hardening of the arteries which roughly corresponds to age very often," answered Carpenter. "When it occurs in the coronary arteries, it obstructs the blood supply to the heart and occludes those vessels, and in this individual's case I estimated with the naked eye occlusion on the order of possibly seventy percent.

"In order to compensate, the heart enlarges, but there is a certain point where compensation is not possible and the usual cause of death is a fibrillation, sudden loss of rhythm of the heart, a sudden amount of twitching. Another cause of death would be actual complete obstruction in part of the heart muscle, which would be called myocardial infarct. Now, we cannot determine whether or not an infarct in fact occurs unless the individual has survived about six hours. Prior to that, there is no evidence of a myocardial infarct. There is indication that he had heart disease, that he has a type of heart disease that would cause sudden death."

"Were you advised, doctor," Teran paused, looking at Carpenter for a long moment, "at the time of the autopsy about some of the suspicions of the investigators and that another psychologist was found in northern California with Dr. Langlos's credit cards and driver's license?"

Slowly Carpenter replied. "I was very much aware of them. I don't believe that matter came out during the original post, but this was a suspicious death from the very beginning, and the problem is to establish a cause of death. Just having an individual's credit cards doesn't indicate you killed them. You may have merely rolled the dead body. It is not my job to determine that. I still agree this is a suspicious death, but I can't make up evidence."

"What was the condition of the brain?" Teran said, his tone sharp.

"There was no damage to the brain or no damage to the skull, and it is unfortunate that the brain for the second autopsy for one reason or another was not present in the body," Carpenter replied.

Teran followed this with his most auspicious comment: "Dr. Carpenter, you agree the circumstances are very suspicious in this case?"

"I certainly do," Carpenter nodded.

"Where a person known to him turned up with his credit cards and driver's license, this would be very suspicious?"

"Yes, indeed." Carpenter wiped his forehead with his handkerchief.

"Have you changed your opinion at all after these many years?"

"The only legitimate cause of death that is in evidence in this case is heart disease," Carpenter said slowly. "It can cause the person to stagger around clutching the pain in his chest. It can cause him to fall on the floor, convulse, get wedged under a desk. Everything can be explained on the basis of a natural death."

Ruth wanted to jump from her seat to object, but she restrained herself.

The reports of Dr. Jindrich and Dr. Billingham strongly disputed Carpenter's explanation.

It was 3:30 P.M. Judge Teran gave the jury instructions and decided to reconvene the next morning. Before he dismissed them he said, "I personally feel apologetic to Mrs. Langlos that she had to wait this long for an inquest on something that happened in 1976. I was not around, I don't know why, and I am not making any explanations. I am just expressing my sympathy to Mrs. Langlos for that."

When the jury returned to the courtroom at 9:30 the next morning, Ruth could scarcely breathe. Her thoughts were agonizing. Her hands fidgeted. She rested them for a moment on her lilac-colored skirt. Not being able to hold them still, she folded them. When this didn't work, she clasped them in the air at waist level.

Finally, Judge Teran started to read: "His death was caused by an undetermined cause . . . "

"Oooh," Ruth threw herself back against the bench in jubilation.

" . . . and from the testimony introduced at this time, we find this death to have been at the hands of another person," Teran concluded.

Ruth raised her clenched fists, tears of joy in her eyes. Then she buried her head in her hands, trying to compose herself.

"Can I thank the jury?" Ruth asked, rising. Her voice cracked with emotion.

Teran nodded. Ruth, tears running down her cheeks, said unsteadily, "After six years and four months, I want to thank every one of you."

That evening, Channel 2 Los Angeles anchorwoman Connie Chung opened the news: "A victory tonight for a woman who's been trying for six years to prove that her husband was murdered."

Reporter Bonnie Strauss recapped the inquest and got Ruth's reaction afterward. "I just had to know how my husband died," Ruth said emotionally.

Then Chung turned to Strauss: "Is she going to pursue the District Attorney?"

"Well, now it's up to the District Attorney's office, and she's going to be monitoring that very closely," Strauss answered.

Very closely indeed.

Chapter 20

Arrest for Murder

Fiery-eyed, prematurely white-haired Sterling Norris prowled back and forth in his king-sized office like a caged tiger.

"This isn't right," muttered the forty-two-year-old Deputy District Attorney. "It just isn't right."

The ex-Marine slammed his fist on the desk, scattering papers. He loathed crime with a passion bordering on obsession. Criminals knew that drawing Norris as their prosecutor left only one undecided issue: How long would they rot in the slammer? Defense attorneys said he was a zealot. Even some of his colleagues said he was too intense. Police described him simply as the toughest D.A. in Los Angeles.

Norris didn't care what anyone said. He worked single-mindedly to avenge victims—victims like Ruth Langlos.

It really was no surprise that the mysterious Jack Langlos case had landed at Norris's door in the fall of 1982. Of the nine hundred prosecutors in the L.A. District Attorney's Office, Norris was a home run hitter.

He headed the Special Trials Unit, an elite corps of five troubleshooters assigned to the county's controversial, high profile cases.

It was his job to prosecute the baddest of the bad—the freeway killers, the execution-style mass murderers, the night stalkers. He reveled in keeping them behind bars.

Norris tried more jury trials than anyone, but he never went stale. Forty-nine out of every fifty cases resulted in convictions. That made Norris something of a legend—and a marked man.

His life had been threatened many times. One December evening, someone fired a bullet through a window at his home while he decorated a Christmas tree. More threats followed. Because of one, he was given a permit to carry a gun while prosecuting those who killed members of the Kermit Alexander family. Alexander was a former UCLA football star.

In Norris's last trial, a thug convicted of assault and rape had pointed his finger at Norris seconds after the verdict was read. "Motherfucker, you are dead," the thug sneered.

"Your honor, the defendant has a statement that should be put in the record," Norris responded casually.

"Motherfucker, I said you are dead!" the thug called out again despite the public defender's efforts to quiet him.

The threat became a part of the court proceedings.

Norris didn't pay much attention to threats on *his* life, but he wasn't so casual about the safety of his loved ones. He zealously guarded the privacy of his wife, who was expecting another child, and his three daughters. They were a close-knit family.

On a warm fall morning, Norris was doing a slow burn. He had just finished his first reading of the entire Langlos file. It had been about as much fun as sitting in a dentist's chair and getting a tooth drilled.

"Bob, we've got a real mess with this Langlos case," Norris complained over the phone to his colleague Bob Perry. "Our paper pushers have done it again, I'm afraid. They didn't file because the coroner said the guy died of a heart attack. But wait till you see the evidence. Everything points to a homicide."

"We'd better get Tomich on this right away."

Al Tomich, a D.A. investigator, also thrived on pressure. His last assignment had been to investigate the circumstances surrounding the twenty-year-old death of Marilyn Monroe. In three months, Tomich had used his bulldog tenacity to accumulate ten volumes of material.

Nearly forgotten for more than six years, the Langlos case now was attracting the heavyweights.

On June 1, the County Board of Supervisors approved the motion of Supervisor Michael Antonovich requesting the District Attorney and the grand jury to investigate the cause and circumstances of Dr. Langlos's death. It was a rare request reserved for special cases. The last time the board sought to reopen a case was that of Marilyn Monroe.

While interviewing police, prosecutors, and pathologists, Norris's first impression grew stronger: The case has been bungled by incompetent prosecutors.

At the county morgue, he found Dr. Carpenter in a damp, cramped office.

"Doctor, I've read your autopsy report," Norris said, "and I'm not convinced your opinion is much different from Dr. Kornblum's. I've interviewed Dr. Kornblum, and he believes that Dr. Langlos died of a fear-induced or scare-induced heart attack." Norris had brought scores of death scene photographs for Carpenter to peruse. "Dr. Kornblum is of the opinion there was a struggle. That would explain the wound on the head, the untucked shirt, and the blood on the wall. During the struggle, Langlos suffered ventricular fibrillation."

He paused, waiting for a reaction.

"That's plausible," Carpenter replied almost inaudibly.

"And it's consistent with the autopsy findings," Norris declared.

"Yes, but so is the scenario I suggested at the inquest," said Carpenter. "He could have died from natural causes. He could have had a sudden pain in his chest, pulled the shirt buttons, hit his head on the corner of the desk, and fallen down. It may be specious. It's just a scenario."

"Well, which scenario is more consistent—natural death or a scare-induced death?"

"They're both reasonable interpretations," answered

Carpenter.

"Both are reasonable?"

Carpenter nodded. "Yes. When you autopsy a body you can conclude a cause of death. Then, if you put other factors into the mix, like photographs of the scene, you can draw other opinions."

"There are a lot of variables to consider in this case," Norris said.

"The cause of death doesn't change, but how it happened is another matter," Carpenter remarked. "I've said all along that the Langlos death was suspicious."

By January 1983, Norris had waded through the complete history of the Jack Langlos case. He found it pockmarked with a systemic incompetence that infuriated him.

He abhorred the lack of trial experience in the D.A.'s office. Because of it, he felt many of the prosecutors were nothing more than professional administrators. Some had never given a summation in front of a jury. But here they were making judgments on which cases to file and which to discard. The result was a bureaucratic quagmire in which were stuck apathetic soldiers who drew their salaries, played it safe, and retired. Their decisions were rarely reviewed by experienced prosecutors. In the Langlos case, Norris felt haste made tragedy.

"So why didn't Schafer and Thompson file it?" inquired Perry, who had helped in the information gathering. Perry had listened attentively to Norris's emotional recitation of all the facts that pointed to homicide.

"Because the police didn't find Hartman over Langlos's body confessing to the crime in front of witnesses," Norris's voice dripped with sarcasm.

"Yeah, the coroner's office made a mistake, but so did we. There's no magic with the coroner's opinion. All you had to do was look at the crime scene, the blood . . . then the guy takes the checks, credit cards, and driver's license."

Norris strode to the window. From the eighteenth floor, he observed the rush of humanity in downtown Los Angeles. He took a deep breath, then let the air escape slowly.

"This isn't an easy case, but we've had fear-induced heart

attacks before. I'm sure Schafer and Thompson looked at this and didn't see an automatic victory, so, they blamed the coroner. How convenient," Norris said contemptuously. "And once Schafer makes up his mind, that's it."

"They settled for a plea on forgery," Perry said.

"Forgery," Norris nearly spit the word out. "What a disgrace! If he's guilty of forgery, he's guilty of murder. Now we've got to prove it."

"The case in San Diego gives us a good M.O.," Perry declared.

"Yeah, there's a great similarity between the assault of that old man in San Diego and the assault in Downey," Norris agreed. "Both were men taken into Hartman's confidence, both were men he borrowed money from, both were men who had come to the conclusion he was taking their money and not paying it back. He tried to get more money, and there was a confrontation. He used a handgun in San Diego, and at the time Langlos died, he had two handguns registered in his name."

"What about Hartman's explanation that Langlos gave him his wallet, checks, and credit cards to withdraw money?"

"A jury won't buy that," Norris smiled wryly. "When you add that to the bloody scene and Hartman's propensity for violence, it's going to be dynamite with the jury."

"You think we'll file?"

"I'm sure as hell going to recommend we do," Norris said decisively.

"What charge?"

Norris's voice cut like a razor. "Murder."

Hartman, meanwhile, was in trouble on another matter.

After his parole in 1980, he had taken a job as an apartment manager in Venice, near Santa Monica. The owner of the complex told police Hartman collected rent from tenants and then embezzled $4,633.50. Hartman claimed he spent the money for building maintenance with the owner's approval.

In August 1982, he was charged in Santa Monica Municipal Court with three counts of grand theft and theft. On December 8, he was convicted of petty theft, placed on three years of probation and ordered to make restitution. He spent twenty-one days in jail and was granted probation in Alameda County, where his parents lived.

On February 6, 1983—exactly seven years after the funeral of Jack Langlos—the Los Angeles District Attorney's office filed a complaint of first-degree murder against Hartman. The former psychologist was arrested ten days later in the Hayward, California, home of his parents.

"On reevaluation, we find that the blow to the head was a contributing factor to the death of Dr. Jack Langlos and that the heart attack was a stress- or fear-induced heart attack," District Attorney Robert Philibosian told the Associated Press.

Other expert witnesses, including Dr. Jindrich and Dr. Billingham, disagreed with the diagnosis, citing strangulation or a blow to the head as more probable causes of death.

Prosecutors and police alike praised Langlos's widow for having the grit to fight for the truth. The fight, however, had cost her great emotional expense and fifty thousand dollars.

At his office, Norris was faced with a tough decision. Although he wanted to prosecute Hartman himself, he couldn't. He was in the midst of handling the case of the Skid Row Stabber. Ten derelicts had been murdered in downtown Los Angeles by a man who wrote on the Greyhound bus station wall: "I'm Lucifer. I kill whinos to put them out of their mercy."

A convict from Tennessee who had collected the derelicts' social security checks was on trial for the murders. He eventually was convicted and given a life sentence.

For the Hartman prosecution, Norris picked Roger Kelly, a skillful interrogator considered one of the five best prosecutors in the county.

Bulldog-like Kelly, a handsome man with thick, curly brown hair, was a body builder. A former Mr. Illinois, he was a physical fitness addict, lifting weights, exercising, and taking vitamins daily.

At the moment he badly needed a tough case to recoup his aggressive reputation. He recently had suffered an ego blow when a judge ordered two deputy attorney generals to prosecute the infamous Hillside Strangler case. Kelly had rejected the case because

207

he thought it wasn't prosecutable. He was proven wrong.

Under siege for not seeking charges, Kelly threw himself into the Langlos case with a vengeance.

On the other side of the aisle would be the deputy public defender, dark, good-looking Mark Jones. He would be a formidable foe.

Jones came out with his legal fists flying. He filed four motions to dismiss the murder charge even before the first witness testified. He sought to have the case thrown out because of unlawful multiple prosecution, denial of due process due to lack of a speedy trial, and invidious prosecution. In the fourth motion, he charged that police had taken items from Hartman's suitcase unlawfully because they didn't have a search warrant.

In mid-February, the county Civil Service Commission had voted to uphold the demotion of Noguchi.

On March 1, the coroner's office became the center of another missing brain controversy involving Dr. Carpenter. Kent County District Attorney Edward Jagels told the *Los Angeles Herald Examiner* he dismissed a murder case against the husband of a deceased twenty-three-year-old woman after a sheriff's sergeant learned the woman's brain was missing.

The woman died following a blow to the head allegedly suffered in an argument with her husband. Dr. Carpenter, who claimed he had been doing various tests on the brain, died in December before completing the case.

The sheriff said the new doctor on the case told him, "I've been looking for the brain for three weeks . . . "

It was an excuse that had been heard before. One of the criticisms that led to Noguchi's demotion was the disappearance of Jack Langlos's brain. Because of Carpenter's death, Kelly figured the prosecution would never learn why that had happened.

◆ ◆ ◆

At 1:50 on the afternoon of Tuesday, March 22, 1983, the preliminary hearing opened in Municipal Court in Los Angeles against a backdrop of continuing public scrutiny of Dr. Noguchi and his staff.

Presiding Judge George Trammell was no stranger to the issues raised in the case against Hartman. In 1966, while a Deputy District Attorney, Trammell had prosecuted the first successful fear-induced first-degree murder case in California.

Included among a handful of spectators in the courtroom was the widow of Jack Langlos. Ruth wanted Hartman to feel her presence. She sat close to the first row. He never looked back.

Deputy District Attorney Peter Thompson, the filing prosecutor in Downey, was the first person to take the witness stand. Ruth glared at him, remembering how he sternly advised her to forget about the case. They had only talked on the phone, but Ruth was determined to meet him face to face.

Thompson testified that he hadn't filed a murder charge against Hartman seven years earlier because of the natural cause of death determined from the autopsy.

As soon as he finished, Ruth headed for the hallway, preparing to ambush Thompson before he left the courthouse. He burst through the courtroom doors and walked swiftly toward the exit. Running to catch him, Ruth shouted, "Deputy D.A. Thompson, you dared me to try to reopen this case. I did it, didn't I?"

He paused, glanced her way, and kept walking.

"Who was that?" asked Penny Hawkins, the clerk from Boy's Market who had cashed the forged check. She was seated on a nearby bench.

"Oh, he's only a deputy D.A.," Ruth said defiantly.

On Wednesday morning, Ruth was called to testify. Although nervous, she was determined not be intimidated by Jones, who stood towering over her. She kept telling herself to be calm.

Jones's voice cut into her thoughts. "Mrs. Langlos, you indicated that your husband's complexion was light, is that right?"

"Yes, sir," Ruth said quietly. She was quite aware that Jones knew that Jindrich had noted the lividity of her husband's face in death scene photos. Such coloring could be due to sun exposure or strangulation.

"When you last saw him on January thirtieth, when he took you to the airport, you are saying he did not have a suntan?"

Ruth shook her head. "No sir, he did not have a suntan."

"Was your husband an alcoholic?" Jones asked.

Ruth wasn't about to fall into Jones's trap. "I can't answer that the way you have asked it," she responded.

"Was he a heavy drinker during that period of time?"

She repeated her comment. "I cannot answer that question the way you have asked it."

Jones was becoming irritated. "How much did your husband drink?"

"I cannot answer that question the way you have asked it."

"Why is that?" Jones asked, his hands in the air in a gesture of exasperation.

"I cannot answer your question the way you have asked it," Ruth insisted.

Jones shook his head and said peevishly, "When you saw him drink, how much did he drink?"

"I can't answer that question the way you have asked it."

"What is it about the way he is asking the question?" inquired Judge Trammell.

"He is not asking the right question," Ruth answered and tried to explain. "If I am not allowed to talk . . . " Ruth pressed her lips in a thin, disapproving manner.

Judge Trammell broke in, "When you are in a court of law we operate differently than we would in your home—"

"I understand that, Judge." There was a slight gleam in her blue eyes.

"May I finish?"

"Yes, sir," she said quietly.

"We proceed on the basis of questions and answers. The attorneys have the right to narrow the scope of the questions to where they want to go, the idea being that there is an attorney for both the prosecution and the defense here," Trammell explained.

"But, judge," Ruth protested, "I can't answer it with a yes or no."

"Can you answer it with an explanation?" the judge asked.

She sighed. "Yes, if I would be given the chance."

"Sure, go ahead," said the judge.

The muscles around Ruth's mouth began to relax. "When we were first married, January 1, 1971, he did drink a lot, and it continued until November 17. He knew he needed help. He entered the V.A. Hospital as an outpatient for treatment. That was the last time he had a drink."

"So, Mrs. Langlos," Jones replied, "your answer is, you did not see him drink at all after the period of the time he went through this treatment program."

"From November 17 of 1971, no sir."

The rest of Ruth's testimony went more easily. Then on Thursday, it was time for one of the State of California's star witnesses.

Smiling and looking dapper in an expensive gray suit, Thomas Noguchi strode to the stand. After the preliminary questions, Jones asked, "Dr. Noguchi, I take it you recall the Langlos case, is that correct, sir?"

Noguchi said courteously, "Yes, I do recall the Langlos case."

Jones continued. "Now, in the original autopsy, Dr. Carpenter indicated the cause of death was occlusive coronary artery disease as a consequence of arteriosclerosis. Now, from the discussion I just had with you, I think you feel that you would be agreeable to live with a cause of death that would be described as undetermined, is that correct?"

Noguchi was at his charming best. "Yes, certainly."

Jones went on, "Dr. Carpenter and yourself were acutely aware that there were circumstances that could be indicative of a possible homicide, is that right?"

Noguchi nodded, smiling faintly. "Yes, we felt the circumstances were very suspicious."

Jones prompted, "So when Dr. Carpenter consulted with you on the original autopsy report, you wanted to be careful as to what the finding was, is that correct?"

Noguchi glanced toward the judge. "No. I was not aware the autopsy was conducted. Certainly Dr. Eugene Carpenter is a qualified forensic pathologist to handle the homicide case. And on many occasions certainly he handled it, and apparently, as I recall, the deceased's family called my office and it was necessary for us

211

to review the case."

Later that morning in the hallway during a recess, Ruth spotted Noguchi standing alone. A volcano of feelings erupted within her.

"Dr. Noguchi," Ruth called out, running toward him.

Less than a foot away from him, Ruth stopped abruptly. "Dr. Noguchi, do you know what you've done to me?" she cried out, pointing her finger in his face. He remained silent.

"You have taken seven years out of my life," Ruth said emotionally.

"Hey, Langlos," yelled Kelly, who heard the exchange from across the hallway, "that's enough."

Ruth didn't have anything else to say. She walked away feeling better.

Back in the courtroom, Jones pressed Noguchi for his opinion on how Jack Langlos died.

"Well, certainly I support my staff doctor, which is Dr. Carpenter," said Noguchi. "After a second autopsy, although it is very highly suspicious circumstances, I recommended not to change the death certificate or wording."

Jones queried, "What is your opinion as to the cause of death? Would you feel that you would want to say undetermined, or say that the cause of death was due to coronary heart disease, or what would be your opinion?"

Noguchi hesitated a moment or two, then said, "Around perhaps the second autopsy, I do agree that injury to the head itself could not explain the cause of death. The result is not enough injury into the deep tissue. There were no marks that we often expect to find . . . bruises on the wrists and hands and so forth were not present. It seemed blood was limited to a certain area, yet not having a distinct cause of death, we all agreed perhaps not to change the death certificate until such time we may have more concrete information whereby our opinion could be strengthened. I certainly received a letter from Dr. Jindrich recommending an undetermined cause that would have been entertained also. Other than in between diagnoses, if a person who has a gunshot wound in the back of the head, execution type, we really don't need other information. In this case the circumstantial evidence was highly suspicious, according to the reports submitted to us, so we were concerned. Yet we didn't have any definite diagnosis, so the certificate of death remained the same."

Kelly stood up and asked in an irritated voice, "Could we have the question read to Dr. Noguchi—the question that was asked of him?"

After the court reporter read back the question seeking Noguchi's opinion on the cause of death, Noguchi answered: "My thought was, although none of the anatomic findings are convincing to certify the death certificate, Dr. Carpenter certified it and I supported it."

"Again that doesn't really answer the question," declared Judge Trammell. "We are asking for your opinion as to the cause of death, if you have an opinion."

Noguchi's face was inscrutable. He said, "I don't think I do in a moment, of course. I don't think I can specifically determine the precise cause of death in this case."

At her seat, Ruth was so engrossed in the testimony that she hadn't noticed the man standing next to her. He motioned for her to come outside. While being escorted out of the courtroom, Ruth walked slowly so she could hear as much as possible.

"Mrs. Langlos," the bailiff said.

"Yes?"

"You've been making facial contortions. You'll have to stop."

Jones continued his line of questioning. "From looking at the evidence, it would be consistent with accidental death, and somebody else coming in later and moving a desk against the body, is that right?"

Noguchi's reply was quiet, restrained. "Yes. In this case it could be accidental, could be natural cause, could be homicide, or otherwise. We were rather conservative . . . we didn't want to do anything that led into interpreting things that may be changed. Especially, we don't want to rely on circumstantial evidence that often changes. We wanted to state a basis of what we find . . . and . . . in the body. . . . "

On cross-examination, Kelly had only one question: "Any

quarrel with an undetermined cause of death, possible homicide?"

"I don't think we had a problem with that. Certainly we have considered that."

A short while later, Judge Trammell summoned Kelly to the bench.

"Mrs. Langlos is becoming a disruptive force in this court-room," Trammell said. "I'm going to let her return, but you'd bet-ter tell her that if she makes one more facial expression or shakes her head one more time, I'm going to bar her from the courtroom."

"Your honor, I think it would be better if it came from you. She'll listen to you more than she will to me," replied Kelly.

Trammell's furrowed brow and stern expression mirrored his displeasure.

"Mrs. Langlos, you're acting like this is a circus," he scolded.

"Judge, there's only one person I wanted to upset on the wit-ness stand and that was Noguchi. I promise I won't do it any-more. Please let me stay."

Trammell nodded. "All right. But one more time and you're out."

Ruth sat quietly.

After three days of testimony from eighteen witnesses, Judge Trammell heard debate that Friday on Jones's motions to have the trial dismissed.

Jones argued that the District Attorney's office had waited far too long to bring Hartman to trial. Because of the delay, Hart-man's memory of events had faded and he would have difficulty locating alibi witnesses, Jones said. The loss of the brain also left Hartman without a chance to press for new evidence through another autopsy.

"From the very start," Jones declared, "it appeared to be a pos-sible homicide. The District Attorney at the time had the power to order the coroner's inquest. They had the power to delay filing the case until other coroners were consulted to examine the origi-nal autopsy findings. They had the power to re-autopsy immedi-ately, and they did not do that. A negligent delay is just as bad as an intentional delay."

When it was his turn, Kelly shifted the blame from the District Attorney's office to the coroner's office.

"Dr. Noguchi testified on the witness stand yesterday that he did not feel uncomfortable with the cause of death being undetermined, possibly homicide. This is virtually 180 degrees from the original 1976 autopsy when, to coin a phrase, the testimony of the coroner's office seemed to be set in stone as to it being accidental or death by natural causes."

Rather than badmouth the prosecutors, Kelly preferred to credit one woman's perseverance.

"What we have here is a woman who had the wherewithal to buck City Hall and win, by bringing what was an injustice to the attention of authorities," Kelly forcefully declared. "What we have is a situation wherein an injustice has finally been brought to the attention of authorities after having gone through the vast labyrinth of City Hall red tape."

On Monday morning, Judge Trammell denied Jones' request to dismiss the charge. He ruled that Hartman had failed to present evidence that his memory was poor or possible witnesses could have been lost.

Trammell said prosecutors could not proceed because of insufficient evidence, partly blaming the negligence of Dr. Carpenter in performing the autopsy. Then he offered his version of what happened in the office of Dr. Jack Langlos.

"The victim was attacked while seated at his desk. In my opinion, it would indicate that the assailant was probably someone he knew, that his assailant attempted to strangle him with his tie, that in the course of the struggle the victim's head somehow went over to one side of the chair that he was seated in and that the head was rammed into the corner of the desk in the struggle. This created the laceration of the head. While the victim was still in his seat during the course of the attempted strangulation, his head was hit up against the wall, as I see it from the photos, at least four times and possibly five."

The judge's gaze shifted to the defendant. His tone became harsher, more formal. "It would be my conclusion that an attack of such violence did, in fact, generate substantial fear and stress in

Mr. Langlos. That fear and stress was the cause of his death. Therefore, the defendant's death would be a homicide."

"The question, however, is not ended there," continued Trammell. "If the homicide is murder, the statute of limitations has not run. However, if the homicide is manslaughter, it is a death that occurred in the heat of passion or sudden quarrel and was not likely to produce great bodily harm or death. If it would be manslaughter, prosecution at this point would be barred by the statute of limitations.

"As to the prosecution's theory of murder in the course of a robbery, which would be murder in the first degree, I just don't see evidence based on what has been introduced here. In order to sustain a felony murder finding, I'd have to find that the intent to rob existed at the very beginning of the struggle, and based on what I have heard here, I cannot.

"I feel the more reasonable inference is that after Mr. Langlos died, the assailant took the opportunity to then steal the credit card, license, and the checks." Trammell paused, scanned the papers in front of him, then began again. This time his voice cut like a knife. "I do find, however, that the viciousness of the attack does supply the requisite implied malice to establish murder. Therefore, I find that the charge of murder has been shown to me, and I make that finding without respect as to degree."

His eyes impaled the defendant.

"Lastly, I find that the defendant's use of the victim's credit card, driver's license, and forgery of the victim's check on the following day is sufficient to cause me to believe that he was the one who assailed Dr. Langlos."

Hartman was bound over to Superior Court. Bond was set at one hundred thousand dollars.

Chapter 21

Ruth's Mystic Power

"Don't cry during the trial," Roger Kelly ordered.

Ruth couldn't believe it. Here was someone who'd obviously never lost a spouse, especially through murder, she thought to herself. If he had, he'd know that emotions aren't like running water you turn on and off at the faucet.

"If you cry, the jury will think you're acting," Kelly reasoned. "Your husband died over seven years ago. It's been too long."

How insensitive, Ruth thought. *How can he know how I feel?* But rather than argue, she nodded.

Kelly was as tough mentally as he was physically. Headstrong and aggressive, he was the type of fighter you wanted in your corner, not pitted against you. When Kelly handled a case, it was his way or no way. Ruth didn't want to antagonize him with her need to shed tears.

It had been seven months since Hartman was bound over for a trial, and the first witness hadn't taken the stand yet. The wheels of justice spun so slowly that Ruth couldn't detect motion most of the time.

Hartman's lawyer, Robert Jones, had filed a mound of

217

paperwork seeking to have the murder charge dismissed under state Penal Code section 995. The grounds: Hartman had been committed without reasonable cause and denied a speedy trial.

Some of Jones's arguments seemed to Ruth to be taken from a spy novel. Jones claimed Hartman was singled out for prosecution simply to appease Ruth Langlos's desire for revenge. He said Ruth had influence in the Attorney General's Office for some unknown reason.

Kelly thundered back his denial: "The present case against Mr. Hartman as being based on arbitrary classification, having its origins in some sort of a mystic power that Mrs. Langlos had over the Attorney General's Office, the Board of Supervisors, the District Attorney's offices, is ridiculous."

"There is no sort of a clandestine conspiracy linking Judge Trammell and District Attorney Robert Philibosian and Attorney General George Deukmejian and the Board of Supervisors in an effort to attack and put Mr. Hartman in jail because of this power that Mrs. Langlos holds over individuals," Kelly argued.

The District Court of Appeals and the state Supreme Court agreed with Kelly. They rejected Jones's pleas.

On the eve of the trial's commencement, Kelly was advising Ruth on the do's and don'ts of courtroom protocol.

"As for how to dress, I'd like you to wear business attire every day," said Kelly. "You have to look like a doctor's wife."

Ruth nodded, eager to help.

"Where should I sit?" she asked.

"Anywhere in the section behind me. Please encourage family and friends to attend, but make sure they sit in our section. It's very important that the jury knows how much people cared for Jack Langlos."

Early the next morning, Jones and Kelly began the process to select twelve jurors and four alternates. There were 115 prospective jurors. The selection process lasted three days. Throughout the questioning, Hartman took notes feverishly on a yellow legal pad. He studied each potential juror, conferring constantly with Jones.

"He's probably trying to use his knowledge of psychology to

help screen them," Kelly said.

The final group that Kelly helped pick was racially mixed; about one-third were black, including the woman who served as jury foreman. Judge Robert Roberson Jr., who also was black, had a reputation for being tough and fair. Ruth felt comfortable with the fact that the final verdict would be decided by an impartial jury instead of bureaucrats trying to avoid controversy, but she wished the case would begin. Each hour dragged by. They were ready.

Finally, at 11:00 a.m., Wednesday, November 2, 1983, Case No. A-3876931, *People of the State of California v. Eugene Clarence Hartman*, opened in Department 122 on the thirteenth floor of the Criminal Courts Building in Los Angeles.

Knowing the emotional impact Ruth's appearance would have, Jones decided to counter it before she said her first word.

By now the courtroom was Ruth's second home. She already had spent fourteen days in courtrooms that year. This would mark the fourth court hearing at which she had testified since her husband's death.

"Could we approach the bench before she comes into the courtroom?" Jones requested fifteen minutes after the trial started. Ruth had been sequestered with other witnesses.

"Approach the bench."

"Mrs. Langlos is going to be a difficult witness in that she will talk or testify very quickly," Jones said. "I would like Mr. Kelly to tell her not to mention the statement about Jack Langlos."

"About what?" Roberson said.

"About Jack Langlos fearing the defendant. Because I don't think it's admissible and I will want to have had a hearing before that question is ever asked of her. Because otherwise she is going to blurt that out."

Roberson excused the jury until 1:45 p.m. but said Ruth was allowed to come into the courtroom to hear Jones's objection.

She returned to hear Jones argue earnestly: "Mrs. Langlos, when she testified at the preliminary hearing—and I assume she would testify the same way at the trial—would testify that on at least one occasion shortly before the death of her husband, he told her he was afraid of Mr. Hartman, and at the preliminary hearing I objected on the ground that, number one, it is hearsay and, number two, it is not relevant to the case and, number three, it was highly prejudicial."

Judge Roberson turned his attention to Ruth. He wanted her to know his ground rules.

"Mrs. Langlos, when you are called as a witness, you should listen to the question very carefully, be responsible only to that question, don't volunteer information. There is some evidence that could be blurted out that could jeopardize everything we have done here as far as selecting a jury. It could result in a mistrial, and we'd have to start all over again. In the event that the particular statement is deemed to be admissible by me, then Mr. Kelly will so inform you and will ask the question to elicit that. Other than that, do not blurt that matter out. I am not saying you will, but an ounce of prevention is worth a pound of cure."

The statement in question was Jack's remark after Hartman paid him with a bad check. Jack had told Ruth he was afraid to press Hartman for the money.

However, the jury never heard it. Roberson ruled that statement inadmissible.

◆ ◆ ◆

From the onset Hartman's court-appointed attorney tried to intimidate Ruth. She knew, however, that he had a job to do and was doing it very well. She didn't like him and let him know it. The truth was she didn't like public defenders. She couldn't understand how they slept at night.

Ruth was on the stand about three hours Wednesday afternoon and Thursday morning. The questioning was long and grueling, especially when Jones was cross-examining her.

At one point Jones asked Ruth about a check she had written to Prudential Insurance. She had given it to Jack to mail when he drove her to the airport the last time Ruth saw him alive. He never had the chance to mail it.

"And you remember him putting it on the visor in the car?"

Jones asked.

Ruth shook her head. "I didn't see him do it but I saw it there."

"Do you recall telling the police about that check?"

"No." She wanted her answers to be clear and concise.

"You got something from Prudential indicating the bill had not been paid?"

"Correct," she said definitively.

"And you wrote them another check?"

"Yes, sir." Their eyes locked. He looked away first. "Did you tell the police that?"

"The parole officer," she said, drawing the words out.

She had meant to say, "The probation officer." Ruth's words infuriated the defense attorney. Jones said disgustedly, "Your Honor, can we approach the bench?"

At the bench, the attorneys and Judge Roberson had an animated conversation.

"I think Mrs. Langlos is determined to sabotage this trial," claimed Jones. "Mr. Kelly told her not to say anything, but that statement about the parole officer—"

Roberson, trying to calm Jones, interrupted: "Let me give you my observation of her. She is very nervous and she is very anxious to get in things that she feels should get in. You might explain to her, Mr. Kelly, the importance of her not slipping in things she feels are important because it's not responsive to the particular question."

"The problem is I feel she's just waiting to pounce and say things," Jones muttered.

"I don't think that's it. Frankly, I think she's nervous," observed Kelly. "She doesn't want a mistrial, I can tell you that. With respect to this, I don't think it's that big a deal, because a jury doesn't know the difference between a parole and probation officer. She didn't talk to a parole officer, but she did talk to a probation officer."

Roberson took a sip of water from the silver canister on the table before him. "Gentlemen, I don't get the impression she is doing something, but I think she's intelligent enough that if you

221

take her aside and explain to her that there are things she should not slip in, . . . I think that will suffice."

On Wednesday night, Ruth took sedatives to get some sleep. She was so nervous, she would have to do so every night of the trial.

The next day she almost made it through the rest of her testimony without incident. Almost.

During Kelly's redirect examination, he showed Ruth a series of bank statements and records pertaining to the forged checks that had been stolen.

"So the two statements you have in front of you, People's 7 and People's 8, what account are these statements for?" Kelly inquired.

As Kelly pursued the line items on the bank records, one line jumped off the page at Ruth: payment for Jack's funeral.

"This was a joint account, and then after he, you know, . . . " Ruth stammered, paused, and began to cry.

Kelly pressed on. "Was it for your personal account or business account?"

"Personal," Ruth whispered. She had promised herself she would be calm and she was crying over a bank record, disobeying the prosecutor's instructions to keep her emotions to herself. She simply couldn't relive the past without shedding tears.

"Maybe we could have a recess, your Honor," said Kelly.

"I'll be all right," Ruth insisted. She didn't want them to stop, not after waiting so long for this trial.

Roberson turned to his recorder, "Lucille, do you have a cup there, she can have some of this water?" he said, indicating the pitcher. The recorder gave Ruth a cup of water. "Just take a deep breath and relax," she said kindly.

The testimony continued. Ruth felt embarrassed, helpless. But as Kelly continued the questioning, she regained her composure.

"Now, was there a point when you felt the Downey Police Department was no longer involved in the case?"

"Yes, sir."

"When was that?"

"Approximately February 24 of '76."

"That would be shortly after the District Attorney's office filed the forgery count."

"That's correct." Ruth nodded affirmatively.

"You told us about getting a report from Jindrich, getting a report from Kornblum. You took those reports to the District Attorney's office, is that correct?"

"D.A. Schafer," she said softly.

"And on each occasion that you saw him, did he refuse to do anything for you?"

"Yes, sir," her voice was gaining force.

"Was his reaction to your request virtually the same?"

"Always the same," she said firmly.

"Did he state a reason for refusing to file more charges?"

Ruth grimaced. "Of course. Hartman just came upon a dead body and robbed him. Deputy D. A. Schafer always said this."

"And Carpenter?"

"And Dr. Carpenter was a good pathologist. He didn't agree with Jindrich or Kornblum."

When Ruth's testimony concluded, the attorneys took their familiar pose in front of Judge Roberson. In hushed voices, they discussed a familiar subject: her. Ruth watched from her seat. Next to her sat a white-haired man named Gabriel who was fast becoming a friend. His hobby was criminal cases. He was known as a court watcher, someone who came to court so frequently to hear the cases he knew what to watch and whom. "Listen to the judge, Ruth," he whispered. "We'll know which way he leans."

It was thanks to Gabriel that Ruth met CBS news anchor Dan Rather during the first week of Hartman's trial.

"Psst, Ruth, there's a great case going on down the hall," Gabriel said one afternoon. "Somebody's suing '60 Minutes' and Dan Rather is scheduled to testify."

When they got to the courtroom, there was a winding line waiting to get inside. Television monitors in the hallway showed the proceedings. As Ruth waited in line with Gabriel, a security guard announced that the case had been adjourned for the day.

Suddenly, Rather and his attorney strode from the courtroom, refusing interview requests. Ruth walked nearby for a while until all the journalists had quit following. Ruth and Rather were now side by side.

"How are you today?" Rather looked at Ruth and smiled.

"Couldn't be better. I hope you win your case. I think you're the best journalist on TV."

"Well, thank you. That's nice of you to say," he said with a big smile.

As Rather strode out the door, a man rushed up to Ruth, pad in hand.

"Do you know Dan Rather personally? You two acted like you knew each other."

"Well, no. Who are you?"

"I'm from *Newsweek*," he said.

Ruth returned to the present and focused on what the judge was saying.

"Is there any reason why Mrs. Langlos should not be allowed to remain?" asked Roberson, his sympathy in the case already showing. "Do either of you intend to call her again as a witness. It's important to her to see what happens."

"Let me explain," Jones replied, "why I want her excluded. At the preliminary hearing when the coroner Dr. Noguchi got up, she would make faces, she would laugh—Judge Trammell was consistently and constantly telling her to stop doing this. My feeling is that Mrs. Langlos will sit there and make faces and do those things whether it's inadvertent or not."

"Well, if that is the only basis for it, I am going to allow her to remain," Roberson declared. "But I want her to fully understand that the first sign of any of that type of conduct, out she goes."

"I will tell her that," Kelly replied.

Early Thursday morning, Westray was studying police reports at the Downey police station. In a few hours, he was scheduled to take the stand as a people's witness. His partner, Miller, had gone to the court to meet Kelly.

"It's a producer from Channel 2 News on line one," said the receptionist.

"I'll take it," Westray replied.

The television crew wanted to set up an interview with the

police to discuss the Langlos case.

"What specifically are you looking for?" Westray asked.

"We want an on-camera interview about what's going on in the courtroom, the police reaction, things like that," the producer replied.

"For the evening news, right?"

"Most likely. This is one of the cases everybody's talking about."

"All right," said Westray. "We've got a lot to say. Can you have a crew outside the courtroom at 9:45?"

"Sure."

"Okay. I'll have someone ready for an interview."

Five minutes before court was to reconvene, Miller and Westray relaxed on a hallway bench.

"Never thought we'd ever get the chance to testify in this case, Wimp," said Miller.

"Yeah, that crime happened a long time ago," Westray remarked.

"You were a peon like me then but now you're a big-time sergeant with big-time responsibilities."

"Big-time headaches, you mean."

"Amazing how some things don't change in seven years though," Westray observed. "You're still ugly, you're still—"

"Wimp, look at this," interrupted Miller, watching the television news crew lugging a camera, tape recorders, and sound equipment down the hallway. A woman in a business suit looked side to side as she hurried along a couple feet in front of two men carrying the equipment.

"Wonder what's going on," Miller said. "There must be a high-profile case someplace."

Behind his back, Westray caught the eye of the woman and motioned toward Miller.

She nodded, walked straight to Miller, and placed a microphone in front of him. "Officer, can you tell us if police think there was a conspiracy between the coroner and the owners of Lakewood Park to cover up the Langlos case?"

Caught off guard, Miller began stuttering, "Uh, uh, I'm not

sure I can comment . . ."

Ten feet away, Westray watched in amusement. The camera lights revealed an anguished look on his partner's face. Westray grinned. This was turning out to be a really good day.

That afternoon, it was Westray's turn to squirm. He was a street cop, not a polished witness. Although he had testified at some trials, Westray didn't like this part of the job. He knew the defense attorney would try to trip him up by twisting his words, and he felt his hands began sweating.

At first everything went well. Kelly asked Westray about his background and role in investigating the office of Jack Langlos on February 2, 1976.

"And was there a point in time when the desk was removed from the victim's head?" Kelly asked.

Westray nodded, "Yes, there was."

Kelly continued his line of questioning. "Was there some sort of an indentation that had been made on the cheek of the victim?"

"Yes," Westray nodded again.

Kelly drew him out, "Do you want to describe that for us?"

Westray took a deep breath and began, "There was a line running from the forehead area down through the cheek portion, running through the eye socket, and the ear piece—the right ear piece of the glasses was forced down into the eye socket."

"Did that line correspond with where the edge of the desk was resting on top of the victim's face?" Kelly asked.

Westray's face was firmly set, "Yes, it did."

Kelly queried, "Was the desk parallel with the north wall or was there a difference between the front edge and the back edge of the desk?"

Westray's voice was firmer but still unsteady. "The front edge of the desk was, as I recall, approximately one inch from the wall, and the back edge was approximately eight inches from the wall."

Public Defender Jones stepped forward. He also was interested in the desk and surrounding area.

"There appeared to be blood on the front left corner of the desk, is that correct?" Jones asked.

"Well, that would be the rear portion of the desk," Westray

responded. "That part where you sit."

Jones's voice cut across Westray's words, "Now, those blood spots on the wall—I think it's better depicted in People's 18—those blood spots appeared to be slightly above the top of the chair, is that correct?"

Westray nodded. "That's correct."

Jones pressed on. "And do you recall whether you or Detective Miller ever sat in the chair and leaned back to see if they would coincide?"

"Yes," Westray said uncertainly, "one of us did. I don't know which one of us."

Jones asked crisply, "Did the head come directly to the side where these blood spots are in People's 17?"

"Yes, approximately," Westray affirmed.

For fifteen minutes, Westray and Jones traded points as they recounted every gruesome detail of the scene: the blood drops on the floor, the torn-off shirt buttons, the dented ink pen, and the desk calendar partially covering a white, bloodied rag on the floor. It was difficult for Ruth to sit still in her seat without crying out.

Jones questioned Westray as if he was ready to pounce should the detective make a mistake.

"Do you recall what kind of rag it was?"

Westray shrugged. "It appeared to be like torn from a sheet, a bed sheet, that type of material."

Jones pressed him. "That rag isn't in the box here, is it?"

Westray was perspiring now. "I don't know."

Kelly interjected, "I think so."

Detective Miller, who was seated next to Kelly, pulled a rag from a small box of exhibits. The unexpected sight of that blood stained cloth was too much for Ruth, who gasped. She hurriedly left the courtroom.

Jones didn't miss the incident. "Could we approach the bench, Your Honor?"

Roberson nodded. "Yes."

At the bench, away from the jury's earshot, Jones said: "Your Honor, again I'm asking for an exclusion of Mrs. Langlos. Whether or not it's an honest reaction by Mrs. Langlos or whether it's a stage reaction, I don't know, but it's very disrupting, and I think she is trying to do it to influence the jury."

Roberson said quietly, "I have noticed that during the course of the trial at various phases of the testimony she does get up and go out. When the rag was brought out, I heard a slight gasp, and she got up and hurriedly moved toward the door with her hands over her mouth, giving me the impression that perhaps she was going to regurgitate." He looked at Jones as if weighing his opinion.

Jones stood his ground. "It is a public trial, she has the right to be here. However, I think it is somewhat disruptive and unfair to the defense. Although I have great sympathy for this lady, it seems to me perhaps if it affects her this way, perhaps she shouldn't be here watching it."

Taking Ruth aside a short time later, Kelly told her he would warn her in advance when graphic testimony or exhibits would be introduced—and she should leave the courtroom beforehand.

The next witness, Dr. Kornblum, was intriguing. When Kornblum first analyzed Jack's autopsy, he was an outsider. Now, as the successor to Dr. Noguchi, he was an insider.

His original testimony, along with Dr. Jindrich and Dr. Billingham, discredited the very coroner's office Kornblum now headed. Like the others, Kornblum had reviewed heart slides—medical slides made from tissue of the heart and coronary arteries.

Ruth's nemesis, Dr. Noguchi, was never called to appear at the trial. But he was appearing in lots of other places—mostly promoting his new book, *Coroner*.

Released in October, the book dissected the deaths of Marilyn Monroe, Robert Kennedy, Sharon Tate, Janis Joplin, William Holden, Natalie Wood, and John Belushi. It sold more that 100,000 copies in hardcover before its release in paperback. According to newspaper reports, Noguchi received a $250,000 contract, including $40,000 from the *National Enquirer* for a two-part excerpt. In the book, Noguchi offered his insight into murder:

"In any case of unusual death, it is the first duty of medical examiners to suspect murder. But I concur with those authorities [forensic science] in one particular: Every death is a homicide, until proven otherwise."

Its jacket cover promotion titillated readers: "The luxurious apartment in which William Holden was discovered . . . The red down jacket that Natalie Wood wore . . . The tiny pinpoints of blood on John Belushi's arm . . . Until now I have been unable to tell the whole story."

Meanwhile, a real-life case that didn't seem to have the same fascination for him was unfolding in Los Angeles.

◆ ◆ ◆

"What is your occupation, sir?" Kelly asked Kornblum.

"I am a physician. I am the Acting Medical Examiner for the County of Los Angeles."

"So you are the person who has taken the place of Dr. Noguchi, is that correct?"

"Yes," Kornblum said watching him.

"About how many autopsies have you performed over your lifetime?"

Kornblum's answers were slow and precise. "Personally, about seven to eight thousand," he said.

"You've become familiar with the lay person's term of heart attack, have you not, sir?" Kelly asked politely.

"Yes," Kornblum replied.

"And you've written some papers on heart attack or death through heart problems, have you not, sir?"

"Yes," Kornblum said.

"And do you want to tell us what the major types of heart attack are?"

Kelly held his usual aggressive manner in check. He matched Kornblum's slow, deliberate pace stroke for stroke, hoping to showcase his witness properly.

"The one that most people are familiar with is known as a coronary occlusion, or sometimes just spoken of as a coronary. And that is a blockage of the coronary arteries, which are the arteries that supply blood vessels that supply blood to the heart." Kornblum paused, looked at Kelly, and continued. "Another major classification would be what is called a myocardial infarction, that means a portion of the heart muscle dies due to lack of blood, lack of oxygen."

Kelly inclined his head, "Is there another classification of heart attack that may be important in this case?"

"Yes," Kornblum nodded affirmatively.

"What is that?" Kelly asked.

"That is known as ventricular fibrillation, and that is an electrical type of a disorder of the heart. The heart normally has nerves inside the muscle which are regulated so that the heart beats in a rhythmic fashion so that it pumps blood out and it opens up and blood comes in and it pumps it out again. If something happens to the electrical, these nerve fibers and the heart no longer pump in an unified fashion but just kind of flutter and fibrillate, is what it's called. Circulation will stop and the individual will die."

"Ventricular fibrillation." Kelly scratched his head. "Is that when you use a pacemaker?"

"A pacemaker is designed to prevent ventricular fibrillation, yes."

"What is the difference between a hospital pathologist and what you are?" Kelly began to set up his argument like a pro, hoping to hammer his point home to the jury.

"Well, a hospital pathologist is based at a hospital, and they examine organs that are removed during surgery and they examine blood and urine. Forensic pathologists usually are attached to a coroner's office and perform autopsies on individuals who die suddenly, die violently, or in a suspicious manner in an attempt to determine the cause and manner of death."

"Now, with respect to ventricular fibrillation, can you through an autopsy see physical signs of a person having had a ventricular fibrillation being the cause of death?"

"No. That's an electrical type of a situation. You can't see that at autopsy, you can only surmise it."

"So unless a person has an EKG on him when he dies of ventricular fibrillation, you would not be able to say for certain that he died of ventricular fibrillation?"

"That's correct," Kornblum affirmed.

"Now, as a result of your investigation into the death of Jack Langlos, did you reach some sort of a conclusion as to the cause of death?"

"Yes."

Kelly raised his eyebrows.

"And what was that?"

"I could not determine a cause of death."

"Did you reach some sort of conclusion as to the mode of death?" Kelly asked quietly.

"Yes."

"What was that?" Kelly's voice rose.

Kornblum met his eyes and said slowly, emphatically, "I thought the mode of death was homicide."

Kelly let Kornblum's words hang in the air a few moments.

This was going well. Kelly could not completely suppress the smile forming at the corners of his mouth. "Now, with respect to the cause of death, in your opinion what would you say the most likely cause of death is?"

"I would think that the most likely cause of death is that he had an episode of ventricular fibrillation during the course of a struggle."

Kelly stopped there, his points made.

However, on cross-examination, Jones zeroed in on Kornblum's relationship with Noguchi, hoping to discredit Kornblum.

"You were the acting coroner at the time of the coroner's inquest?"

"Yes, I was," Kornblum said apologetically.

Jones didn't wait more than an instant before firing his next question.

"And you were aware that there was a second autopsy in which the cause of death was still listed as natural, is that right?"

"Yes," Kornblum nodded.

"Were you aware that at the second autopsy the cause of death was kept the same with the approval of Dr. Noguchi?" Before Kornblum could answer, Kelly stood up, "We object to that as assuming facts not in evidence."

Roberson said tartly, "Sustained."

Barely acknowledging the ruling, Jones began again.

"The coroner of Los Angeles County, how does he become coroner of the county?"

"He's appointed by the Board of Supervisors," Kornblum said blandly.

Jones didn't hesitate.

"So he sits at the privilege of the Board of Supervisors, is that correct? He is not an elected official?"

"He is not an elected official," Kornblum agreed.

"And I take it that there is no love lost between you and Dr. Noguchi, is that correct?"

Kornblum shook his head.

"I don't think that's true at all."

"Do you have a good working relationship or do you—"

Kelly interrupted, "We object to that as being irrelevant."

"Overruled," Roberson's sonorous voice declared.

"Specifically, what do you need to know?" asked Kornblum.

Jones shot back, "You have the job that he wants back, is that right?"

"Yes." Kornblum was unruffled.

"And part of the ongoing thing against Dr. Noguchi is the way he ran the office, is that right?"

"That's correct," Kornblum reluctantly agreed.

Kelly had his opening. He could make his point that because he was the acting coroner, Kornblum could shed light on how the office operated. On redirect examination, Kelly seized his opportunity.

"You're familiar with the procedures of the Los Angeles County Coroner's office relative to keeping track of evidence?"

"Yes."

"Have they been changed since you became in charge of the coroner's office to some extent?"

"Considerably."

Kelly insisted, "In changing them, did you become aware of the manner in which evidence was kept track of under the auspices of Dr. Noguchi?"

232

"Yes," Kornblum acknowledged.

Kelly launched a frontal attack.

"Was the coroner who was in charge of the autopsy and who took organs out of a body, would he be the one that would be responsible for making up some sort of a card that would index where the organ went and what was done with it, et cetera?"

"He should have been," Kornblum said quietly. "The problem is that nobody really was in charge."

Kelly pursed his lips doubtfully. "And in your checking for the heart in this case, did you find any cards or anything that indicated what happened to the heart or anything like that?"

"The sheet that is normally marked, it's not marked," Kornblum said.

"How about the brain? That's also missing."

"That, I understand, is also missing," Kornblum admitted.

"And you have no indication as to where that went?" Kelly said, enunciating each word carefully.

"I have none."

"And the urinary bladder is also missing?"

"I also understand that that's missing."

"And one of the kidneys?"

"Yes," Kornblum replied.

"And all of those are things that Dr. Carpenter supposedly made out a sheet on and you don't find any sheets that have been made out?"

"That's correct," Kornblum grumbled.

In his second day of testimony, Kornblum was being bounced back and forth like a ping pong ball.

It was Jones's turn to fire a shot.

"Now, a person that has a heart attack or some other cause, if they fell down on the ground, hypothetically, they could go into a spasm, is that correct?" asked Jones.

"What do you mean by a spasm?" Kornblum asked.

"They could be moving around very vehemently."

The older man's features stiffened. "I'm not sure what you mean. An individual having a fatal heart attack or just a non-fatal heart attack?"

"Let's say a non-fatal heart attack," Jones said, moving closer to the witness.

"Well, then," Kornblum replied dryly, "of course, it's variable and the person having severe chest pains would be moving, yes. A person with a fatal heart attack probably would not."

"So there's a whole range of how a person struck by a heart attack could react, is that correct?"

"Yes," Kornblum had to agree.

"And I take it again it's very hard to generalize or to make any statement one way or the other about how a person reacts, is that right?"

"Yes, every person is different," Kornblum said flatly.

"So I take it you've seen cases where a person is hit with a massive heart attack and they would literally just drop dead, is that right?"

Kornblum shrugged and then said, "Yes."

Jones was emoting now. "Just collapse. Other people might put up a struggle, is that right?"

"Some people grab their chest and go down slowly, other people just seem to drop. Sometimes it takes minutes, sometimes it takes hours. It's variable," Kornblum said matter-of-factly.

"And sometimes, I imagine from what you said, it could take a second or less than a second, right?"

"Yes, it can," Kornblum replied quietly.

Jones smiled, "Thank you, Dr. Kornblum. No more questions."

"Any redirect?" said Roberson.

Echoing Jones's flair for the dramatic, Kelly went him one better. He finished his questioning by showing Kornblum People's Exhibit 16, a photograph of Dr. Langlos as he was discovered in his office.

"Ever had a situation, Doctor, where a person has jammed his head underneath a desk as a result of a massive heart attack?" he said, locking eyes with the doctor.

"No, I haven't," Kornblum said firmly.

"Ever seen a person in a death position like People's 16 as the result of a massive heart attack?"

"No, I haven't," Kornblum voice was quiet, steady, and decisive.

After his testimony, Kornblum approached Ruth outside the courtroom. He looked exhausted from the grilling.

He hugged her and said: "I think you're going to win."

Kelly thought so, too. "I have a feeling for juries. This one is slowly coming around to our side," he said smiling. He walked over to the other prosecutor. "Sterling, you should have seen this guy Hernandez from the coroner's office. . . . "

Whenever possible Sterling Norris and Kelly conferred on how the case against Hartman was proceeding. Sometimes it lasted two minutes at the department coffee machine. Other times, they talked for hours in the late afternoon following the day's testimony.

Today both prosecutors were in a good mood, comfortable with the progress of their case.

"Hernandez asks Jones if he can demonstrate how he thinks Langlos hit his head on the desk corner. Before you know it, he grabs Jones by the necktie and starts shoving his head downward. It was great for the jury to see, and Jones got his hair messed up. I enjoyed that," Kelly said laughing.

"It sounds like we're in control," Norris replied, looking for a cup to pour some coffee into.

"Well, we've had a couple of problems," Kelly mused. "The judge won't let us use what Miller and Westray found in Hartman's suitcase."

"You mean those books about how to escape and beat the bill collectors?"

"Yeah, he ruled the cops should have gotten a search warrant."

"Figures." Norris shook his head.

"And then we found out that a judge in 1978 ordered all the MasterCharge invoices Hartman forged to be destroyed after the forgery conviction."

"Have you brought up the Monheit beating yet?"

"No, but we've had the transcripts of Hartman's testimony at his psychology hearing in San Diego read into the record.

Dynamite stuff."

"Okay, but don't forget the Monheit case. It shows a pattern of violence, and that's important. The jury has got to see that Hartman is capable of a vicious attack."

"Yeah."

Norris was satisfied. Jindrich, Billingham, and the Downey police had been powerful witnesses. More important, Kelly was his old, aggressive self, despite personal problems.

He had attacked the Hartman case like an unrelenting bull-dog. Kelly at his ferocious best was too much for any public defender to handle, Norris believed.

With the trial in its third week, Ruth was happy to still be allowed in the courtroom considering Jones's preoccupation with her.

A few days later when court recessed after one of the endless conferences at the bench, Kelly rushed over to Ruth, a huge smile lit up his face.

"Hartman's going to testify!" he said excitedly.

"You're kidding."

"Well, I can't believe it myself, but Jones just told the judge that chances are ninety percent Hartman's going to take the stand on Monday."

"Finally," Ruth said emotionally.

Kelly nodded. "They're saving their best for last, and I'm going to stomp all over him."

Chapter 22

In the Jury's Hands

Captain Frank Sanders was finishing one of his least favorite chores: grocery shopping.

On a Saturday morning, the market near his home in Downey was a beehive of confusion. Clerks moved boxes of cans to block exactly the shelves he needed to get to—or so he believed. Then there were the long lines at the meat counter, the whining youngsters wanting to ride in the carts, and the shoppers with fifteen items in the eight-items-or-less line.

No wonder he forgot to buy all the groceries. Sanders's knack for forgetting at least one item on the shopping list was a family joke. A former FBI agent, Sanders could recall in minute detail the types and numbers of weapons seized in a raid fifteen years ago. But ask him to purchase seven things at the market and invariably he returned with six.

This day he made his usual mental check while looking in the cart. Steaks. Potatoes. Beer. Napkins. Lettuce. Tomatoes.

Ah-ha, no salad dressing. Sanders started to veer out of the produce section when he heard a familiar voice.

"So your wife has you shopping, too."

Across the aisle, a grinning deputy D.A. Joe Schafer was testing the cucumbers.

"Don't you just love picking up a few things on a Saturday," Sanders moaned. "I swear I'm not coming here on Saturday and then here I am."

"What's new?"

"Nothing much. Thinking about getting out and doing the Christmas shopping early this year."

"Yeah, right," Schafer replied. "We'll both be shoulder-to-shoulder in some mob on Christmas Eve."

"I can at least have good intentions," Sanders smiled.

"What do you think about this Langlos case?" asked Schafer.

"That's a one-in-a-lifetime case," Sanders declared. "No use talking about it. You and I haven't agreed on this since day one."

"You still believe it was a murder, don't you?"

"Never had a doubt."

"How do you think the trial is going?"

"Well, Miller has been there every day, and he seems satisfied with the witnesses. Kelly is one tough S.O.B."

"Tougher than the widow?" Schafer deadpanned. They both laughed.

"Not quite that tough," Sanders replied.

"I still think Langlos is going to lose," said Schafer. "Hartman will go free. How much do you want to bet?"

Sanders grimaced, "Oh no, after everything that's happened, this is one case I wouldn't bet a penny on."

◆ ◆ ◆

At 10:25 A.M., Monday, November 21, half of Judge Roberson's courtroom was packed. The other side was empty.

Eighteen of Jack's friends had come from as far away as Arizona to witness Hartman's testimony. They sat with Ruth behind the prosecutor's table, eagerly awaiting the start of the proceedings.

Hartman, clad in a light-colored windbreaker, shirt, and slacks, had nobody beside him offering moral support. He didn't show any signs that this bothered him, though. As on every other day, he smiled a lot, took pages of notes, and avoided looking at the spectators.

Before the jury was brought out, Kelly, Jones, and Roberson met at the bench. Ruth and her friends couldn't hear a thing, which added to their suspense.

The three men were locked in conversation. "Your honor, I was down talking to Mr. Hartman at the county jail on Friday. We were going over his anticipated testimony, and portions of his testimony evidently would contradict the testimony he gave at his psychology board hearing in San Diego," Jones explained.

"You say part of his testimony here on the stand would be contra?" Roberson asked.

"Would be contra, yes," Jones admitted. "He said, 'Could they file perjury?' and I said, 'I don't think so.' And, of course, I read the statute and the statute says the three-year limitation is from the date of discovery, not the date of the occurrence.

"This morning I said to Mr. Kelly, 'Mr. Hartman wants to get up and tell the truth this time and would like to know what will happen.' I think it's very important that he testify. The testimony was in San Diego County, and Mr. Kelly, being a representative of the L.A. County D.A.'s office, could not give immunity. So I asked Mr. Kelly if he would graciously call up the San Diego D.A.'s office and get him a grant of immunity on any perjury prosecution. Mr. Kelly said, 'Quite the contrary. If the defendant was acquitted, I would file perjury.' So I don't expect a grant of immunity from Mr. Kelly."

"I'm a dirty bird," Kelly said with a grin.

Jones flashed him a look.

"So I went back and told Mr. Hartman that they could conceivably file perjury," Jones continued, "and this morning Mr. Hartman thought it over for about an hour and said: 'I don't want to testify and take the chance of having a pure victory of being found not guilty of murder and immediately having a perjury charge filed by San Diego County.' He asked if I could assure him that would not happen, and I told him I couldn't. He has reluctantly decided not to testify.

"The reason I'm up here right now is to relate that history. I would like to put Mr. Hartman on the stand and have him indicate to the jury that he would like to tell his story, but he has been informed that if his story contradicted anything that was testified to at the psychology administrative hearing, perjury could be filed. For that reason he has elected not to say anything else to the jury.

"I'm asking if your honor will allow Mr. Hartman to do that."

"Mr. Kelly?" Roberson said.

"There would be an objection."

"What is the objection?" Roberson asked.

"I don't know. I'll have to think about it. But I'm sure there is an objection to it," Kelly said. "I think it's kind of irrelevant and not the type of thing that comes before the jury."

Jones, sensing Judge Roberson's reluctance to approve his unusual proposal, said: "I'm not trying to sandbag the court. The statute-of-limitations thing is something that didn't enter my mind."

In his long career, Kelly had never heard a request like this. The defendant basically wanted to tell the jury he would like to testify but couldn't because of his past lies under oath.

Kelly frowned. "The inference from the witness saying, 'I'd like to take the stand and testify but I can't,' puts us at the disadvantage. The only inference we derive from that is there is a denial that he did it. And then where do we go from there?"

"Yes. All right," declared Roberson, "that objection will be sustained."

Ten minutes later, Kelly walked dejectedly to his seat, summoning Ruth to the prosecutor's table.

"Hartman isn't going to testify," he whispered in Ruth's ear. "He's afraid we'll charge him with perjury when he contradicts his testimony at the San Diego hearing."

Ruth felt her heart skip a beat. "Does that make any sense to you?"

Kelly shook his head. "Not really. I just think he knows what would happen if we had the chance to question him. By the way,

240

Hernandez is supposed to testify again this afternoon—it could get pretty graphic."

"If I had a gun, I think I would shoot Hartman myself," Ruth blurted out.

Kelly looked at her sympathetically. "You're under a lot of stress. Why don't you take a break?"

Glumly, Ruth made her way back to her seat. She knew Jones was desperately looking for a way to have her tossed out of the courtroom, and she wasn't about to give him the opportunity. Three days ago, he had accused Ruth of smiling at one of the jurors. Unknown to Ruth, he had a spy in the back of the courtroom watching her every movement. Fortunately, Judge Roberson wasn't impressed with his report on Ruth's smile.

It was time to find her friend Gabriel again.

Gabriel had helped Ruth pass lots of time during the trial, and she had found his perceptions very astute.

Each morning Gabriel, who was retired, studied the court schedules and mapped out his day. He knew where to be and when to be there to hear the riveting portions of the testimony.

On the last day of testimony in Hartman's trial, Gabriel, who was seated in the back of Roberson's courtroom, found another hot spot.

Ruth walked up to him. "Where's the best courtroom today, Gabriel?" she asked.

"I thought it was going to be here," he said, rising from his seat in the last row. "Isn't Hartman going to testify?"

"No." Ruth shook her head.

"Then, I'd say the next choice is the Hillside Strangler case. They're supposed to sentence Angelo Buono today."

Ruth couldn't help smiling, "You really enjoy being here, don't you?"

"It's better than watching a TV soap opera," he declared.

"So it is," she laughed.

The next afternoon, Gabriel was back in Judge Roberson's courtroom waiting for the fireworks. Because the burden of proof rested with the prosecution, Kelly would give his closing argument first. After Jones's summation, Kelly would have a final chance to respond.

Kelly appeared relaxed. Public speaking was one of his strong suits.

"Ladies and gentlemen of the jury, we've now reached the final portion of a jury trial which is known as the argument. You can always tell when there's going to be an argument or summation in a case because all the lawyers come with their good suits and make as though they're very believable individuals. I wear a black suit, somber for the occasion; Mr. Jones wears a blue suit, they're not quite so somber.

"Normally we wear a sport coat, but when it comes to argument, you want the jury to be impressed with your very professional nature and you start it by selecting a wardrobe in the morning.

"The jury is usually called upon to determine whether it was the defendant or some unknown third person that committed the crime that killed the individual. That's the normal thing in a murder case where identity is an issue."

Kelly stood legs apart, ready to attack.

"In this case it's considerably different in that there are really only two suspects as to who could have killed the deceased. Both of them we know, both of them suspects. The suspects are, number one, the defendant, and number two, God. Those are the two people or entities that could have killed the deceased, and your task is to determine which one is responsible for the death of Jack Langlos. If it was God, obviously no crime was committed. If it was the defendant, on the other hand, then we have a homicide."

His voice gathered force.

"Let's take a look at the evidence, which shows that the defendant, Eugene Hartman, is the one that killed Jack Langlos and it was not God. You could come up with some Laurel and Hardy scenario of events with respect to the injuries that may be, you might say, a death by natural causes, but the scenario is so absurd that it is not a rational conclusion."

With a flourish of his hand Kelly pulled a four-by-six-foot chart from the table and put it on an easel. It described the condition of Dr. Langlos's body:

- Laceration to the skull
- Bruise to the right eye
- Blood on wall (three locations)
- Bruise on inside of mouth
- Hemorrhage in neck
- Shirt pulled out/buttons ripped off
- Flushed face
- Head jammed underneath desk

Kelly read each one dramatically as if it was a nugget to savor. He studied the jury as he did so.

"There is only one rational explanation that covers all of those injuries and that is that the victim was killed during a fight, during an altercation in which the defendant was attempting to get money from him."

His voice crescendoed.

"It's a homicide. That is the explanation that covers every one of those injuries. Every one of them."

He paused and let his words hang in the air. The entire courtroom was silent as if holding its breath. Then Kelly dropped his voice and said quietly, "Now I've left another column here for Mr. Jones to utilize, in giving us one reasonable rational explanation that is going to cover all of these things. Tell us about a series of events that is going to result in all of these things that anybody would believe."

He gestured toward Hartman.

"A struggle arose because of the defendant's need for money as evidenced by the fact that he'd already given a bum check to Mr. Langlos. For his need for money, this struggle resulted in the defendant banging the victim's head against the desk in the manner indicated by Hernandez and then forcing it against the wall with the resultant splotches of blood on the wall.

"Hartman may not have intended, may very well not have intended, and, probably, in all honesty, in all candor, did not intend to kill his victim."

Kelly walked back and forth in front of the jury box, pausing every now and then for emphasis.

"But, when you consider the evidence presented in this case, he acted with a callous disregard for the life of the victim, Mr. Langlos, and was willing to use, really, whatever force was necessary in order to accomplish his purpose.

"I don't think there is any evidence that he intended to kill. But when you look at it, he really didn't care one way or the other under circumstances where there is a high probability that a death would result.

"He lied about the contention that he had called the hospital on February 2. Hartman stated at the hearing that he had called the hospital February 2, 3, and 4, and at that time he was told by whoever answered the phone that they would buzz Mr. Langlos and they didn't.

"Now, there's no doubt in my mind that the death of Jack Langlos at the Lakewood Park Health Center was an event that was being talked about constantly and known by everybody in that facility. To say that he called and he got a message that they would attempt to call Langlos is absurd. The entire story reeks of inept creativity on the part of Mr. Hartman.

"The checks are really of critical significance. Why? Assume you don't say right off, 'The story is preposterous, this is ridiculous.' Assume you might say, 'Gee, there might be some truth to that.' The checks are of critical significance. Why? Because the checks, unbeknownst to Hartman, were on two separate accounts, one having less than one hundred dollars in it, the other having in excess of five thousand dollars.

"The check," Kelly paused ominously on the word then went on, "that Hartman cashed at Boy's Market was the sole check he possessed for the account with the five thousand dollars. The remaining check—the one Hartman said he was to use to deplete the account of eighteen hundred dollars—was only applicable to the account with less than one hundred dollars in it.

"Now," Kelly said gravely, "if Jack Langlos had been engaging in such a scheme to defraud his wife out of the balance of the bank account and he gave Mr. Hartman two checks, don't you think that one further thing Jack Langlos would have done—I mean, after all, he does have his doctorate, so he has an IQ over thirty-five at least—don't you think he would have said, 'Now be sure when you get to depleting the entire bank account, be sure and use this check right here because this is the only account with a lot of money in it'?"

Kelly waited for a few seconds, beads of sweat dotting his forehead. He looked at the members of the jury one by one as if to say, "There, that should settle matters."

Then he continued.

"Finally," Kelly's voice was strong and clear, "ladies and gentlemen of the jury, the attempted commission of a robbery is so inherently dangerous to life that whenever there is a death that results, even if it's unintentional, it is a robbery-murder and murder in the first degree. With respect to this case, the defendant's intention to rob permeates the entire case. The missing money, the checks, the wallet gone, credit cards gone."

Kelly waited immeasurable seconds before starting his last plea.

"There really is no justifiable verdict in this case other than guilty of murder in the first degree. And I ask that you return a verdict that is commensurate with that."

There was a murmur of satisfaction throughout the courtroom.

Watching and listening closely, Mark Jones sighed deeply. Kelly's skill as an orator was enviable; he had scored big with the jury. Jones was no slouch himself in his ability to impress a jury. As he stood up, he knew he would have to be at his best.

Meticulously dressed and self-assured, the tall, attractive public defender quickly stepped forward.

"Ladies and gentlemen of the jury, I would like to congratulate Mr. Kelly on what I consider a typical prosecuting attorney's argument. It's like a Hawaiian muumuu—it covers all but reveals nothing."

Jones moved toward the diagram Kelly had used. Instead of concentrating on the injuries as Kelly had, Jones began talking of the passage of time and the various steps initiated or influenced by Langlos's widow—her hiring of Dr. Jindrich and Dr. Kornblum, the second autopsy, the coroner's inquest.

Jones motioned toward the jury. "Mrs. Langlos spent fifty thousand dollars of her own money, but nothing was ever filed until February of 1983."

He paused and smiled in the direction of the prosecutor.

"I think even Mr. Kelly would grant me that it's a very unusual case." He paused, letting silence fill the room, and then, with the people's attention fixed on him, he said dramatically, "Probably the most unusual that I've seen. And I'm sure Mr. Kelly would say one of the most unusual, if not the most unusual, he's seen.

"In a period of over seven years, nothing new has been revealed. Unlike Mr. Kelly, I want to look at the facts, but I don't want to do the muumuu with you. I want you to see what's there."

Jones's voice was pitched low and serious. "Mr. Kelly would have you believe that this was a situation where a life and death struggle ensued." Picking up People's Exhibit 20, a photograph of Langlos's office, Jones approached the jury box. "But it's a room where you look inside and there is not one thing amiss. Not one thing from that view. Mr. Miller said from the outward appearance nothing seemed out of place except for the items we have talked about consistently. Mr. Westray said when you first walked in, nothing appeared to be out of place."

Jones studied the jury's faces as he began a seemingly reasoned approach.

"Saturday afternoon would probably be the probable time of death. What difference does that make here? Mr. Hartman used the cards in a flourish of activity on Sunday afternoon. If indeed he killed Langlos Saturday afternoon, why did he not do a flourish of activity Saturday afternoon and Saturday evening?

"Mr. Hartman knew Mrs. Langlos was in Texas that weekend, according to the transcript Mr. Kelly read to you. The checks had the Pacific Palisades address. The house keys and car keys were still in Mr. Langlos's pockets when Mr. Hernandez removed them."

Listening to him, Ruth felt slightly sick. Would the jury believe him?

Jones was talking intently now.

"Why is that important? If someone is going to kill and rob somebody, and he knows the house is vacant, would not the one thing he would do—if he's already killed and robbed—be to go over and burglarize the place?"

Jones then pointed to one of the photographs.

"Look at the blood distribution in the photographs. It is consistent with somebody that had a head injury that sat in the chair and was resting his head against the telephone about to make a telephone call.

"What at first blush seems to be a homicide can be an accident. What can be or what appears to be an accident can be a suicide. Most of the experts testified that at worst it could be a probable homicide. And Mr. Kelly is saying, you as lay people are to reject all their testimony and say you feel they're all wrong and you have been convinced beyond a reasonable doubt for some ungodly reason. Now that is something out of *Star Wars*.

"The only thing that makes sense—if you were in the position where you felt Mr. Hartman was present—is that he came over there, they were talking or arguing, and they started shouting at each other about money, borrowing money, or pay back the money. And maybe there was a push and shove. Or maybe he bumped him. And Jack Langlos slipped or fell or got pushed and hit his head, was helped up in the chair, something happened, assistance was given by whoever that person was there. Mr. Hartman or some other person opened the shirt to allow breathing, and then Mr. Langlos died of a heart attack, which was precipitated by a coughing, asthmatic, stress-induced type bleeding. That makes more sense. And then he's dead and the property is removed."

He looked at each of the jurors in turn. Then he said slowly and with emphasis, "Now that's reprehensible but it's not murder."

Jones had polished his closing the previous night, and it was good. He continued.

"In summary, I think Mr. Kelly is asking you to put that muumuu on. Nothing's been revealed; I would say it was wearing a muumuu in a room full of smoke. He's asking you to convict Mr. Hartman because one coroner was sloppy, and granted, he was sloppy. The Los Angeles County Coroner's office was sloppy. He's asking you to convict him because seven years later, after no new evidence has been developed, the District Attorney has elected to file a charge.

"I think he's asking you to convict him to appease Mrs. Langlos, who is present in the court. Her burning desire is for revenge, not justice. And I think if you do that, then I don't think you'll ever be able to live with yourself. It's a difficult case, and there is no other conclusion but not guilty."

"Mr. Kelly," Roberson called.

It was Kelly's last chance to convince the jury Hartman was a murderer. Ruth prayed that the jury found his case as convincing as she did. Kelly's voice broke into her thoughts.

"Mr. Jones attacked the case from the aspect that there was a five-year time lapse between the time Dr. Jindrich performed his functions in the case and the time we finally filed the case," Kelly said. His rasping tone conveyed his irritation.

"I think that's regrettable, but if anybody has ever been involved with trying to budge the bloated carcass of bureaucracy—and by that I include the District Attorney's office—they recognize how time consuming it is to make them change a decision already made. Even if the initial decision is erroneous. It is only someone with great fortitude, great stick-to-it-iveness, and a worthwhile cause that one is able to do something like that.

"To get people who are, quote, in-house or in-club, to change their viewpoint so they disagree with other persons in-club is virtually impossible. If you were confronted with the same situation with your wife or husband, you would have absolutely no idea where to start, what to do, or how to do it. Mrs. Langlos was confronted with the same situation, and it took that length of time before the error—the error of Dr. Carpenter, Dr. Noguchi, and some district attorneys involved in the case—was rectified. Justice was only served by the filing of the case."

Kelly walked slowly to his seat.

After three and a half weeks, the case was ready for the jury.

Eighteen witnesses had testified. There had been sixty-nine exhibits, including photos, medical slides, clothing, police and autopsy reports, and composite drawings.

Ruth, her family, and friends returned to listen to the final jury instructions on the Monday after Thanksgiving following a four-day holiday break.

Ruth was combing her hair in the ladies room when a woman on the jury entered.

As the woman went to wash her hands, Ruth nodded and said, "Good morning."

"Good morning," she responded.

"I wish I could talk to you but I can't," Ruth declared. Without replying, the woman went out the door and headed straight for Judge Roberson's chambers.

In the courtroom, Ruth reported the exchange to Kelly. "I think I might have made a mistake," Ruth said sheepishly, and related the incident.

"I should have warned you," Kelly grimaced. "The only things you can say to a juror are 'Good morning,' 'Good evening,' and 'Hello.' But we should be all right. You didn't say anything specific."

Ruth breathed a sigh of relief when Roberson made no mention of the exchange and continued waiting.

On the third day of deliberations, the jury requested a rereading of Hartman's testimony given at his psychology license hearing in San Diego.

Except for going home to eat and sleep, Ruth wouldn't leave the courtroom—not after waiting all that time. Nothing would deter her from being there when the jury returned. The hours inched by. No word came.

At the end of the day there was still no verdict. The jurors were excused for the night.

In the hallway, Jones walked up to Ruth. He was smiling.

"Mrs. Langlos, I think we have a hung jury," he said gleefully.

Chapter 23

The Moment of
Truth

Jones was a bright, articulate attorney, but he was not an accurate fortuneteller.

At 11:35 the next morning, the jury asked to see the bailiff.

They had reached a verdict.

Because Kelly was involved in another court case somewhere else, Judge Roberson ordered the verdict sealed and delivered to the court clerk for safekeeping. It would be unsealed and read after lunch.

Ruth had no appetite. For the next two hours, she sat on a bench in the courthouse with a close friend from North Hollywood, Phyllis McSwain. They had worked together at the Loretta Young Finishing School.

"Whatever the decision, Ruth, you've done your best to get this case to trial," McSwain said. "Jack would be proud of you."

"All I ever wanted was justice," Ruth replied. "I truly believe God has walked with me every step of the way. Sometimes He had to carry me. I'm fortunate to have friends like you. You have stood beside me, too." Her eyes were misty.

McSwain tried to make small talk about Christmas, which was twenty-five days away, but it was no use. For most of the time, they sat in silence.

When the lunch was over the two women walked back to the courtroom. As Ruth took a seat, her heart seemed to be pumping against her chest. Scattered thoughts shot through her mind like missiles.

How would she react if the verdict was not guilty? What would she do? Would she lose her temper? Scream? Cry? Shout? Phyllis sat on Ruth's left, a reporter from the *Los Angeles Times* to her right. Ruth knew they wanted to support her. Frightened, she clutched a handkerchief, winding it into a ball.

Hartman entered the room smiling. He was still clad in a windbreaker, chinos, and a sport shirt. A family member had purchased a new powder-blue suit for him, but Roberson would not let Hartman wear it. There wasn't enough time to check it for weapons or contraband, the judge ruled.

The clock on the wall showed a couple of minutes before two o'clock. The scene took on a surreal aura.

The woman Ruth had talked to handed the envelope to the court clerk, a gray-haired woman. Her square face was inscrutable. Opening it, she took out a piece of paper and nestled it in both hands. "We, the jury in the above-entitled action," her voice droned, "find the defendant, Eugene Clarence Hartman, guilty of murder . . ."

Guilty. Guilty. Guilty.

The word banged against Ruth's temples. A sensation of ice stung her body.

". . . in violation of Section 187 Penal Code, a felony, as charged in the information and we find it to be murder of the second degree."

Ruth buried her head in her hands to stop the room from spinning. The handkerchief crumpled in her hands was moist. When she looked up, a pair of arms wrapped around her. "You did it, Ruth," McSwain cried.

In the background, Jones asked for the jury to be polled.
The court clerk's voice droned on:

"Hong?"

"Yes."

"McInerny?"

"Yes."

"Stein?"

"Yes."

As each of the jurors answered, Hartman sat expressionless.
So did Jones. However, Ruth's face was jubilant.

Later that day, down the Pacific coast at Manhattan Beach,
psychiatrist Mary Brenneman, who was reading and watching
television at the same time, glanced up from her book to see a
longtime friend and client talking to reporter Ruth Ashton Taylor
on the five o'clock news.

"It was worth the seven years and ten months of fighting for
justice," the woman smiled. "I want to let other people know that
there is hope. Just don't sit back and say, 'Oh, you can't do anything about it.' Get at it and do something. You can fight and
win."

"Donna," Brenneman said to her daughter who was seated on
the sofa. Brenneman nodded toward the screen. "There is a real
heroine."

"Like Joan of Arc?" her daughter asked.

Brenneman smiled. "A heroine is someone who does something super against all obstacles. She goes beyond the usual de-
mands of life. Society didn't listen to her. Neither did the coroner,
the judicial system, the newspapers, the city. She was alone against
them. It's always tragic to be a heroine, because you're trying to
right a wrong. The coroner's office was her Waterloo. More of us
could try to do it if we decided to."

Brenneman smiled at her daughter.

"Yes, I consider Ruth Langlos a heroine."

Less than a month later on January 5, 1984, the courtroom of
Judge Roberson was packed with Langlos family and friends.
They were there for Hartman's sentencing.

The overwhelming sentiment favored a harsh prison term.

Hartman told Robert Kang, an investigator for the Superior Court probation department, that he did not commit the crime and would appeal his conviction.

"I don't know why my second wife asked me for a divorce," he said in a brief statement to the probation officer. "Actually, the two major factors were probably her new status and independence as a college instructor and my three hospitalizations for treatment of multiple sclerosis attacks."

Hartman's eighty-three-year-old father, whom Hartman said he would live with and care for when he was released, described his son as peace-loving and gentle. "His mother was an invalid the last two years of her life. When Eugene heard I was caring for her twenty-four hours a day, he volunteered to care for her during the day and I took care of her at night. My wife died one month after Eugene was arrested."

One brother, a retired commander in the Naval Intelligence Service, wrote in a letter: "When Eugene is living in a structured environment among family and friends, he is relaxed, disciplined, and in control." The brother described Hartman as a master bridge player who was active in church and community groups. Hartman's disability income was below poverty level, preventing him from adequately supporting himself, the brother said later in the same letter.

"Eugene seems to have more than his share of borrowed trouble," another brother wrote to the probation department. "He has serious emotional difficulties and a great deal of anger bottled up. He is probably, as a result, his own worst enemy."

Roberson skimmed the report for the last time. It said Hartman was a highly educated, intelligent man. He shook his head. The investigator recommended denial of probation and a sentence to state prison.

According to the state's Victims Bill of Rights, the widow was allowed to address the court at sentencing.

Ruth had plenty to say. She walked to the front of the courtroom as people in the courtroom watched intently and whispered. The podium was between the tables where the prosecution and defense sat. It was slightly behind the tables, leaving Hartman in front of her and to her right. Ruth didn't care if he looked at her; she stared at him, a handkerchief clutched in her hand.

The slight hum in the room stopped abruptly as the beautiful blond widow began to speak. Her voice was strong and clear.

"Clarence Eugene Hartman, I received a life sentence the day you killed Jack. I will receive no time off for good behavior, nor will I ever get probation or go on parole. You took Jack away from me suddenly and permanently. It was a shattering loss to lose the man I dearly loved.

"Now it's difficult for me to survive the senseless act of Jack's murder. I was traumatized by many emotions: frustration, hurt, anxiety, resentment, hostility, sadness, depression, pain, and confusion. I am devastated and I wonder why my darling husband Jack had to die by your hands."

Ruth was shaking now, but it felt good to let the anger out. "Why did you kill this living, breathing creature of God? How could you kill him? How could you be so violent and brutal?"

"Mrs. Langlos," Roberson interrupted, "if you will address the comments to the court."

She nodded and paused as if to get more control of her emotions.

"All right. I'm sorry."

Ruth turned to face the judge, but her words were still directed at the man who had taken so much from her. "You took my whole future away from me. My financial support became zero the day he was killed. My future was to face life alone with everything taken from me," she stammered, tears choking out her words.

"One of the biggest shocks is when I found out that you had applied for Jack's job on March 24 of 1976. Now, how could you apply for Jack's job only fifty-four days after you killed him and robbed him?

"I have signed one statement that if I die or disappear, the prime suspect would be Hartman. And if he is ever free again I will write out a new one. I am extremely afraid of him.

"I do have one thing that I want to say to Mr. Jones. There was no clandestine conspiracy to appease what you say is my desire for revenge. Mr. Jones, for your information, I don't have any mystic powers.

"I wish to thank everyone for their support. Justice has been achieved, and with God's help I can begin to live again."

Ruth's son Dr. Chad Emrick had flown in from Denver to address the judge. He came forward now.

"I speak in behalf of my brothers as well as myself. Our mother had sought for years to find security and love in an intimate relationship, and she did find that in Jack Langlos.

"Before our stepfather's death she was happy, vibrant, and hopeful. That was all taken away from her. She spent years in anguish, feeling helpless. She was in despair. She needed to be hospitalized for depression. But certainly through support of her friends, many of whom are in the courtroom today, and excellent medical attention, our mother was able to survive the subsequent years. And now with the conviction of Mr. Hartman she has regained her security. For the first time in seven years she was able to celebrate Christmas.

"Today you will decide whether her newly regained security will be preserved or again taken away. Today you will decide who is sentenced: our mother or Mr. Hartman."

Chad's eyes began to water. His voice cracked.

"Our mother will either be sentenced to a lifetime of fear for her life or be set free to live in safety. We have heard the violence that Mr. Hartman is capable of. I hope you will decide to set our mother free by sentencing Mr. Hartman to the state penitentiary. Should he be granted probation, I can only foresee more anguish for her. I hope that does not occur." Chad looked searchingly at the judge. Their eyes locked, and then he walked back to his seat.

"The defendant is a vicious, violent person, and a danger to the public," Judge Roberson declared in a somber voice. "The court therefore sentences the defendant to the state prison for the time prescribed by law."

He set Hartman's prison term at five years to life, according to the sentencing guidelines in effect at the time of the crime. Kelly figured Hartman would be incarcerated for eight to ten years because of his violent past.

Watching as Hartman was being escorted out of the courtroom, a feeling of intense satisfaction came over Ruth. Largely because of her efforts, a very dangerous person was headed to state prison. It was a cause for celebration. Ruth treated all her close supporters to lunch at a fancy downtown restaurant.

Hartman immediately appealed the conviction for many of the same reasons that his lawyer had stated earlier, notably that he was denied a speedy trial. Only this time he added a new objection—failure to exclude Mrs. Langlos as a witness.

The day after sentencing, Ruth went to visit Jack's grave. The Veterans Administration cemetery in Riverside was situated near a lake. It was a tranquil site with preening white swans gracing the area. Ruth felt at peace.

Sitting on Jack's grave, she cried. "Darling, I didn't give up. The man who murdered you is in jail. It's all over now. You can rest in peace."

But for Ruth, the fanfare was just starting. The media latched onto her story like hungry birds to morsels of bread.

People magazine did a profile on Ruth that ended with Downey Captain Sanders saying: "I've told Mrs. Langlos that if she ever reads that anyone has done away with me, I want her to be on the case."

Other newspaper and magazine stories followed suit. And Ruth was asked to guest on television talk shows in Los Angeles, San Francisco, Pittsburgh, and Philadelphia. At first, she agreed, hoping her commitment to gaining justice for her dead husband would help others. Soon, however, it became apparent that it was time to get on with her life. And she knew exactly what she wanted to do.

A few months earlier while waiting for Hartman's murder trial to begin, Ruth's friend UCLA professor Elizabeth Aaron had taken her to a luncheon meeting of a support group called Parents of Murdered Children. Founded in Cincinnati, Ohio, in 1978, POMC expanded in 1982 to the Los Angeles area to become the only national agency at the time to exist solely to aid those who have lost a loved one to murder. It filled an obvious need, as the number of murders worldwide rose to staggering heights.

Aaron had convinced Ruth that the experience would be beneficial even though she had not lost a child. The group, which has since changed its name to Parents of Murdered Children & Other Survivors of Homicide Victims, met on a sweltering July day in Los Angeles. Forty people with a deep void in their lives gathered in a meeting room at a bank to hear Doris Tate speak.

The 1969 murder of Doris's daughter, actress Sharon Tate, had shocked a nation. Under the orders of their messiah, Charles Manson, a gang of drugged cult followers butchered Sharon in her and her husband Roman Polanski's Hollywood Hills home along with six other victims throughout Los Angeles. Tate, who was 8½ months pregnant with a baby boy, was stabbed sixteen times. Both she and the baby died. To mark their deed, the gang scrawled "pig" in the victim's blood on the front door.

Ruth listened intently as Tate described the emotional roller coaster she had ridden after losing her daughter and grandson. Then people around the room said a few words about the person they'd lost and their experiences. Some showed pictures of their children.

Ruth briefly told how she had lost her husband and spent more than seven years trying to get his killer sent to prison. It felt strange to be sharing her feelings so openly with strangers.

Most people don't want to discuss homicide, unless the crime has touched their family. Although most of Ruth's friends and relatives were supportive, some treated Jack's murder as though it were a disease.

"Ruth, I can't stand to talk about it, because I loved Jack, too," one friend explained. "I can't bear to think about the horrible way he died."

After the POMC luncheon, Ruth was introduced to Doris Tate. She was a warm and friendly woman.

"I hope you get Hartman convicted," she had said with a hug.

During the trial, Tate had called to offer encouragement. An energetic woman, she wanted to understand the problems other survivors were experiencing in case the organization could help.

During a meeting in her home after Hartman's conviction, Tate talked about the need for parole reform in California.

Although Charles Manson and his followers had received the death penalty, that penalty was overturned by the State Supreme Court. She said that the family members now came up for parole periodically, prompting the need for campaigns to keep them imprisoned.

"Last year, we found out that a group had formed calling themselves Friends of the Manson Family," she told the twenty-five people sitting in her living room. "So we gathered more than ten thousand signatures. If we're not vigilant, I fear they'll be set free."

After the talk, Ruth and Doris Tate sat at a dining room table comparing experiences. "Are you afraid of Hartman?" she asked.

"Extremely. I've signed a statement that says he's the prime suspect if anything happens to me. I get my mail at a post office box in another city to try to hide my whereabouts. I don't have a telephone in my name. What else can I do, wear a bullet-proof vest?"

"My greatest fear is that Manson and the others will outlive me and go free, and murder others. As long as I'm alive I'll fight it, but they're a lot younger than I.

"The judicial system needs a major overhaul, Ruth," Tate sighed. "There's so much to do. Victims like you and me have got to keep speaking out."

They hugged that night, two souls bonded by a common cause.

Joining POMC helped Ruth realize a new purpose in life. She dedicated herself to helping other survivors of violent crimes.

There was more to be done than Ruth had ever imagined.

Chapter 24

A Stunning Twist

Over two years had passed, during which Ruth slowly began to reclaim her life. Then late one evening the telephone rang.

"Sterling? What's wrong?"

"Ruth, I'm afraid I've got some bad news," Norris said dejectedly. She could tell by the sound of his voice that this was serious. Her mind raced back nearly a decade to another voice bearing bad news—news about the death of her beloved husband. Nothing could be worse than that.

"What is it, Sterling?" There was only silence. "Sterling, please tell me."

"The District Court of Appeals reversed Hartman's conviction today on a legal technicality," Norris declared. "I wanted you to know before it hits the papers and TV."

Ruth felt as if she was going mad. "Why would they do that?" she shouted into the phone.

Norris was apologetic. "They ruled that Hartman was denied due process, because it took us too long to bring him to trial."

She thought that she could not stand it anymore, that this time her heart would surely break. "I thought there was no statute of limitations on murder."

"There isn't," Norris replied. "But they ruled that the seven-year delay harmed Hartman's defense. They said the District Attorney's office had no reason for waiting so long to file charges after you had come up with the expert opinions of Jindrich, Billingham, and Kornblum."

"But Noguchi wouldn't listen to any of us," Ruth said angrily. "Didn't they read the transcript?"

"They ruled that Hartman could have had trouble finding alibi witnesses after all those years had passed."

"But he never had an alibi witness or a character witness at any of the trials. Never."

"I know. I know. It's a bad decision."

"The court doubted Hartman's guilt?" Ruth asked quizzically.

"No, that's not it. The issue is due process. He's got a right to a speedy trial."

"God knows, I wanted him to have a speedy trial."

"The system messed up," Norris replied. "The coroner messed up. The D.A.'s office messed up. There's plenty of guilt to go around, Ruth. I'm certainly going to push for an appeal to the Supreme Court."

"Didn't they know what Hartman did to Monheit?"

"I know, it would have shown what he was up to when he was on probation," Norris said. "I told the prosecutor several times to use it, and I didn't find out he hadn't until after the case was decided. Kelly said he had enough evidence without it. But it never hurts to get as much on the record as possible. I should have kept closer tabs on him. I'm sorry."

"Sterling, you have nothing to apologize for. I just wish I had known you nine years ago."

Ruth was furious at the system.

Later, when Ruth read the twenty-one-page opinion of the Second Appellate District Court, she became even more furious. The three-member judicial panel set Hartman free essentially because of the incompetence of the coroner's office and the District Attorney's office. The vote was unanimous.

"Delay of justice is injustice," wrote Justice Armand Arabian.

He noted that "pathetically, the coroner's office misplaced the victim's brain after the initial autopsy."

Arabian, who wrote the court's opinion, said Hartman had been prejudiced by the missing evidence. Hartman's memory possibly could have faded because of the lapse of time, the judges ruled.

Concluded Arabian: "The primary function of the office of prosecutor is to diligently and vigilantly pursue those who are believed to have violated the criminal codes of the state. The combination of circumstances chronicled here violated fundamental fairness, the touchstone of due process."

Hartman's attorney had made the same due process argument before the trial. The Court of Appeals and the State Supreme Court had rejected it. Now, after the conviction, the same plea was accepted.

For Ruth, it was another chapter in a comedy of errors. But there was nothing funny about it.

Instead of accepting defeat, Ruth went on the offensive again. She collected hundreds of signatures on petitions urging State Attorney General John Van de Kamp to seek a rehearing. She wrote letters to Governor George Deukmejian, State Supreme Court Chief Justice Rose Bird, and the deputy Attorney General assigned to appeal the case to the State Supreme Court. Twice, Ruth's friend Louise McCord went with her to the Attorney General's office seeking action. Victims advocacy groups joined in the effort.

The State Attorney General's office appealed the decision, claiming the seven-year delay "arose when, despite highly incriminating circumstances, the examining deputy coroner opined that death was from natural causes. The case was not filed in 1978 because the corner's office refused to change the cause of death to homicide despite contrary expert opinions."

This time, the decision was irreversible.

If Dr. Noguchi was bothered by any of this, he never let on. Actually, he had more intriguing matters to deal with.

Noguchi had written a new book and was involved in making more media appearances to publicize it. *Coroner at Large* dissected the deaths of another set of celebrities—Beach Boy Dennis Wilson, Sal Mineo, Freddie Prinze, and Elvis Presley. The book jacket titillated readers: "We see forensic science in action, unraveling mysteries of death—both natural and unnatural—in real-life cases that might have baffled even the great Sherlock Holmes."

◆ ◆ ◆

On December 5, Hartman wore a blue jacket and a big smile as he strode out of Los Angeles Superior Court. For the first time since his arrest in February 1983, he was free. The parole board had set Hartman's release date from the California Institution for Men at Chino for February 10, 1986, but the Court of Appeals ruling was cutting a couple months off that timetable.

His early release was a formality, because the State Supreme Court refused to hear the case. Nevertheless, the Criminal Courts Building was abuzz with electricity. Hordes of reporters waited outside the courtroom for reactions from the prosecutor, Sterling Norris.

Norris didn't disappoint them. His face flushed with emotion, Norris didn't mince words.

"The man has committed murder, and in essence he has gotten away with it. I think it's a travesty of justice—they've put a dangerous man back on the street. He's a walking time bomb."

Ruth didn't have much more to say. In a way, the sudden twist had only firmed her resolve to help reform the criminal justice system. This wasn't only about Hartman anymore. She couldn't walk away now.

"Are you afraid?" one television reporter asked.

"I'm afraid, but I can't be an Annie Oakley gun-toting woman," Ruth said with a shrug of her shoulders. "I did think about wearing a bullet-proof vest today."

In a Downey diner, Miller and Westray were having breakfast. Westray was reading a newspaper with Hartman's picture on the front page, and cursing.

"It's at times like this I think we're fighting a losing battle."

"Hartman?" Miller asked, buttering his toast.

"Yeah, figure this." Westray threw the paper across the table at his partner. "Here's a guy with a conviction for forgery of a hundred-dollar check, a conviction for assault with a deadly weapon, a conviction for theft, and then a conviction for second-degree murder. See any pattern, partner?"

"Wimp, I see a pattern," Miller mimicked.

Westray grimaced. "Okay. So let's forget about this legal technicality bullshit. Even without that, the parole board in its infinite wisdom had decided this guy should be out in three years for good behavior."

Miller slammed the paper down. "Three years. Obviously, the only place he shows any good behavior is in prison. Wasn't his sentence five years to life?"

"And they settled on three years. Imagine, if that had been his first offense . . . probably would have served, oh, six to seven hours," Miller said tartly. "They obviously don't care that we're risking our lives to catch these criminals."

"How many times does a guy have to do this sort of thing before people wake up!" Westray was seething.

"But if they wake up, the streets would be safer. They'd cut our hours," Miller said, tongue firmly in cheek.

"Geez, partner, I never thought of that. I feel better already."

Ruth harnessed her fury by immersing herself in a number of projects. Her goals were twofold: help make the system more accountable to victims of crime, and assist victims in coping with their losses.

The number of advocacy groups for crime victims was growing. Ruth jumped in with both feet. At various times, she was a trustee for POMC and an active volunteer for Crime Victims for Court Reform, Victims for Victims, Justice for Homicide Victims, Family and Friends of Homicide Survivors, and Memory of Victims Everywhere.

After the Court of Appeals reversed Hartman's conviction, it prompted a storm of protest.

Among her staunchest supporters was Ellen Griffin Dunne, the founder of Justice for Homicide Victims. Lenny, as she is affectionately called by family and friends, has multiple sclerosis and has been in a wheelchair for many years. Her drive and determination has helped educate the public on the injustices in the justice system. Her organization, like Doris Tate's, spawned from tragedy.

Her daughter with Dominick Dunne, actress Dominique Dunne, had been murdered by her ex-boyfriend. Because of the sometimes curious machinations of the criminal justice system, the murderer was convicted of manslaughter. He was released from prison after serving three years.

Dominique had portrayed the older sister in *Poltergeist* and had made guest appearances on "Hill Street Blues" and "Fame." When she was strangled to death, Dominique was scheduled to make a pilot for NBC.

Lenny was incensed by Ruth's tragedy. She wrote a letter to Governor Deukmejian seeking his help in keeping Hartman in prison. "Too many people have been released from prison who are a danger to society," she wrote.

Ruth attended meetings and get-togethers in Lenny's Beverly Hills home. Lenny's garden parties to promote the cause of Justice for Homicide Victims attracted such Hollywood notables as Jimmy and Gloria Stewart, Robert Wagner, and Jill St. John, who also were horrified at Ruth's story.

In November 1986, the organization scored their first major victory for victims in helping to defeat the re-election of Chief Justice Bird of the State Supreme Court. During the campaign, Ruth worked the hotline for the Orange County chapter of Victims for Victims against Bird and two of her associate justices. Ruth celebrated their defeats with other homicide survivors and celebrities at the Century Plaza Hotel in Century City.

When Ruth sent a letter to Bird after Hartman's conviction was overturned, it was returned to Ruth because she was considered a non-party. The court clerk suggested Ruth file a brief of amicus curiae. To the average citizen, that type of legalese is tantamount to telling one to get lost.

In Ruth's opinion, Bird was a criminal-coddling judge who was out of touch with the public. The overwhelming defeat of Bird and her associates was historic—the first time a California state justice had lost a bid for re-election.

During this same time, Ruth was often asked to speak to civic and political clubs about her experiences. One of the most lively sessions occurred at UCLA in front of Professor Aaron's graduate class, Public Health 486, a study of death, suicide, and homicide.

Many of the students were in their twenties, and Ruth felt compelled to appeal to their youthful idealism. After a brief history of the Jack Langlos case, Ruth wanted to challenge them to challenge our bureaucracies, to fight as she had.

"Don't walk away when you know there's been a great injustice," she said decisively. "How can you fight?" a girl with waist-length hair asked. "First of all," said Ruth, her voice gathering force, "put things in writing. People can deny things said over the telephone. And when you write, keep it short. If it's more than a couple of pages, people won't take the time to read it. Of the hundreds of letters I sent, the only one who did not respond was Warren Burger, Chief Justice of the United States Supreme Court.

"I recommend carbon copies to at least two or three other people. One time, I cc'd seven people on one letter. That way, the person can never say he or she didn't receive the communication.

"Secondly, always follow up on your request. Don't assume they'll follow through. In fact, assume they won't. Third, always go to the top."

"How did you get a meeting with Thomas Noguchi?" asked a red-haired young man with freckles splashed across his face.

Ruth smiled. "Getting a meeting with Dr. Noguchi took some doing. His aides would tell me, 'He's very busy. He's out of town. He's testifying at a trial. He's doing this. He's doing that.' I got the perfect runaround until Professor Aaron here gave me some sound advice. She told me to be more specific with the aides who were giving me the excuses. Instead of just listening to the excuses, I started asking things like 'Why won't Dr. Noguchi see me? I want a list of the reasons why he won't see me.' Pretty soon, I had my appointment. A little pressure on the person making excuses for their boss doesn't hurt.

"Fourth, and by far the most important bit of advice I can offer, is this: Pray every night that God will direct you and give you

265

the perserverence to endure roadblocks. Deputy D.A. Schafer didn't like it when I kept coming to his office. He said I was a pest. Actually, I always felt good about bugging a paper-pusher like him."

Laughter broke out in the room. Ruth waited for the class to quiet down. Then she went on. "A lot of young people don't think you can fight City Hall. If you don't get results there, go to the county, or the state, or Washington, D.C. Do your homework, then let the system know that you're not going away.

"Remember, you can fight City Hall. Thank you."

There was lengthy applause. The subsequent question-and-answer session brought out several good queries.

"Looking back on the case, is there anything you'd do differently now?" asked a pert-faced young woman.

"Oh yes. I should have gone directly to the District Attorney in Los Angeles instead of relying on Deputy D.A. Schafer to do it. He said he had talked to the D.A. about the death of my husband, and I accepted that. I never followed up to see if he really had."

"You're an outgoing person," a lanky young man observed. "Isn't the average Joe going to be intimidated even if they get a meeting with someone at the top?"

Ruth smiled at him. "Well, let me share a secret I was taught many years ago," Ruth answered. "Nobody is better than you are. Everybody excels in some area. That person you're talking to may be a big wheel, but you can do some things better than he can.

"Now, if that person still makes you uneasy, imagine how awful he would look if he were nude!"

The class howled. The room was filled with chatter and giggling. Ruth smiled again.

"In some cases, imagining them naked isn't a pleasant thought," Ruth said, rolling her eyes. "But it'll relax you. More importantly, it'll remind you that we're all human beings. Their position doesn't make them better than anyone else. I didn't back down to anybody."

Again, there was applause rocking around Ruth. She hoped their response would translate to a boost in their own self-confidence.

"The man you helped convict is back on the streets because of a legal technicality. Didn't the system finally beat you?" a pretty Asian student in the front row broke into Ruth's thoughts.

"Good question," Ruth congratulated her. "At first I was furious. The system had victimized me again. But I wasn't devastated. The court didn't say he wasn't guilty, it said he should have been tried years ago. He spent almost three years in prison for Jack's murder. He lost his means to earn a living, his psychology and teaching licenses. A twelve-member jury said he murdered my husband. I saw him taken to jail, and that was the most important thing for me."

The evening ended with the students gathered around her to shake her hand.

Ruth loved speaking to young people because it was they who had the opportunity to change society and so she attended every engagement to which she was asked. But as the year went on, her health was deteriorating and the antibiotic medication she was taking for upper respiratory problems wasn't helping. She continued as an Orange County trustee for POMC and worked for the hotline for Victims for Victims, receiving a service award from Theresa Saldana's organization. Saldana, star of the TV series "The Commish," started Victims for Victims after she was brutally stabbed in 1982 while walking to her car near her apartment.

But Ruth was slowing down. Her chest ached and she was tired more and more frequently. Finally, she was hospitalized for a month at the UCLA Medical Center for what was diagnosed as reactive depression. The death of her husband and all that followed had taken its toll, the doctors said.

As always, Francois Toussaint helped her through the ordeal. Whenever she could leave the center, he'd be there. They would go for a walk around the UCLA campus, find an arts and crafts show, or go for a drive by the ocean. And it was again to his apartment that Ruth returned.

On August 5, she awakened Toussaint at 2:30 A.M.

"There's something wrong, Francois," Ruth said.

"What's the matter?"

"I thought it was my stomach, so I took some Pepto-Bismol.

But it didn't help. I'm so cold."

Francois took her temperature. It was 96.6 degrees.

"My left arm and chest are starting to hurt, too. So is my back. I may be having a heart attack." Ruth said, frightened.

He bundled her up. "I'm taking you to the hospital," he said.

When they reached the hospital, Ruth fainted as they put her in a wheelchair. When she awoke, a sea of faces peered down at her. Ruth looked around for a few seconds, then everything turned black again.

"You really gave them a scare in ER last night," a nurse told Ruth when she awoke the next morning. "You slumped over when they were trying to take an X-ray."

Although at first everyone thought Ruth was too young to have a heart attack and that it very probably was something else, it was indeed a heart attack.

Afterward, Ruth had to have an angiogram and angioplasty. When she returned to Toussaint's apartment, things seemed to be going better.

But on August 24, many of the same symptoms returned. It was 9:30 A.M. Francois was at work. Ruth called 911 and was taken to the hospital by an ambulance with intensive care equipment.

She had suffered another heart attack. Her son Thad flew in from Memphis, Tennessee, to be with her. They did another angiogram and angioplasty.

"We had trouble with your mother," the doctor told Thad after the surgery. "Her heart stopped, but we brought her back."

"How long was it stopped?" Thad asked.

"One minute."

This time Ruth was in the hospital for a few weeks. Because Toussaint had scheduled a trip to Belgium to visit his elderly mother, Ruth's daughter-in-law, Cathy, came from Texas to take care of her.

In October, Ruth had a third heart attack. Doctors put her on heavy medication that left her close to non-functional. Each morning she woke up feeling almost as tired as when she went to bed. All she could do was rest on the couch and watch television or read. Still she convalesced as best she could and tried to keep a positive attitude.

While visiting Thad in Memphis in April, Ruth thought she was having yet another heart attack. The doctors said it was an angina attack and that Ruth needed triple-bypass surgery. Afraid she wouldn't make it back to California, Ruth opted to have the surgery in Memphis.

"Thad, make sure the chaplain comes to give me communion before surgery," Ruth said sitting up in the hospital bed. It was the day before the surgery and she wanted to be prepared.

"Of course, you know if I die I am to be buried with Jack at the Riverside Cemetery." Thad began taking notes. "I want the 139th Psalm read. And I'd like some organ music at the service. I think the best hymns would be—"

"What are you talking about?" said the doctor who would perform the surgery. They hadn't noticed him come into the room.

"I'm just making funeral arrangements," Ruth said matter-of-factly.

"Mrs. Langlos, you're far too young to die. Don't you have any faith in me?" the doctor said with a grin. "I certainly don't want to lose a celebrity patient from California and ruin my reputation."

They all laughed.

The triple-bypass surgery was successful. But Ruth's heart had sustained a lot of damage in the past.

"Mrs. Langlos, before your heart attacks, you were hitting on eight cylinders," the doctor explained, "now you're hitting on six. It'll be that way the rest of your life. You can always get somewhere on six cylinders, but your life span isn't going to be as long because of the heart damage."

Ruth spent twenty-nine days in the hospital because of a kidney infection and a fluid buildup around her heart. Her sons visited her. Thad, Francois, and Cathy took turns caring for her. With their support, she began making plans to return to the victims' rights movement. Even on six cylinders.

Near the end of Ruth's hospital stay, a minister from a Presbyterian church stopped in for a chat.

It had been preying on Ruth's mind that at the end of life, one is supposed to forgive their enemies, and she was still unable to do so in Eugene Hartman's case.

"I am unable to forgive the man who murdered my husband," Ruth said sadly.

"That's not your job," he reasoned. "That's between the man and God."

After his visit, Ruth felt a serenity she had not experienced in many years.

Chapter 25

A Get-Well Gift?

On a Sunday morning in late August, there was a knock at the door. Francois Toussaint looked at his watch: 8:45. He rose slowly, newspaper in hand, and opened the door.

"Is Ruth Langlos here?" said a young woman with long brown hair who flashed a big, bright smile. In her hands rested a fourteen-by-fourteen-inch gold box with a huge white ribbon on top.

"Oh yes, just a minute, please," Toussaint answered.

Ruth was resting on the couch, reading a book. Four months after heart surgery, she was just learning how to cope on six cylinders.

The kitchen table looked like a pharmacy, with bottles of pills in neat rows. There was Tenormin for high blood pressure. Mevacor to lower cholesterol. Halcion for sleep. Valium for nerves. Ecotrin for aspirin. Nitrostat in case of an angina attack. Sorbitrate for angina pain. Tagamet for an ulcer. And Transderm-Nitro patches to prevent angina.

If she took her medication and got plenty of rest, the doctors said she could soon ease into normal activities. She was feeling antsy.

"I think there's a get-well gift for you," Toussaint called.

Wearing her pink flowered robe, nightgown, and slippers, Ruth went to the door.

"I have a package for Ruth Langlos," the young woman smiled again, exposing perfect white teeth.

"That's me," Ruth said smiling back.

"Would you please sign here." She handed Ruth a receipt.

After Ruth did so, the young woman quickly pulled out a paper from under the box. "This is for you," she said, putting the paper in Ruth's hand. Startled, Ruth looked at it as the woman ran away clutching the box.

Ruth's eyes widened in astonishment as she read. "This is a court summons!" she exclaimed.

Without a word, Toussaint bolted out of the apartment in pursuit of the woman. But instead of using the elevator, she had raced down the stairs and disappeared.

When he came back, Ruth was still standing in the same place he had left her staring at the paper she held in her hands.

"Francois, I'm being sued for half a million dollars by the man who murdered my husband," Ruth said incredulously.

Eugene Hartman had filed a lawsuit in Los Angeles Superior Court seeking three million dollars in damages for malicious prosecution. In addition to Ruth, the other defendants were the State of California and the County of Los Angeles. He was seeking two million dollars from the county and half a million dollars from the state.

Hartman's suit accused them of conspiring to have him charged with the murder of Jack Langlos.

Ruth's motive, according to Hartman, was "to victimize, harass, intimidate, annoy, and injure him in order to make a claim with the state's victims assistance fund and as a manifestation of her personal hatred and ill will towards the plaintiff."

Ruth read the court documents again and again. "How can he do this to me?" she protested.

Toussaint paced around the living room angrily. "Why did I open that door?" he kept saying.

Ruth contacted Sterling Norris at home.

"It's a worthless suit, Ruth," he declared after hearing the particulars. "But you're still going to have to hire an attorney to defend you."

"I'm being victimized again," Ruth said. "Not once, but twice. I wasn't on the jury. I'm not a part of the criminal justice system. I had no way of convicting him."

"The judge will see through this, I'm confident," replied Norris. "This isn't fair to you. The county and the state have their own attorneys, but you're going to have to bear the expense yourself."

The television tabloids had a feeding frenzy. "Crimewatch Tonight" and "Inside Edition" featured a history of the bizarre case. "Inside Edition" reporter Cynthia Allison asked Hartman for his reaction to the jury's verdict in his murder trial.

"I felt a little bit relieved it was murder-two," answered Hartman. He was seated on a couch and nattily clad in a striped tie and short-sleeve white shirt. "They had found me not guilty of murder-one."

"Did you murder Jack Langlos?" the reporter asked.

"No," deadpanned Hartman.

"Do you think someone else did?"

"No," he repeated in a monotone.

Allison then asked, "How did he die?"

"He died of a heart attack," Hartman coolly replied.

Asked why he filed the lawsuits, Hartman said matter-of-factly: "I would like to be able to afford to live in LaJolla . . . with its Mediterranean climate."

"Will winning the lawsuit make that possible?"

"Yes, of course," he smiled.

"That's why you're doing it?"

"Yes."

"Inside Report" called the litigation a "case of the hunted stalking the hunter." On that show Hartman said he would drop the lawsuit against Ruth Langlos if she would give him access to her files.

"No chance," Ruth said when she heard the comment. "All

my records are public documents that Hartman or anyone else can obtain by their own efforts. I'm not about to make it easy for him."

Ruth had no money to worry about losing. Her life savings had been exhausted long before. Fortunately, she qualified for a free legal aid service in Orange County.

The lawyer to whom she was assigned, blond and well-built Burt Mills, was fresh out of school. At twenty-five, his exuberance hadn't been tainted yet. He enjoyed helping people who couldn't afford $125 an hour for legal services.

"I've never heard of such a thing," Mills said while poring over Hartman's lawsuit. "You say this guy was convicted of killing your husband?"

"Yes, but I was the one who got the life sentence," Ruth replied dejectedly.

"He's claiming humiliation, injury to reputation, emotional distress and anguish, loss of personal liberty . . ." Mills read.

Ruth nodded, "He spent almost three years in prison, but I wasn't on the jury."

"This guy was convicted, freed on a legal technicality, and now he sues the widow for damages. We never discussed this at law school," he said with a smile.

"I can't believe he can legally do this to me," Ruth protested. "If he wins, does that mean criminals can sue their accusers when they get out of jail?"

"The bizarre thing is, Mrs. Langlos, I don't know of a law that prevents Hartman from doing this," Mills said, shaking his head.

By the time of Ruth's October 18 hearing, Judge Raymond Lopez had dismissed the cases against the county and the state on grounds of governmental immunity.

That left Ruth the lone defendant.

On the morning of the hearing, security was unusually tight. The District Attorney's office did not know what to expect from Hartman. They prepared for the worst. A plain-clothes investigator drove Ruth and her friends Louise McCord and Phyllis McSwain to the courthouse from the nearby motel at which they met. They parked in a restricted underground area used for judges and police.

At the command post they were introduced to seven uniformed police officers.

"Mrs. Langlos and her friends will be coming out this way after the hearing," the investigator told the police who guarded the halls.

Ruth entered the courtroom flanked by an investigator and a uniformed officer. "There's Hartman," the investigator pointed him out to the police officer.

Hartman, sitting alone, looked away as soon as he saw Ruth and her protectors enter the courtroom. He was his own lawyer.

"Your honor, these charges are totally without merit," Mills said to Judge Lopez when the case was called. "We'd like to know what basis he has for bringing this action. Mrs. Langlos is a private citizen who had no authority in this matter."

Judge Lopez's eyes impaled Hartman.

"Mr. Hartman, this is the third time you've been here with this," Judge Lopez admonished. "I've already dismissed it twice. What is the purpose of this?"

"She was a key factor in this whole thing taking place," Hartman pleaded.

"Enough is enough," Lopez declared. "You've introduced no evidence to support any of your allegations."

The complaint against Ruth was dismissed within fifteen minutes. There would be no trial.

Outside the courtroom, Mills and Ruth spoke to the waiting media reporters. Afterwards, Mills told Ruth that Hartman had threatened to appeal the ruling.

"Sometimes it's wonderful not to have any money," Ruth responded. "There's nothing to get."

The irony of Hartman's lawsuit was not lost on then-California State Senator Edward Royce, whom Sterling Norris had talked to on Ruth's behalf. On March 2, 1990, Royce introduced Senate Bill 2766 to fill a legal loophole.

"Existing law does not restrict any person convicted of a felony from pursuing any cause of action against any other person who was injured or became a victim as a result of the crime or crimes for which the felon was convicted," Royce explained to his colleagues.

The legislation sought to add Section 43:56 to the civil code. It read:

> Any person convicted of a felony is prohibited from bringing any suit for damages or filing any action, in any manner relating to the act or acts for which he or she had been found guilty, against any or all victims of any of his or her crimes, or the victims' heirs, relatives, estate, or personal representatives.

Ruth and the members of victims' organizations of which she was now a member besieged the governor with further pleas for justice for victims and their families, and on September 18, 1990, California Governor George Deukmejian signed Senate Bill 2766 into law. It was nearly fifteen years after Ruth's husband's death. No victim or victim's family would ever be put through such litigation again in California.

Besides the passage of this law, the year 1990 marked another precedent-setting victory for the victims' rights movement.

In June 1990, California voters approved Proposition 115, the most far-reaching reform of the criminal justice system in state history. Ruth had worked hard to get voters to sign petitions to put the reforms on the ballot.

The mood of the public was obviously angry—the pendulum of justice had swung too far in favor of the criminals.

Proposition 115 reforms have dramatically evened the odds so that crime victims rights now count. Among the things the reforms accomplished:

- Gave crime victims the right to a speedy trial. Only the accused had the right previously.
- Allowed persons convicted of torture to be imprisoned for life.
- Permitted one trial for a person charged with several crimes or several people charged with the same crime.

- Sent a person charged by the grand jury directly to trial, eliminating preliminary hearings.
- Increased penalties for murders.
- Streamlined preliminary hearings.
- Required the defendant in a criminal case to reveal the evidence he intends to use in court to the prosecutor. Previously, only the prosecution had to reveal evidence to the defense attorney.
- Required court-appointed defense attorneys to prepare cases in reasonable time limits set by a judge.

In July 1992, almost nine years to the day after she and Ruth had first met at a POMC meeting, Doris Tate died. Francois and Ruth attended the memorial service. Crime victims had lost a beacon of hope and encouragement. Ruth had lost a friend.

Chapter 26

Further Good-byes

On a spring Saturday morning in 1993, Ruth and Francois Toussaint sat side by side, watching while from the cloudless heavens black and purple-chinned hummingbirds swooped onto their apartment balcony for a refreshing respite.

Amid an inviting lush green bed of plants, a tube of watery nectar awaited their sun-parched beaks. Some came alone, others in pairs and threesomes to drink and rest. Then, as quickly as they appeared, they were gone.

Francois treated the hummingbirds with great love. At least once a week, he'd mix a quarter cup of sugar and a cup of water for the feeder. He followed the formula meticulously—too little or too much sugar would not please his feathered friends.

After a while Francois and Ruth got up and went back inside the apartment.

The personality of Francois Toussaint was everywhere. Shelves of history, nature, and photography books lined the living room. There were books on the coffee table and on the kitchen counter too. Ruth called him a walking encyclopedia because of the way he devoured the written word. The apartment's color scheme reflected his conservative taste in dark wood and brownish hues.

When Ruth looked around, she didn't see much of her own tastes. She preferred white leather furniture with lots of stainless steel, modern lamps, and bright red draperies. In the Palisades, she and Jack had a marble-topped table in the dinette. On the walls, a large, boldly colored scenic picture warmed the room. Their trumpets served as wall decorations. And of course, Ruth's Hammond organ was the centerpiece.

But Ruth's possessions, including the organ, remained in storage because of Toussaint and her cramped quarters.

For years, fighting the criminal justice system had been Ruth's only priority. Lifestyle and residence didn't seem to matter. Without much notice of her surroundings, Ruth had lived in a bachelor's pad. But that was now ending.

Toussaint was leaving his job in the importing and exporting business. But to receive his pension for the many years he had done the same work in Belgium, Toussaint had to live in Belgium.

Shortly before his departure, Ruth and he discussed their futures.

"You're sure you wouldn't like living in Belgium?" Toussaint asked plaintively, knowing the answer.

"Francois, my sons are here, my friends are here," Ruth replied. "If something happened to me, I'd be too far from my family."

They sat close together on the couch and stared outside in silence. So many memories. So much to say. But how to say it?

"Why didn't you do something to make me mad at you? That would have made parting so much easier," Ruth said finally.

"Why didn't you do something that made me mad enough to throw you out?" Toussaint replied. They laughed.

"Remember when you drove to see me in LaJolla, then got so angry that you turned around and went back to Los Angeles?" Ruth recalled.

"Yeah, our one and only argument," Toussaint said. "You were really upset, and I was, too. What was that fight all about?"

"You mean, after all these years, you don't remember?" Ruth

teased.

"I don't have a clue."

"Well," Ruth paused and looked at him, "neither do I."
They howled like school kids.

"Friends?" he said, a twinkle in his eyes.

"Yes, friends," Ruth answered, her own eyes misty.

They embraced warmly. As always, Ruth felt secure in his strong arms.

"I just might be back, you know," Toussaint said with a wink.

"You've done that before." Ruth laughed. "If you return, you'd better be planning for marriage."

Toussaint returned to his homeland on June 30, 1993. Despite her sadness at his departure, Ruth resolved to once again move forward. Taking a new apartment, she got her possessions out of storage. She was especially heartened to see once again her Hammond organ. Putting it in a special place in her living room, Ruth began playing her music again.

Ruth returned to her work for POMC. A few nights later she heard guest speaker John Gillis, chief of the state's parole board, speak. It was as though she had never left. In a hotel conference room in Orange County, Ruth was sandwiched between two girls whose mothers had been murdered.

"Has the case been solved?" Ruth asked the woman on her left.

"My dad did it, and he's still walking around," she cried.

The other woman was too distraught to talk. She just wept.

Their tears reminded Ruth of the ongoing challenge all of us face to help the victims of homicide.

If listening to their innermost feelings will comfort them, she thought, *we must do so as often as needed. If more laws must be changed to achieve fair treatment for victims, we must change them. And if the criminal justice system needs shaking to respond, we must shake it.*

These were the things she had tried to do and would still do if and when her efforts were needed.

◆ ◆ ◆

In Brea, California, a five-foot marble monument stands in a beautiful park setting of rose trees, flowers, and shrubs. The inscription reads: "Dedicated to Those Who Lost Their Lives in Violent Crimes." An oval panel with a pink carved flame is above the inscription. Below is a partially open carved rosebud.

It truly is a monument of love, built through a grassroots fund-raising effort by the Orange County chapter of POMC of which Ruth is a devoted member.

Along the nearby walkways, granite markers bear the names of 144 victims. A new set of names will be added during a ceremony in the spring of 1994. Ruth plans to attend.

Among the new names will be Dr. Jack Langlos.

He rests in peace.

Epilogue

Fifteen years.

That's a long time. Long enough for a child to mature into adulthood. Longer than the careers of most professional athletes. And longer than most criminals ever spend in jail.

For Ruth Langlos, it was an eternity.

During that period Langlos lived and relived the brutal death of her beloved husband, Jack Langlos. Her ordeal finally ended with the changing of a California state law to protect crime victims from lawsuits filed by convicted felons.

To quote from Hamlet, "How is it that the clouds still hang on?" In the case of Ruth Langlos, the answer is excruciatingly complex.

Instead of grieving and moving on, Ruth Langlos felt she had to know how her husband died. To find out, she stared eye to eye with a criminal justice system grounded in inertia.

Her story of incredible perseverance was chronicled through interviews and nearly fifty pounds of public documents, including police reports, court transcripts, and medical reports. Ruth Langlos's extensive private letters, personal notes, and media reports also stand as further evidence of her commitment.

Ruth Langlos touched many lives during her fight for justice. And many people touched her. Well over one hundred characters appear in this book. All are real people in real situations, although some names have been changed to protect their privacy. Real names have been used for a majority of the key figures. Today, many are active in their professions.

Dr. Ervin Jindrich is the coroner of Marin County, California. He has won election five times. Dr. Margaret Billingham is a professor at Stanford University in the Department of Pathology. Dr. Ronald Kornblum, who resigned as coroner of Los Angeles County, is in private practice.

Sterling Norris remains a deputy District Attorney for Los Angeles County.

Dr. Mary Brenneman is on the staff of Metro State Hospital in California.

Mike Miller is the captain of field operations for the Downey Police Department. Mike Westray is a Downey police officer.

Dr. Thomas Noguchi, a deputy medical examiner for Los Angeles County, now performs autopsies at USC County Hospital. He declined to be interviewed for this book.

Dr. Eugene Hartman lives in California. At the last moment, Hartman agreed to be interviewed, and his comments are included in a postscript to this book.

Jan Baker Emrick, Ruth's oldest son, graduated with honors from Austin College with a double major. He is employed by IBM, from whom he recently received an award for loyal service. His specialty is to develop computer projects for the company. He programmed the projection plotter for the shuttle project for NASA. Jan is married to Cathy and has two children, Cherie and Jeffrey.

Chad Duane Emrick has a Ph.D. in psychology with honors from Columbia University and is in private practice. Recently he was guest lecturer at the Institute of Psychiatry in London. His expertise is alcoholism and related disorders. Chad is married to Carol and has three children, Jason, Tara, and Matthew.

Thad Evan Emrick, Chad's twin brother, has a master's degree in psychology with honors from Memphis State University.

He travels extensively all over the world as Director of Automation for Omega Travel, Inc. He is single.

As for Ruth Langlos, she lives in Orange County, California. Active in victims' rights and anti-crime organizations, she is now planning a video to help families and relatives of homicide victims who are facing the trial of the person charged with the murder of their loved ones.

Postscript

While writing the manuscript of this book, co-author and Detroit Free Press *reporter Dennis Niemiec attempted to contact Eugene Hartman for his perspective on the death of Jack Langlos. Mr. Niemiec received no response from Mr. Hartman. As the manuscript was being typeset, Mr. Niemiec tried again, this time by telephone. Mr. Hartman answered, and they discussed the Langlos case, the publishing of this book, and Hartman's life during and since the events of this book. The complete, unedited transcript of that conversation follows. —Ed.*

Hartman: Hello, Gene Hartman here.

Niemiec: Hi, Mr. Hartman. Hi, this is Dennis Niemiec from the *Detroit Free Press.*

H: Oh, yes.

N: How are you? I didn't know if I would catch you this week. I got your note you were at Vegas World.

H: Well, I'm back here now.

N: I take it you won a couple million dollars at least.

H: Of course.

N: How did you like it?

H: I was busy, relatives mainly.

N: Okay, well Mr. Hartman, as my note said I was hired by a publisher in New Jersey to work on a book with Ruth Langlos on the story of her life, and obviously you're a big part of that, especially with your relationship with her husband, Jack Langlos. I've seen you interviewed a couple times . . . I think it was "Inside Edition," that's the last time I saw. . . . Have you done any interviews since then?

H: I did three of them way back then.

N: That was the late '80s, right?

H: Yeah, right.

N: Well, actually my questions are pretty similar to those. I guess the thing that intrigues me about the case is just . . . well, we're pretty familiar with what happened to her, but your side of the story isn't. You didn't testify. I read the transcript, and you didn't testify at the main trial. From what I gathered in looking at the transcript you didn't testify because you were afraid of what your attorney said was perjuring yourself. Is that right?

H: Right, that's in the records, right.

N: Yes. It had something to do with the psychology hearing. When you had that hearing there were some things you wanted to retract. Am I reading that was the reason why you didn't testify?

H: No.

N: Well, how did you feel you were going to perjure yourself? I was confused at that.

H: Well, I can't tell you that. This is a thing between myself and my attorney.

N: Okay, okay. Well, in going over the case the first thing that comes to mind is that, we're talking now—gosh it's got to be '76—we're talking seventeen years ago. You know Ruth has talked about what she felt happened and I just want to try to get from your side what you feel happened or what you know happened.

H: Well, that would be a long and difficult thing, wouldn't it?

N: Well, you can't be—

H: Very complicated.

N: Well, certainly for one thing you can't be tried again for anything, so you can be comfortable. You can say pretty much what happened without any fear or—

H: I tried to do that. You know those interviews you saw on TV?

N: Yes.

H: Well, I got a telegram to go down to catch a plane, go down to Los Angeles, tell my side of the story. I did.

N: You did.

H: It went on for several hours, but when the actual thing comes out on TV, it's just the way they had it set up and the way they wanted it.

N: Oh, you weren't on—if we're talking about the same show, and I think we probably are—you were probably on it for all of about thirty seconds.

H: Well, more than that.

N: Not much more.

H: Long interview, and we went over a lot of things, but nothing was in it except the way they already had it set up what they wanted it to say.

N: I think—

H: I imagine they . . . see, what happens was they said this one's going to go this way. The three of them did three interviews, but I've never told my story, no.

N: Just because you haven't had the opportunity or because you feel it's private and you don't want to tell the story?

H: No, I want to tell my story. I told you I told my story in the interviews and they went very well but they weren't shown on TV. Two or three hours of talking and filming.

N: Tell me basically what you told them. I'm sure one of the questions they wanted to know was the weekend the coroner ruled Mr. Langlos had died. . . . What I saw in the reports looked like it was probably the Saturday before the Monday that he was found, I think it was something like February 2. Were you with him at all that weekend? Did you see him?

H: With who?

N: With Dr. Langlos.

H: No, I didn't see him that weekend.

N: You didn't see him that weekend?

H: I think it was the Thursday before.

N: You weren't in there, his office, saw him having a heart attack or saw him being beaten or anything like that?

H: No.

N: I know you said it on the show, but I've got to ask you again: You had nothing to do with his death?

H: No, nothing at all.

N: How do you think he died then?

H: I said the same thing, I said it on TV, I don't know how he died, but the coroner said he died of a heart attack.

N: Mr. Hartman, have you seen any of the pictures of the death scene at all? Maybe on TV?

H: Yes, I probably have. Were they in evidence in court?

N: Yes. Do you believe that from those pictures—I guess I'm asking just your opinion—do you believe that that looked like Dr. Langlos died of a heart attack or without any kind of, . . . at least . . . ?

H: You kidding me? The coroner had the body to perform an autopsy, right? They had two more autopsies and four different coroners and the physicians gave four different opinions. The death certificate said natural causes. So what am I suppose to tell from a picture?

N: Well, it was later changed, as you know, the death certificate.

H: Well, actually a lot of the pictures were lost by Dr. Noguchi.

N: Mrs. Langlos has obviously felt that she was wronged by the system. Do you feel you were wronged?

H: Of course.

N: Tell me about that. Do you feel you should have been brought to trial immediately?

H: For what?

N: Well, you were tried on a murder charge.

H: I was arrested for killing Dr. Langlos, and the coroner said he died of natural causes. Why should I be tried immediately? What are you talking about?

N: Wasn't the Court of Appeals . . . from what I'm reading, the decision—

H: Is this being taped, by the way?

N: Pardon me?

H: Is this conversation being taped?

N: Yes.

H: I haven't heard a beeper.

N: I'm taping it for accuracy purposes. Does that concern you?

H: Of course it concerns me. You started this conversation, you're taping and not beeping. Another thing, Mrs. Langlos's book is coming out in October. The title is, you probably know the title, *Murder, No Doubt: A Widow's Nightmare.*

N: Well, that's a working title.

H: That's what it is right now. That's what it's being booked into the bookstores as the title. So the book's already been published.

N: No, it's not been published.

H: It's going to come out October 1993.

N: That's when it's slated to, yes.

H: Right.

N: But I'm still writing. I'll tell you right up front, so there's no misunderstanding, the reason I want an interview with you is I want your side, I'm going to put it in the book. I'm not putting you through this because I like to or I—

H: I'd be happy to arrange that, yes.

N: We'd certainly like to get your side of the story.

H: It's not going to go into a book called *Murder, No Doubt: A Widow's Nightmare* by Ruth Langlos. In fact, I'm sure that Mrs. Langlos doesn't even want you to talk to me.

N: Why do you feel I wouldn't put it in? We don't know each other, obviously. I'm a professional reporter.

H: You were hired by the publisher?

N: Yes.

H: Okay.

N: To do a book with Mrs. Langlos. We're collaborating on a book.

H: Yes, I got that. There's a book due for publication in October. The title is *Murder, No Doubt: A Widow's Nightmare.*

N: That is the working title of the book. My background: I'm an investigative reporter, so that's why I'm talking to you, trying to get your side. I will put everything you tell me into the book, I promise you that. That's my intent. That's one of the reasons I'm taping you, so that I can quote you accurately. I don't want any misunderstanding at all. If you did a two-hour interview and none of your stuff was aired, I had nothing to do with that.

H: In one, I got a lot of money and was living and Mrs. Langlos was wronged, that was a point of view. The second one was I was stalking her—I think that's what Mrs. Langlos told you—I was interested in . . . hurting her or something. That's a lot of bullshit.

N: I've done a lot of interviews with her. I don't recall her ever saying you stalked her.

H: She said this to me on other occasions. And that was sort of the theme of the "Inside Report." It was on TV a half an hour, fifteen minutes.

N: The Court of Appeals ruled that you weren't given a speedy trial. Basically, they said due process was not served.

H: I'll tell you exactly what happened. There was no trial for murder. And the District Attorney at the time told me he's not going to charge me, he's not going to hold me. The death certificate says natural causes. That's the way it was. And then Mrs. Langlos with Gov. Deukmejian and a number of medical people that she hired got the inquest—that was Deukmejian's doing. And then after that the Board of Supervisors with Mr. Antonovich—who had a lot of conversations I guess with Mrs. Langlos, I don't know—ordered a trial. The Attorney General—excuse me, the District Attorney—said no. Then he was elected Attorney General in California. Deukmejian and Antonovich, the Board of Supervisors in California appointed a new

293

temporary District Attorney. So they went ahead and made a trial.

N: That was Philibosian, I believe.

H: That was Philibosian, right. It was political.

[*Note: In 1982 George Deukmejian was elected Governor of California and John Van de Kamp was elected Attorney General. Robert Philibosian was then appointed District Attorney to succeed Van de Kamp. All three are now in private law practice. Michael Antonovich is still a L.A. County Supervisor. Hartman was arrested and charged in early 1983.*]

N: You think it was all political.

H: Well, with the aid of Mrs. Langlos, yes. She had a different motive than they did, I'm sure.

N: What do you feel her motive was?

H: I don't know. But I know that when Republicans run on a law and order . . . they like to have a favorable trial like this. It was political, yes, on the part of Deukmejian, Antonovich, and Philibosian.

N: Didn't you end up spending more than two years in prison because of that?

H: Yes.

N: So you feel you were a victim of politics?

H: I feel I was a victim of Mrs. Langlos and politics, and they were using each other.

N: You had described in your psychology hearing that basically Dr. Langlos had given you the checks and his cards and you were going to get some money so he could claim his cards had been stolen and take some money that way. Is that what really happened?

H: Well, this is the same thing you asked me earlier about. I can't talk about that.

N: Okay.

H: This is the reason I couldn't testify.

N: I'm reading between the lines and I think our readers will, too. I sense that some of the things you said at that time were not true.

H: No, that's one possibility. Another possibility is that some of the things I was going to say in testimony— . . . That's the problem of the defense.

N: Some of the things you could have said would have incriminated you?

H: No, I don't think so.

N: I believe your attorney said you wanted to basically testify at the main trial.

H: Right, and he discouraged me from doing that, so we did not do that.

N: The problem he was having . . . if you were going to tell the truth as you intended to do, some of the things you would have said there would have been in conflict with some of the things you said at the psychology hearing.

H: My attorney recommended that I do not testify because of the difficulty and because Kelly wouldn't make any kind of waivers or anything like that.

N: Did everything you testified to at the psychology hearing, was that accurate?

H: I don't think everything was. I think most of it was, yes. I haven't read that.

N: Hindsight is 20/20. If you had to do it over again, would you have testified at the main trial?

H: No.

N: No. Why?

H: Because my attorney advised me not to.

N: On what grounds? You can't talk about that.

H: Exactly. And the trial didn't come out so badly, as you may know, in that respect.

N: You got convicted, Mr. Hartman.

H: I was accused of . . . well, you know what I was accused of.

N: You were accused of first-degree murder.

H: Right. What was I convicted of?

N: Second-degree.

H: That meant three years in prison, right?

N: Uh-huh.

H: How did that conviction come by? There's where the story is. What happened in that trial? Why was I lost? Why was I not allowed to go to court one day? Why did they delay it over the Thanksgiving holiday? Why did they keep me in prison for six days after the judge ordered the case dismissed? I have a lot of complaints.

N: Again, this whole thing was political?

H: No, I think a big factor was the activities of Mrs. Langlos. I don't know anything about this, but she did appear before the Board of Supervisors in Los Angeles, right?

N: Uh-huh.

H: And she probably did have conversations with Gov. Deukmejian.

N: Right.

H: I don't know what they said.

N: The coroner's report ruled it natural causes, but they later changed it. The majority of medical experts that testified said it was most likely a homicide.

H: That wasn't it at all. The testimony of the medical people was divided about six different ways. About five or six guesses or assumptions about what the cause of death was: fibrillation . . .

N: Fear-induced.

H: Fear-induced, asphyxiation.

N: With the brain having been lost, a lot of that was speculative. They couldn't prove asphyxiation without a brain.

H: Well, what happened to that brain? I think the coroner's office just lost it. He had a brain at the first autopsy, and that finding was he died of natural causes. That's what the death report said.

N: Again, the deputy D.A.'s theory was that you just robbed a dead body.

H: That was one of the theories, yes.

N: That's not true?

H: Well, I'm not going to say about that.

N: If that's what had happened, and if you had said that right at the beginning, probably a lot of this would have never happened.

H: Are you sure? I copped a plea and I walked out of jail and that was one of the happiest days of my life. I wanted to forget the whole thing. Mrs. Langlos hired people, talked to people I knew without my knowledge for several years, and paid a lot of money ending up because of the election of Deukmejian as Governor and the former District Attorney as Attorney General. Then an order by the Board of Supervisors, Los Angeles County, for a trial. Years later. Under the guise or disguise that something new had come up, which was not true. That was one of several things that the Appeals Court said violated due process.

N: Does this thing still bother you?

H: What thing?

N: The whole ordeal.

H: Of course.

N: Do you still think about it a lot? Does it still have any impact on your life?

H: I don't think about it except when something pops up, somebody asks me about it. I thought about it again when I started this suit.

N: Your purpose in that was you thought you were maliciously prosecuted?

H: Yes. Political reasons.

N: This is personal, so you tell me if you want to answer this or not. You're obviously a very intelligent man, very learned, was a psychologist at the time. Yet I have this sense you were always having financial problems. Why would a guy with your background and a good job be having financial problems?

H: Mainly because I have multiple sclerosis.

N: Does that cause you to not be able to work as many hours as you'd like or slows you down?

H: Once you're diagnosed with that you can't work because you can't get any insurance.

N: But you were working.

H: Well, I worked in the same hospitals John Langlos was working.

N: But even at that time you weren't in good shape financially?

H: That was because Medi-Cal would pull—God knows for what reason—would not make payments to hospitals or individuals.

N: They were slow pays?

H: This bankrupted hospitals in the state of California. I think

Blue Cross was handling the computers then.

N: It was the slow payments that were causing the problem?

H: Exactly.

N: You copped a plea. Then you tried to start anew in the San Diego area and you get into all that trouble with Monheit. It's kind of like you're back in the soup again.

H: That had nothing to do with this Langlos thing. But I wasn't well off. At that time I was getting what I'm getting right now.

N: Social Security?

H: Social Security.

N: How is your health? Are you doing okay?

H: Yes.

N: I just have an instinct that there's something here that hasn't been told. There's some secret here.

H: Yes, there's lots of them. There's a lot of questions I have. A lot of things I don't understand.

N: Tell me some of them.

H: You're working for this book.

N: There's no doubt about that. But I'm telling you again, I will do everything in my power to not be like those TV people that didn't give you your full say.

H: If you can write something up for me and I can check it over...

N: I can't do that.

H: You do that for Mrs. Langlos. You work for her.

N: I don't work for her. I'm collaborating with her. I work for a publisher, New Horizon Press. That's who my employer is. If you tell me, I will do everything in my power to put it in there.

H: You will do everything in your power to put it in there?

N: To put anything you tell me into the book.

H: Okay. Put in the book that the trial and my imprisonment came as a result of the election that sent Deukmejian to the governorship and the District Attorney Van de Kamp to the Attorney General's office and brought in Philibosian, who was appointed by the Republican political leadership and then ordered by the Supervisors of Los Angeles County to bring me to trial.

N: Why would they do that to you? Because they were on some kind of get-tough-on-crime kick?

H: Not a kick. A political policy.

N: But why you, Mr. Hartman?

H: The idea is to bring in a Republican District Attorney and keep him there.

N: But why you?

H: Anybody who is charged with something and . . . it's possible to do this in . . . a political situation would be used. I just happened to be there. There isn't anything particular about me. It's not even personal, I don't think. It's just political tactics.

N: Again, you had nothing to do with Mr. Langlos's death?

H: That is right.

N: You didn't even see him die?

H: That is right.

N: And you didn't rob him at all?

H: This particular part that we're getting into, I'm not going to talk about. I didn't testify at the trial because my attorney recommended that I didn't.

N: If you came upon his body and robbed him, I don't see at this point why you'd be hesitant in saying that.

H: When you started this conversation, you said I couldn't be tried. But you know better than that. People can be tried for all sorts of things.

N: You can't be tried for the same crime twice.

H: That is correct. But you can be tried—and this is why we had trouble in the trial—you can be tried for perjury. So I already said one thing about what happened in that sworn statement in the hearing before the trial and everything else.

N: So, in other words, the answer to the question "Did you rob Dr. Langlos when he had already been deceased?" is you can't answer that question.

H: On the instruction of my attorney, that is correct.

N: Aren't you answering it by saying that?

H: I don't know.

N: You're saying you can't answer that because of the possibility of being tried. If it wasn't for that, would you want to answer that question?

H: You said you would put what I say on certain things down and get it published somewhere, right?

N: Yes.

H: I told you what my side basically was at trial.

N: The political.

H: Right.

N: Is there anything else you'd want published?

H: Yes, lots of things.

N: Start running them by me.

H: Look, I'm not going to run anything more by you. I'm writing a book myself.

N: Are you?

H: Don't give me that, "Are you?"

N: No, I didn't know that. How would I know that?

H: I've been sending proposals out all over the place.

N: Are you working with a writer or doing it yourself?

H: Doing it myself.

N: How's it going?

H: I had trouble at the very start. Somehow my attorney lost his files on the trial. I tried to get them for a long time. Then I called the state board. Then he came back with: It's lost.

N: What do you think of Noguchi?

H: I don't know Noguchi. He testified twice.

N: How far along are you with your manuscript?

H: I've been sending proposals to different publishers. A few years ago, I was working real, real hard on this.

N: Did you get any kind of contracts?

H: No, I have no contracts.

N: It's a difficult field.

H: It's very difficult, you're right.

N: Your book is primarily about your life story?

H: The book was primarily on the Langlos problem. My relationship with him, his death, the trial.

N: Were you going to tell everything in it?

H: Everything.

N: Even if it caused you a perjury charge?

H: If you write it in a book, it doesn't mean you've sworn about something. It just means you're writing a book. I'm going to tell everything.

N: What was your relationship with Dr. Langlos?

H: We had a friendly relationship. We were co-workers . . . in different hospitals in southern California. We had lunch the Thursday before he died.

N: The thing that wasn't credible to me in your testimony about him giving you the checks—

H: Giving me the checks?

N: Where he gave you his credit cards.

H: Nobody believed that. Nobody believed that. It's not credible. Nobody believed that.

N: The two checks, one had several thousand dollars in the account, and the one account had very little money in it.

H: But see, I don't know anything about the Langlos account? Which check does what, which has money . . .

N: But if there had been that "scheme" that Dr. Langlos had concocted like you were talking about to have you draw out the money, he would have told you.

H: In fact, he did. We'll get to that some other time.

N: You were drawing the money on the wrong account.

H: That's not true.

N: You wrote the check that had several thousand dollars on it, like six thousand dollars. The other account had like one hundred dollars on it.

H: Have you read that story that nobody believed—it's far-fetched, I know—but it tells exactly what happened in that file you have on the hearing.

N: The psychology hearing?

H: Right.

N: You still stand by that testimony you gave at that hearing?

H: I stand by the testimony I gave at that hearing, yes.

N: You know something that hasn't been told. As a reporter I'm looking for the missing piece of the puzzle.

H: You haven't told *me* something. For example, you sent me this letter. You didn't say a word about the fact that this book was already written and ready to be published. You said, quote, you're working on a book.

N: That's true.

H: You didn't tell me it was going to come out in October.

N: That's true.

H: You didn't say you were working for a publisher. You just said you were working in conjunction with Ruth Langlos. I put your name in a computer and it popped up with this printout: "Title: *Murder, No Doubt: A Widow's Nightmare.*" I should believe you play straight and narrow about everything after that?

N: Wait a minute. There's no lies in there, Gene. I'm working in collaboration—

H [*reading from letter*]: "I am an investigative reporter working in conjunction with Ruth Langlos about her life."

N: That is true.

H: "The book will include a history of events that transpired before and after the death of her husband."

N: That's true.

H: Primarily, that's what the book is about, right? That's what the title says. It's not about her life. It's about this.

N: Oh, no. Obviously that's a big part of her life. But it's about her entire life all the way back from her childhood. No, I didn't deceive you on that.

H [*reading again from letter*]: "If you wish to be interviewed by me for inclusion in the book. . . " No way is Ruth Langlos going to have you go to a publisher with a book that includes me and her in it.

N: That's where you're a little confused. You're right about that if I was working for her she would never want me to interview you. But I'm not working for her. I'm an investigative reporter. I'm hired to write this story in collaboration with her. She tells me her side of the story. You know most of her story anyway.

H: I'm going to rush down and buy the book as soon as it hits the bookstore here in Sacramento.

N: But the thing is, just because she for instance doesn't want you interviewed, that doesn't mean we don't want to interview you. The publisher wants you interviewed. I want to interview you. That's why I made the contact.

H: I know, but she has a book contract with the publisher, right?

N: That's right. We both do. It would be like if I was going to help you do your book, for instance.

H: When should we start?

N: Let me explain this to you. You may tell me: "Dennis, don't interview Ruth Langlos." Okay, but that doesn't mean I'm going to listen to you. I don't work for you. I could work in collaboration with you, which means we're like partners.

H: So actually the publisher is helping in the writing of the book.

N: No, the publisher isn't helping writing, but the publisher does the editing and the publisher is the boss.

H: That's right.

N: So the publisher says: "If there's another side to this story, we want you to get it." That's what I'm trying to do. That's what the boss says. And they may do the same thing to you for your book. You may turn in your manuscript, your proposal, and you might write it, and they may say, "We want you to get a professional reporter to help you with it, and we want

Deukmejian interviewed, and we want Langlos interviewed, and we want Philibosian interviewed," or whatever. They'll tell you what to do. They're your boss. That's what it is all about, and that's why I'm interviewing you.

H: When do they plan to publish the book? At which stage in all this procedure?

N: We're still months away. We'll get it in the book. We're not doing this as an exercise to make you feel good. We're going to put this in. I sense you think the book is done. If the book was done, I wouldn't be having this conversation with you.

H: The working title says the whole thing: *Murder, No Doubt.* This is exactly what I'm talking about with my attorneys. The title.

N: That is based on mostly that there were medical experts that thought it was a probable homicide.

H: They volunteered to work with Mrs. Langlos. That's my understanding. And she didn't even pay for their expenses. That's my understanding.

N: Well, she had Jindrich, Billingham, Kornblum—

H: Kornblum, who took over for Noguchi, and you wonder why I think it was political.

N: Weldon Walker, and there were others.

H: Kornblum was essentially working for the supervisors, particularly for Antonovich. And he was working with Mrs. Langlos and Gov. Deukmejian. Political. In the last analysis, the trial only came about because the Democratic District Attorney was not going to charge me, not going to hold me even though they had that inquest . . . and then he got elected Attorney General and Philibosian was appointed District Attorney. Van de Kamp talked to me personally. "I'm not going to hold you. I'm not going to charge you."

N: How long after that were you charged?

H: After the election, naturally.

N: When he was the District Attorney, he personally told you he wouldn't charge you?

H: I'll talk to him about this before I say anything more about that. You should interview him if you wanted to.

N: You keep coming back to this having nothing to do with anything but politics.

H: No. I was charged with murder and tried because the Democratic District Attorney was elected Attorney General, a Republican District Attorney was appointed in his place, and this person and Deukmejian and Antonovich went to the Board of Supervisors and ordered this trial. And Mrs. Langlos appeared with them.

N: You're saying Mrs. Langlos had a lot of power within the Republican Party.

H: With certain people. I think mainly Mr. Deukmejian.

N: But, politics aside, they did have a trial, and based on the evidence a jury convicted you.

H: No. That is not true.

N: What's inaccurate about that? The jury was out something like three days, and they came back with a guilty of second-degree.

H: That's correct.

N: There's no politics in that.

H: There's politics in that. I told you earlier. At the time this was supposed to go to the jury, why was I delayed and not delivered to the courthouse until after Thanksgiving? And why during that particular period, between that and Thanksgiving, was there an article in the *Los Angeles Times* that told what a good guy the head of the prosecution was. If you think the *Los Angeles Times* doesn't have anything to do with all this politics in southern California . . . well, you know they do. They can also influence a trial, can't they?

N: But the jury is hearing testimony, and based on that they're making a decision. And they judged you guilty of second-degree murder.

H: That's right. And you know why? Because the judge would not allow a hearing on, for example, lesser charges. Manslaughter, for example. Were you aware of that?

N: Yes.

H: My attorney wanted that included in the instructions. I wanted that included in the instructions.

N: What are you guilty of, in that case?

H: Oh God, in what case?

N: The Langlos case. Forget the jury . . . forget the politics. What are you guilty of? You are a very learned man. You know the system. You know what the different charges are. You know what manslaughter is.

H: You're using the term *guilt* in a court sense. I'm guilty of none of the charges, including manslaughter.

N: Are you a religious man?

H: That would be great. We're talking about guilt in a legal sense in a case of murder in Los Angeles County.

N: Maybe I'm out in left field. I've been in left field before.

H: I'm left field myself.

N: I think we're playing semantics. What is it in the Langlos case you're guilty of?

H: I just told you, nothing.

N: Not even robbery?

H: Should we go around again? I'm guilty of nothing.

N: You've said that before. You're working on a book. I'm

confused what you would have new to tell people? Would politics of L.A. County be the basis of your book?

H: No, how a trial and conclusion that violates fundamental due process can be brought about and put an innocent man in prison.

N: In a nutshell, how politics can, in your words, put an innocent man in prison.

H: Well, that's not the way I would put it. I'd be saying this is what happened in this particular case. As soon as I see Ruth's book, I'm going to read it right away, 'cause I want to see if she has anything about her talking with Mr. Deukmejian at an Armenian yearly meeting or things like this.

N: I don't know how much she knew Deukmejian. I think that's pretty high up the totem pole. Wasn't he Governor at the time?

H: He was Attorney General and then elected Governor.

N: From what I see, she appealed to everybody on this case.

H: I think she also had help from a group, I think it's called Victims of Crime, something like that.

N: A lot of groups were aiding her cause, because they felt her husband had been murdered. And those people wanted to see some justice. It took over seven years to get you to a trial.

H: Because Van de Kamp was elected Attorney General.

N: If Van de Kamp had stayed as D.A., you would never have been brought to trial?

H: That's exactly right. In fact, Mr. Van de Kamp was ordered to bring me to trial and he refused, as you may know. District Attorneys are elected officials, so they can be ordered to do things like that, and they shouldn't be.

[Ruth says she has never had a conversation with Gov. Deukmejian. Deputy D.A. Sterling Norris, who recommended the prosecution of

Hartman, says he never even talked to Philibosian about the matter. Antonovich opposed Philibosian's appointment as District Attorney.]

N: Do you have any regrets about this case?

H: Oh, God. Regrets?

N: Is there anything you could have done differently?

H: Yeah, not cop a plea that very first time.

N: What should you have done?

H: I shouldn't have listened to the advice of that public defender in that first situation. The trial was not for murder, as you know.

N: By copping a plea to the forgery you feel that—

H: That put a sort of string around my neck.

N: A stigma?

H: Absolutely. It made a big difference. I wasn't even aware that this was a felony, matter of fact. But I was anxious to get out of Los Angeles County Jail. I wanted to stay out and forget it. In fact, I talked with a reporter in Sacramento, and she said, "Why don't you just forget about this?" That's exactly what I did do, but Mrs. Langlos never did.

N: I think you said in one of the hearings that you didn't even know that he had died until several days afterwards.

H: That's correct.

N: She made the point that you never sent any sympathy cards.

H: I heard her say that on the same TV show you saw.

N: You didn't send a card because you didn't know he was deceased?

H: That's correct. I was in Hayward at the time. That's exactly right.

N: If you hadn't copped a plea to the forgery, I sense you feel they couldn't have convicted you of it?

H: No. We're speculating, aren't we? I don't think they would have.

N: You don't think they had that strong of a case at the time?

H: There's a lot of things involved in that. They had no case at all.

N: They had your checks, they had witnesses that you had signed—

H: No, they had no case at all, because all of their evidence was tainted, as I found out as I learned more about law. Do you know about opening people's suitcases without a warrant? This is exactly what happened.

N: But they would have had the check at the market where you signed Dr. Langlos's name. They had that. That's probably good enough for a forgery. I don't claim to be a lawyer. I saw the check, but I see your point—

H: If I hadn't copped a plea, I don't think anything that was involved in the early thing would have gone to trial. I think it would have been dismissed because of tainted evidence.

N: Then you wouldn't have had this, as you said, this string around our neck. Why do you think the jury in the main trial convicted you of second-degree murder? They didn't know about the politics of the situation.

H: They weren't allowed to convict me of manslaughter, for example, as a part of it. Another reason they convicted me is because they delayed the trial by holding me back so I couldn't appear in court at the time they were supposed to start when the charges were made to the jury. I wasn't there when they were supposed to start going over this. During that time, the *Los Angeles Times* printed an article that said what a great guy the prosecutor was—just before the jury started deliberations.

N: You talk about being held back in the jail and not getting to court on time. That was only one day, wasn't it?

H: That's right. The day before the Thanksgiving vacation. The day that the jury was supposed to start deliberations.

N: What happened that day?

H: They didn't take me to court. Incidentally, the sheriff runs the jail.

N: Why were you delayed that day?

H: For the same reason they kept me in jail after the case was dismissed . . . at a crucial time they didn't deliver me to the courthouse, which is a very short distance from the county jail, as you know. And, generally speaking, a judge could have ordered my delivery there even though they forgot to put me on the bus.

N: About the working title of the book: In Ruth Langlos's eyes and in other eyes they do believe it was a murder without any doubt. You agree to that, don't you? In their eyes?

H: Of course. Look, you saw these TV things. "Come down here, Hartman, and tell your side of the story." Of course. I never told my side of the story.

N: The title *Murder, No Doubt* is a reference to the fact that in their eyes this was murder no doubt.

H: In whose eyes?

N: The co-author of the book, Ruth Langlos, and other people's opinions, too. That it was a murder.

H: I don't doubt that it was Ruth Langlos's opinion. I don't doubt that people seeing the TV programs would, depending on what thing they read in which paper, I have no doubt whatsoever.

N: Have you been interviewed since those shows—"First Edition," "Crimewatch" . . .

H: I didn't see "Crimewatch." I'd appreciate you sending me one.

N: They aired right about the time you were filing suit. You haven't been interviewed since then?

H: No.

N: You don't feel your side came out in those TV interviews?

H: I know damn well my side didn't come out in those TV interviews. The reporter who interviewed me for "Inside Edition" sent me a telegram—I still have ten copies—that said: We'd like to tell your story, come on down, hop on a plane, and I'll meet you at the airport.

N: The main thing you told her in the interview that did not come out in the TV show was this political—

H: Right, all this other stuff, being kept in jail, the whole works.

N: You're right. I never saw any of the political stuff or the jail stuff. Are we talking about, in your mind, a political conspiracy?

H: We're talking about electoral practices. And we're talking about Willie Horton–type things. Is that a conspiracy? I think it is.

N: Were there any other cases at that time that you feel got handled the same way as yours?

H: I don't know. I wasn't paying attention. There are cases like this that happen all the time. There are books written about this . . .

N: I'm certainly going to write it. The things you described here, the political machinations that you feel were going on that led to you being brought to trial. Is there anything else I should get in here?

H: How are you going to get this into a book about Ruth Langlos? Or New Horizon Press?

N: New Horizon Press is the publisher. Your trial for the second-degree murder of her husband is a part of the book. And the lawsuit you filed against her is a part of the book. So you certainly deserve to give your side of the story.

H: Well, maybe I will someday.

N: It sounds like you prefer to give the entire story in a book that you're going to do.

H: No, I gave a good part of what I've talked to you about to all the people who've interviewed me, including you, and I never heard it on TV.

N: I can't promise anything. As the writer you can't promise anything. You can just write it. The editor and publisher comes in, and if they don't like it they edit it, and if they like it they leave it in. What I'm telling you is I'm going to write the political stuff you've told me this evening.

H: Would you do me a favor? Send me a copy . . .

N: I can't send you anything before publication. It's a journalistic practice not to send your writings to the subjects before it appeared. But I'm telling you now, I'm going to write the thing about the political machinations—

H: Just because you send me a copy doesn't mean I can edit it.

N: Is there anything else you want me to put in here besides the political stuff?

H: Oh, if I think about it, I'll give you a call.

N: Okay, and you want me to put in here that you basically are innocent. That's what readers want to know the most.

H: Yes, right. That is right.

N: And you were never with him in the office?

H: That weekend, that is correct. We had lunch two days before.

N: What did you talk about that day, by the way?

H: Oh, I don't remember.

N: It wasn't anything significant?

H: He wanted me to give a test of some kind, short form, an IQ test.

N: How did you get the news that he was deceased?

H: I don't remember. Wait a minute. When I was arrested . . . in San Jose. That's when I got the news. That was the first I heard, right there. I was visiting my parents in Hayward, and I was arrested in San Jose. That's when I was told. The officer said: "We are arresting you for the murder of John Langlos." He said: "Do you know who John Langlos was?" And I said yes.

N: That had to be a double shock.

H: It also was a shock when he said if I tried to run, he'd shoot me.

N: [*Laughs*] I shouldn't laugh.

H: We can laugh about it now.

N: It's a double shock. You're told somebody you were friendly with is dead, one. And number two, you killed him.

H: Right. One more particular item. John Langlos, or Jack, wrote me a letter about ten days before he died.

N: What did he say in that?

H: That's something I want to publish some time.

N: You don't want to tell me what was in it?

H: I'll tell you generally. Hi, just to talk. Good news. We're going to get some of that money released from Blue Cross.

N: You don't sound particularly bitter?

H: I'm not bitter. I'm not bitter.

N: You seemed to be when you filed the lawsuits.

H: No. Filing lawsuits doesn't mean that you're bitter.

N: You served almost three years in jail, and you're telling me you're not bitter at all. You served three years in jail for a crime you're telling me you didn't commit, and you're not bitter.

H: Exactly. Right now it's an opportunity.

N: You mean the book, right?

H: Right. In fact, Ruth Langlos publishing a book will help me be able to tell my story. Sometime. Someday.

N: If I think of any more questions, I'll be in touch. Good luck to you on your book and finding a publisher. We'll get the political stuff—I will certainly write it and turn it in.

H: I look forward to reading it.

N: Okay. Thanks a lot, sir.

About the Authors

Ruth Langlos, an advocate for the rights of homicide survivors, resides in Huntington Beach, California, fifty miles from the home she once shared with her husband.

Dennis Niemiec is an investigative reporter for *The Detroit Free Press*. He lives in the Detroit area with his wife and three sons.